PRACTICAL
FOODSERVICE
SPREADSHEETS
WITH
LOTUS 1-2-3

PRACTICAL

FOODSERVICE

SPREADSHEETS

WITH

LOTUS 1-2-3

Joel Chaban

 Van Nostrand Reinhold
New York

To my wife, Pat, whose love and patience has helped to make this book a reality and whom I love dearly.

Copyright © 1987 by Van Nostrand Reinhold
Library of Congress Catalog Card Number 86-26797
ISBN 0-442-21798-6

Printed in the United States of America

Designed by Beth Tondreau

Van Nostrand Reinhold
115 Fifth Avenue
New York, New York 10003

Van Nostrand Reinhold International Company Limited
11 New Fetter Lane
London EC4P 4EE, England

Van Nostrand Reinhold
480 La Trobe Street
Melbourne, Victoria 3000, Australia

Macmillan of Canada
Division of Canada Publishing Corporation
164 Commander Boulevard
Agincourt, Ontario M1S 3C7, Canada

16   15   14   13   12   11   10   9   8   7   6   5   4   3

Library of Congress Cataloging-in-Publication Data
Chaban, Joel, 1944-
    Practical foodservice spreadsheets with Lotus 1-2-3.

    Includes index.
    1. Food service—Data processing.   2. Electronic spreadsheets.   3. LOTUS 1-2-3 (Computer program)
I. Title.
TX911.3.E9C47 1987   647'.95'0285   86-26797
ISBN 0-442-21798-6

Contents

Spreadsheet Availability on Disk

The spreadsheets contained in this book may be purchased as templates on a 5¼-inch double-sided, double-density floppy diskette in PC-DOS format for IBM-PCs, PC/XTs, ATs, and PC clones and compatibles. They are also available for SuperCalc, SuperCalc 2, and SuperCalc 3 in PC-DOS format (as described above) and in CP/M format in template versions that have been modified for the features of SuperCalc.

For more information about purchasing these templates or to purchase these templates on disk, send your inquiry to Food ABCS, P.O. Box 294, Sausalito, CA 94966-0294. Please specify your computer model, operating system format, and Lotus 1-2-3 or SuperCalc version.

Acknowledgments

Special thanks to Bob Small, of the School of Hotel, Restaurant and Travel Management at Cal Poly Pomona, and to Earl Austin, dean of Hotel and Restaurant Management at Golden Gate University, San Francisco, for their suggestions and encouragement.

Introduction

The trouble with most theories of teaching is that the parts of the body you want to have learn don't understand English.

—Tim Gallwey, *The Inner Game of Tennis*

Learning by Building and Playing with Models

This book was originally conceived to help foodservice operators learn to use spreadsheet software to create spreadsheets that could be used in the management of their restaurant. This original idea has grown to include instruction for students of the foodservice business who want to expand their knowledge of restaurant principles and procedures.

The power of this volume lies in its ability to provide an interactive learning environment using models that are developed through exercises. Learning through spreadsheet model building reinforces cognitive processes through actual doing and through the associated visual imagery. These models allow you to practice foodservice principles and procedures and simultaneously to learn how to use Lotus 1-2-3 spreadsheet software.

While building each spreadsheet presented in this book, concentrate. Get absorbed in the operation of each spreadsheet as you work through the exercise—not so much in the step-by-step instructions, but in how you will use the spreadsheet and how you might want to change it.

Do not be nervous or afraid of making errors. One purpose of this book is to have you learn by making errors. If you follow the step-by-step instructions, you should avoid any disastrous events. Feel free to play and experiment with Lotus 1-2-3. The Lotus software was designed to double-check with you before executing a command that might have disastrous effects. Try different things out. Lotus may be likened to a video game: the more you play, the more you know, and the better your chances of winning become.

The Purpose of This Book

Practical Foodservice Spreadsheets offers the following things:

- A tutorial for learning Lotus 1-2-3 spreadsheet software and for learning principles and procedures of financial and operational foodservice management
- Spreadsheets designed specifically for foodservice applications
- Spreadsheet examples that you can use as a basis for developing spreadsheets suited to your specific requirements
- Insight into the advantages and disadvantages of using spreadsheet software for foodservice modeling, analysis, and reporting
- An environment for learning and practicing many of the principles and procedures of foodservice management

Why Use Spreadsheet Software in Foodservice Management?

Every restaurant owner or manager should have a computer equipped with spreadsheet software on his or her desk. This brazen statement is not an expression of personal bias or computer mania; it is simply an acknowledgment of what a powerful tool a spreadsheet program such as Lotus 1-2-3 is.

Of course, spreadsheet software is not the end-all in computer software. There are many applications for which spreadsheets are inappropriate. For example, they are not very practical for word processing, although some people do use Lotus 1-2-3 as a word processor. In addition, spreadsheets can be cumbersome to use for any sort of sophisticated double-entry bookkeeping or for applications that require data to be stored across multiple files. Although some people undoubtedly have the patience, fortitude, tolerance, and time to use spreadsheet software to do their accounting, the practice is not recommended.

Spreadsheets are terrific for forecasts, budgets, "what if" analyses (such as sales projections), and many non-double-entry accounting functions. They are especially suited to the task of computerizing daily and periodic forms that require mathematical calculations—for example, the daily sales/cash report used in thousands of foodservice operations to record and reconcile actual cash and cash-drawer vouchers with what the cash register says should be in the cash drawer. The computed result of most daily sales/cash reports is a dollar amount, referred to as an *overage* or *shortage* of cash, that indicates the discrepancy between what is actually in the cash drawer and what ought to be there at the end of the day.

Some daily sales reports are simple; others are complex. In addition to reconciling actual cash with records of cash transactions, they may analyze food and labor costs, calculate figures relating to server productivity, analyze menu sales, and even provide sales/expense ratios through comparative sales analysis.

Like Batman and Robin, the dynamic duo of computer and spreadsheet can rescue nonmathematician foodservice managers from laboring over an out-of-balance daily report, no matter how simple or complex it is. A spreadsheet can be constructed that automatically performs most daily report calculations, pinpoints discrepancies between actual and theoretical items on the daily report, flags results to indicate special conditions, generates graphic representations of data for making visual comparisons, and provides decision-making messages predicated on conditional outcomes. In other words, a spreadsheet will enable you to generate all the information you are getting from your present daily report, plus additional information you are not now getting.

Now the smallest independent restaurateur or foodservice manager with spreadsheet software can single-handedly generate daily reports that, if done manually, would require a staff of several full-time bookkeepers. Information can be generated about food, labor, and sales at a level of sophistication on a par with that of a large, multiunit operation.

So hang your coat on your pencil sharpener, put your eraser in the same cabinet with your box of candles (for emergency use in case of electrical power failures), push your adding machine to the back of your desk, get out your computer and your Lotus 1-2-3 spreadsheet software, and get set to design new daily reports.

How This Book Is Organized

If you are a new computer user or a Lotus 1-2-3 spreadsheet beginner, you will want to start with part I (chapters 1 and 2) of this book, which is designed to help you get started. Chapter 1 is an introduction to computer use and to the DOS operating system. Chapter 2 is an introduction to the features of Lotus 1-2-3. Having read them, you can begin building the Daily Purchases Register described in chapter 3, moving on to each subsequent chapter in consecutive order.

If you are an intermediate or advanced Lotus 1-2-3 user, you may begin with any chapter in part II. The first five chapters of part II, however, are interrelated. In particular, chapter 7 presumes your having already built all of the spreadsheets introduced in the previous four chapters.

Each of the first four spreadsheets (in chapters 3 through 6) involves input of data based on your operation's daily activities, and each becomes an integral part of the Daily and Period-to-date Report spreadsheet prepared in chapter 7.

Chapter 3 explains the Daily Purchases Register spreadsheet, which is used to record daily delivery invoices for food, beverages, and supplies, and for inventory transfers in and out of your operation.

Chapter 4 describes how to create a Physical Inventory and Valuation spreadsheet. This form can be used monthly (or over the period of your choice) to take a physical inventory and to price, extend, and total your physical inventory. It calculates a total inventory value (used in the computation of cost of goods sold) and a value for each inventory subcategory.

Chapter 5 explains how to set up a Daily Labor Report spreadsheet, which—based on your input from employees' time cards—calculates regular pay, overtime pay, gross pay, and other information used to analyze daily labor.

Chapter 6 explains how to set up a Daily Cash Report spreadsheet, which compares your actual (manual) cash count to the record of your cash register's journal tape. It locates discrepancies and errors between these two cash counts (actual and journal tape), determines your daily bank deposit, calculates cash overage or shortage, and provides other miscellaneous information.

Chapter 7 is a compilation of data from each of the previous four spreadsheets. By automatically consolidating certain data from the spreadsheets developed in chapters 3 through 7, the Daily and Period-to-date Report spreadsheet is able to analyze and compare these data, after which it generates a final, abbreviated daily and period-to-date financial statement.

Creating the Daily and Period-to-date Report spreadsheet described in chapter 7 depends on your constructing the spreadsheets in chapters 3 through 7 exactly as described in those chapters. If you change the construction of any spreadsheet in chapters 3 through 6, the spreadsheet in chapter 7 may not work. If you *do* make changes to any spreadsheet in the earlier chapters, make sure that you note your changes and adjust the spreadsheet in chapter 7 accordingly.

Chapter 8 explains how to construct a spreadsheet that can be used to calculate your employees' tip allocations and shortfalls. It is based on the IRS's standard tip allocation formulas as of April 15, 1984. The IRS's recommended formulas

are the Hours Worked method and the Gross Receipts method. The spreadsheet does not test to see if you qualify for tip reporting, however, nor does it consider special tip allocation formulas your company may have adopted through a good-faith agreement.

Chapter 9 is primarily concerned with developing an annual operational budget by means of a Budget spreadsheet. All parts of the budget are explained, including forecasting, sales, fixed and variable expenses, the seasonal index, and controllable and noncontrollable expenses. In addition, this chapter covers budget analyses such as break-even analysis, gross profit per customer, seat turnover, and inventory turnover.

Chapter 10 explains how to construct a Recipe Costing and Menu Pricing spreadsheet. This spreadsheet allows you to paint your recipe on the screen by entering inventory item codes and the quantities used in recipes. The remaining costing and pricing work is done automatically, as the spreadsheet finds the name and the price of each recipe ingredient, extends and totals the recipe cost, calculates per-serving costs, and calculates menu prices based on two different menu-pricing philosophies.

Assumptions Made in This Book

The two most basic assumptions made in this book are that you own Lotus 1-2-3 spreadsheet application software, and that you own an IBM PC, PC/XT, or AT, an IBM PC clone or compatible computer, or one of the many computers approved for 1-2-3 by Lotus Development Corporation.

Lotus 1-2-3 version 2 was used to develop the spreadsheets presented in this book. If you are using Lotus 1-2-3 version 1 or 1A, you may encounter some functions in this book that are not supported by these earlier versions. Most commands and functions used here are common to all Lotus 1-2-3 versions; however, certain powerful enhancements to version 2, as well as the version's ease of use, have justified resorting to some features only available on version 2. It is well worth your while to upgrade your Lotus 1-2-3 software to version 2, if you have not done so already.

This book is not intended to explain all the features of Lotus 1-2-3, but to supplement the Lotus 1-2-3 manual. Thus, although part I provides a general review of basic computer use and Lotus 1-2-3 use, you are expected to have at least a general understanding of how to use your computer and 1-2-3 from reading or reviewing the manuals accompanying these tools.

Part I.

COMPUTER

HARDWARE

AND

SOFTWARE

1. Introduction to Computer Systems and DOS

It would be convenient if computers and software were like a simple electrical appliance that you could purchase, bring home, plug in, and use without first having to read an instruction booklet. Unfortunately, the personal computer (or PC) is less "personal" than much of the public and press seem to imagine.

Learning to use computers and software may be likened to learning to play the piano. In order to gain command of the piano, you must first become familiar with the instrument's physical attributes—its keys, strings, and foot pedals. Then you need to learn the musical notes, clefs, and signatures (the programming language of the piano); or if you play by ear, you may begin with an already-programmed software package known in the music business as a song. Most pianists begin learning the software of the piano by learning to play scales and simple songs such as "Twinkle, Twinkle, Little Star." Then they advance to more sophisticated songs.

And so it is with learning to run the computer—although many people find that learning to operate a computer is much easier than learning to play the piano because the ideas and skills needed for computer software applications have already been acquired from school, work, and play. In other words, you do not have to learn the notes or how to program a computer; you may begin playing songs immediately.

But in learning to use a computer, as in learning to play the piano, you need to practice. Performing the exercises in this book will give you needed practice, beginning with this introductory chapter. As your reading progresses through this chapter, you will learn that your "Twinkle, Twinkle, Little Star" of computer exercises is called DOS (pronounced *dahss*). By carefully and systematically doing all the exercises in this book, you will be able to create your own music—or rather, spreadsheets—and will soon be able to say, "Roll over, Beethoven."

Before you learn to play your first piece by the famous composer, Lotus 1-2-3, you will look at some of the physical attributes of the hardware and software required for the performance. The hardware and software components used in running Lotus 1-2-3 may be organized as follows:

- An IBM PC or PC-compatible computer, which consists of:
  - A keyboard, much like one for a typewriter
  - A video screen (also called a monitor)
  - Primary memory, also called random access memory (RAM)
  - Secondary storage, which typically includes one or more floppy disk drives and a hard disk drive
- Operating system software, called the disk operating system (DOS); necessary for running the Lotus software package
- A printer (optional, but highly desirable)

FUNCTION KEYS   **NUMBER/CURSOR MOVEMENT KEYS**

1-1. Typical PC keyboard.

Hardware

The Lotus 1-2-3 spreadsheet software was designed to run on the IBM family of personal and small business computers, such as the IBM PCjr, XT, AT, and 3270-PC; it also runs on computers modeled on the IBM PC but produced by competitors of IBM. These computers, commonly called clones or IBM PC–compatibles, include COMPAQ and the AT&T PC 6300.

You do not need to know how a computer operates internally in order to use Lotus 1-2-3—any more than you need to know how the innards of a Steinway work in order to play the piano. A general understanding of what the different essential hardware components do, however, will help you get an idea of how each fits into the big picture.

The Keyboard

The keyboard is the channel through which you communicate with your computer. On a piano keyboard, you strike a key and the piano responds by making a sound called a note. On a computer keyboard, you strike a key and the computer responds by executing an instruction of the software program you are using. If you are not using a software program, the computer will do nothing when you strike a key.

The keyboard has all of the keys found on a typewriter, plus a few more. Some of these additional keys may be grouped into categories. The keys (pictured on the right side of the keyboard in figure 1-1) that look like the numeric keypad of an adding machine are just that—a numeric keypad for quickly entering numeric data.

If you look closely at these same numeric keys, you will see that they are also marked with arrows and abbreviations such as PgUp (for page up), PgDn (for page down), Home, and End. These markings indicate how the numeric keys are used to move the cursor on the screen. The cursor is the tiny, movable square of light that indicates where you are on the screen.

On the left side of the keyboard shown in figure 1-1 are ten special keys, called *function keys,* that are numbered F1 through F10. These are usually assigned special meanings by the software you are using and typically are used to set off a series of special instructions or to condense several manual keystrokes into a single keystroke. You will learn more about how Lotus 1-2-3 uses these special keys in the next chapter.

The Screen

The screen or monitor is the vehicle by which the software communicates and presents itself to you. When the Lotus 1-2-3 software wants to make you aware of something, it displays a message on the screen. If it wants you to enter information, it prompts you with a question displayed on the screen.

The screen echoes what you enter on the keyboard, displaying the characters associated with your keystrokes. It provides immediate feedback by mirroring the entry of your keystrokes so that you can see what you are typing and can monitor your work for errors.

The two basic types of monitors are black-and-white and color. The term *black-and-white* applies to monitors that are actually black-and-green, black-and-amber, or black-and-white. Black-and-white monitors only display alphanumeric text (characters from your keyboard) unless your computer has special hardware to allow it to display graphics, including drawings and graphs. Lotus 1-2-3 comes with the built-in ability to draw graphs. Unless your black-and-white monitor has access to a special add-on graphics board necessary for displaying graphs, however, you may not be able to use this feature of Lotus 1-2-3. All the other features of Lotus 1-2-3 are available to all black-and-white monitors.

Color monitors can display more than one color at a time. Most color monitors can display graphs and drawings.

Whatever type of monitor you have, be sure to adjust its brightness and contrast to levels that are most comfortable for your eyes. Some monitors only have a knob for adjusting brightness; do not be concerned if you cannot find a knob for adjusting contrast.

Memory

Most microcomputers come with a rectangular box that contains the guts of the computer and is frequently used as a pedestal for the monitor. This box usually contains the disk drives; wires coming out of the rear of the case go to the monitor and the printer. All such boxes contain a thin board that has many chips—commonly called microchips or integrated circuits—plugged into sockets on it. The board invariably has (usually in one corner) a group of eight or more chips that are called memory chips and are commonly referred to as RAM (for *random access memory*). Each chip may be about the length of your thumbnail, the width of the nail on your little finger, and the thickness of the tip of your tongue. Physically, this is the memory in your computer.

Until you turn your computer on, these chips are inactive; they do nothing and contain no information. But when you turn your computer on, they become active. Everything you see on your screen is held in these chips. Even more wonderful is the enormous amount of information these chips can hold. Less wonderful is the fact that the chips need electricity in order to contain any information input to them. Horror stories abound of electrical power failures that have caused computers to lose information contained in these chips.

The volatility of RAM renders it a temporary place for holding information. You do not want to keep information there too long because it can be lost so easily. Moreover, the amount of memory (the quantity of information these chips can hold) is limited—although the more memory chips you have in your computer, the more information your computer can contain. The solution to the insecurity and space limitation problems is to move information from the memory chips to a permanent storage medium such as a floppy disk or a hard disk.

When you want to see information previously stored on a floppy or hard disk, the information is moved from the permanent storage medium to memory chips, from which it can be accessed for display on your monitor. In fact, when you use a computer, there is usually a continual movement of information between memory chips and storage disks. All of these memory management activities are handled automatically by the computer and by the software you are using.

The quantity of information that can be contained in the memory chips is expressed in units called *kilobytes*. A kilobyte is 1,000 bytes; a byte is equivalent to one keyboard character. You may have heard or read that a particular computer comes with 256K RAM. This means that it only has enough memory chips to store 256,000 alphabetic, numeric, and punctuation characters—the number of characters in approximately 128 pages of a typical mass-market paperback book.

Besides containing the information you enter and plan to store on a disk, RAM must contain the software program you are using. Thus, the information held in the memory chips at a given time may include the software program you are using, the information you are entering from the keyboard, old information retrieved from a storage disk (this may be displayed on your screen), and the DOS software program. When you use Lotus 1-2-3, the 1-2-3 software program is placed in RAM along with the information contained in the particular spreadsheet you are creating, using, changing, or displaying.

Lotus 1-2-3 is a large program that consumes approximately 190K of your computer's available memory. The manufacturer specifically states that, to use 1-2-3, your computer must have a minimum capacity of 256K RAM; otherwise, there will not be enough memory to hold everything you need. And even with 256K, there is a limit to the size of spreadsheet you can create. If memory chips become full while you are creating a spreadsheet, the Lotus 1-2-3 software displays a message saying that you are out of memory. This creates a big problem if you have not finished creating your spreadsheet. Once you have run out of memory, you must either use your unfinished spreadsheet as is or redesign your spreadsheet as two smaller but interrelated spreadsheets—a solution that can be cumbersome to work with and less efficient than one large spreadsheet.

Storage

Floppy disks and hard disks are the physical media used with most computers today for permanent storage. They provide a permanent place to store computer-generated information, as opposed to RAM, which is temporary. A floppy disk may be removed from the computer's disk drive for external storage, for mailing to a friend, or for use in another computer. The advantages of floppy disks (as opposed to hard disks) are that they are inexpensive and that they can be removed and transported from one place to another. Their chief disadvantage is that they cannot store as much information as hard disks can. A typical floppy disk used with an IBM PC can store 360K—about 180 to 220 pages of a book.

A hard disk is nonremovable. Most hard disks are permanently installed inside the computer case and are contained in an airtight enclosure

that prevents dust from entering the actual disk environment. The minimum acceptable memory capacity of hard disks used today on PCs is 10 megabytes, which is equivalent to 10,000,000K or 6,000 to 8,000 pages of your favorite encyclopedia. Unfortunately, a 10MB hard disk typically costs from $300 to $800, whereas floppy disks cost $2 to $5 each. The advantages of hard disks (as opposed to floppy disks) include much faster transfer of stored information to and from memory chips, easy management of stored information, easier access to stored information, and the ability to store information in files that are too big to fit on a single floppy disk.

Everything stored on floppy or hard disks is stored in files. Like files in a filing cabinet, the files on a disk contain related information. Each file on a disk has a unique name that must conform to certain rules. There are two basic kinds of files: program files, which contain the software program that provides instructions to the computer on how to perform a specific application; and data files, which contain data and information that you have entered in the computer yourself, to be manipulated by the instructions in program files. When you purchase Lotus 1-2-3, you receive several floppy disks containing program files that are used by the Lotus software. A file called 123.COM contains many of Lotus's program instructions that allow you to develop the spreadsheet applications used in this book. You create the name for each data file that contains a spreadsheet you are developing.

Floppy disks must be placed in a disk drive before they can be used. A disk drive contains a read/write device that moves over the disk surface to "read" data or program files already stored on the disk into memory chips (where your computer may directly access the data and programs) or to "write" data from memory chips onto the disk for permanent storage. When the read/write head reads data or programs from the surface of a disk into memory, it transfers a copy (a mirror image) of what is on the disk into memory; it does not permanently remove or erase the original information on the disk.

Disk Operating System (DOS)

DOS is a combination of several software programs. When you purchase a PC, you must purchase DOS, since software programs will not work without it. One of its functions is to allow other software programs to run on your computer. There are two popular versions of DOS: PC DOS, which is sold by IBM; and MS DOS, which is sold by Microsoft Corporation of Bellevue, Washington. The two DOS systems are virtually identical, and both were developed by Microsoft.

When you turn your computer on, one of the first things it does is to search the disk in drive A of your computer for a DOS program file called COMMAND.COM. If it cannot find this file, you will not be able to do a thing with your computer.

The DOS programs come on one or two floppy disks, as do most other software programs. You must insert a copy of this disk into disk drive A before turning your computer on, to enable your computer to find the COMMAND.COM file it needs to get started.

Besides letting you start your computer and allowing other software programs to operate properly, DOS provides programs that enable you to manipulate the files stored on floppy and hard disks. You will learn how to use several of these programs to manipulate files later in this chapter.

Printers

Although you do not need to have a printer in order to use Lotus 1-2-3, a printer is necessary if you want to print out your spreadsheets to obtain a permanent paper record of your work.

Various types of printers are available on today's market. The printer most commonly used with spreadsheets is the dot-matrix printer, because it is fast. The quality of printing is sometimes less than desirable because the typed characters consist of tiny visible dots. Spreadsheets usually are not required to look especially attractive or typewritten, however; speed is the key. When you want to use spreadsheet information in a formal presentation, a slower-printing letter-quality printer may be the solution.

Letter-quality printers produce copy that looks typewritten. Ink-jet printers are similar to dot-matrix printers in printing appearance and work by spraying a small jet of ink on the paper surface. Plotters and graphics dot-matrix printers allow you to print graphs and pictures in addition to the standard alphanumeric and punctuation characters. Laser printers are used to produce documents with a professional, typeset appearance.

Turning Your Computer On

Insert the DOS disk into disk drive A of your computer. Disk drives on a computer, whether they are for floppy disks or hard disks, are assigned identifying letters by the computer. If you have a single floppy disk drive, this will be drive A. If you have two floppy disk drives on your computer, the one on the left (if they are side-by-side) or the one on top (if they are stacked) is usually drive A, and the other is drive B. This is not always the case, however; if you are not sure, check your computer manual.

When you have inserted the DOS disk into drive A, turn your computer on. Watch the lights on your disk drive go on and off as your computer searches for the COMMAND.COM program file and loads it into memory.

The first thing the DOS program will do after the necessary DOS program files are loaded into memory is ask you (via a monitor display) to enter today's date, as follows:

```
Current date is Tue 1-01-80
Enter new date: _
```

Do as requested. Enter today's date, using dashes (–) or slashes (/) to separate the month, day, and year, as shown on the screen. When you have entered the date, press the <Return> key.

Next, you will be requested to enter the current time, as follows:

```
Current time is 0:01:25:11
Enter new time: _
```

Enter the current time, indicating the hour and the minute only, and separating these with a colon. For example, if the current time is 8:33 A.M., enter:

```
8:33    <Return>
```

Do not type the characters *<Return>*; <Return>—and any other combination of characters in this book that appears in angle brackets—indicates that you should press the appropriate command key on the keyboard (in this case, the <Return> key) after entering 8:33. If the time is after 12:00 P.M. (noon), DOS will expect you to enter the time as 24-hour clock time and not as 12-hour clock time. For instance, if it is 4:15 P.M., you should enter the following as the current time:

```
16:15    <Return>
```

If you have entered the date and time correctly, DOS will display what is called the *DOS prompt*—a letter followed by a > character—as follows:

```
A>_
```

The letter identifies the disk drive that is currently in use. DOS is now waiting for you to tell it what to do. The cursor poised in front of the DOS prompt is waiting for you either to type in the name of a software program (such as LO-TUS) for it to execute or to type in a DOS command.

Using DOS Commands

All DOS commands can be executed only from the DOS prompt. You can not use them while you are inside (that is, in the midst of using) Lotus 1-2-3 spreadsheet software.

Displaying a Directory of Files Stored on a Disk

Frequently you will want the monitor to display a list of all the files contained on a floppy or hard disk. For example, you may create a spreadsheet, save it in a file, and then forget the name you gave it; or you may forget which floppy disk you stored a particular spreadsheet file on. In either case, you will want to see a display of the names of the files so that you can find the spreadsheet file you

want to use. To get the monitor to display a directory list of files on a disk, enter the Directory (DIR) command at the DOS prompt, so the screen reads:

```
A>DIR    <Return>
```

The names of the files on the disk in drive A will then be displayed (remember, the A> means that drive A is the active disk drive). Your display will look similar to this:

```
Volume in drive A has no label
Directory of A:\
AUTOEXEC BAT     358  10-15-85  2:56p
COMMAND  COM   18128  10-18-84  9:43a
CONFIG   SYS      80  10-15-85  3:10p
ANSI     SYS    1963  10-22-84  9:31a
4 File(s)     314090 bytes free
```

If the disk in drive A contains no files, DOS will display the following message:

```
Volume in drive A has no label
Directory of A:\
File not found
```

File names are displayed in the left-most column of the four columns of information displayed by the DIR command. The next column to the right indicates the size of each file (in bytes). In the previous example, the first file (AUTOEXEC.BAT) is 358 bytes long. The third and fourth columns, respectively, identify the last date and the last time at which information was written and stored in that file. The message at the bottom of the directory tells you the total number of files in use on the disk and the total number of bytes left on the disk. Remember that a typical PC floppy disk can hold 360,000 bytes of data. The available storage space (in bytes) remaining on the disk in the preceding example is specified at the bottom of the directory as 314,090 bytes. You must frequently check floppy disks using the DIR command to be sure they have enough room left to store your spreadsheet and other files.

If you have a second floppy disk drive, insert into it a disk that contains files. To see a directory of files on a disk drive other than the active referenced drive, you must specify the new drive by its identifying letter, followed by a colon. For instance, to see the files on drive B, you must enter the DIR command plus the drive identification:

`A>DIR B:    <Return>`

A directory for the disk on drive B will then appear.

Play with the DIR command until you feel confident that you understand its use.

Rules for Naming Files

When you create a Lotus 1-2-3 spreadsheet, you have to give the file containing that spreadsheet a name before you can save it onto disk. When it is saved onto disk, it will be stored under the name you give it. All information stored on a disk is stored in files with unique names; no two files can have identical names. Any time you feel insecure about whether or not your spreadsheet file has been saved, you may use the DIR command to display the disk's directory of files; if the file has been saved, it will be listed there under the name you gave it.

File names are divided by a period into two parts. The part to the left of the period is called the *file name*, and the part to the right of the period is called the *file name extension*. In the file name COMMAND.COM, for example, COMMAND is the file name, and COM is the file name extension. (You may have noticed that, in the directory listing on your monitor, no periods are shown between the file names and the file name extensions of the various files. This is because the DOS program is written to produce directory lists that show file names and file name extensions in separate columns, with one or more character spaces between them. This programming decision does *not* affect the way you are to enter the names of files into the computer when accessing or naming them.)

The file name may be from one to eight characters long. The file name extension may be from one to three characters long and is optional; a file name does not need to have a period or the three allowable characters following the period. Within the eight-character limit, you may use

almost any combination of characters in composing spreadsheet names, but there are some restrictions. You may not put blank spaces between, before, or after any characters in a file name, and you may not use any of the following characters in a file name:

```
+
[
]
.
^
*
=
<
>
?
:
;
|
.
~
' '
```

When naming 1-2-3 spreadsheets, you should use no more than the eight character spaces set aside for the file name. Lotus will automatically add the period and file name extension WK1, identifying the file to Lotus as one containing spreadsheet data and not program instructions. If you name a 1-2-3 spreadsheet BUDGET, for example, Lotus will automatically add .WK1 to the file name when it saves the file onto disk, and a directory listing will show the file `BUDGET WK1`.

If you enter the file name of a program file in response to the DOS prompt (A>), DOS will execute the software program in that file. When you type LOTUS in response to the DOS prompt, for example, DOS will execute the Lotus 1-2-3 spreadsheet application software, just as the DIR command causes DOS to execute the directory listing application. If you are working from drive A and the Lotus program file is on a disk in a currently inactive drive (such as drive B), you must indicate to DOS where the desired program file is by prefacing the file name with the drive letter and a colon, as follows:

`A>B:LOTUS    <Return>`

Alternatively, you may proceed in two steps. First, change the active drive to B by entering the drive letter and a colon, in response to the A> prompt:

```
A>B:    <Return>
```

Second, enter the file name, in response to the B> prompt:

```
B>LOTUS    <Return>
```

Formatting a Disk

Computer neophytes are frequently shocked to learn that new floppy disks are not ready to use when they are purchased. Before disks can be used to store files, they must be formatted by the user. You can format a disk by using a DOS program file called FORMAT.COM.

When floppy disks are manufactured, the manufacturer does not know whether you, the end user, will be using them on a computer that has the PC DOS operating system, the MS DOS operating system, the Apple DOS operating system, or one of the other operating systems available. Each computer operating system has its own unique method of reading, writing, and finding files on a disk; and before it can read, write, or find files on a disk, it must place markers on the disk that establish its own unique fingerprint there. The process is similar to making a map: first a grid is laid out to allow the cartographer to place features in the proper place, and their features are filled in.

DOS's format program begins by completely erasing everything on the disk; then it proceeds to format the disk from beginning to end, using its own unique markers. Because everything is first erased from the disk, you must take care not to format a disk containing data that should not be erased. To prevent a disaster like this from occurring, always check the files on the disk using the DIR command to make sure that it does not hold valuable files. If you use the DIR command to view the file names of a new, unformatted disk, DOS will not be able to read the disk, and your monitor will display the following error message:

```
Disk error reading drive B
Abort, Retry, Ignore? _
```

If you get this message, press A to abort and return to the DOS prompt.

The DOS FORMAT.COM program is on the DOS program files disk. To format a floppy disk, place the DOS disk containing the file FORMAT.COM in disk drive A, and place the disk you want to format in disk drive B. Check the disk in drive B to make sure that it does not have valuable files on it, by responding to the DOS prompt with a DIR command:

```
A>DIR B:    <Return>
```

If you are certain that it is safe to proceed with the formatting of the disk in drive B, enter the following response to the DOS prompt:

```
A>FORMAT B:    <Return>
```

DOS will then cause your monitor to display the following message:

```
Insert new diskette for drive B:
and strike any key when ready_
```

Because you already have a disk in drive B, you do not need to follow the Insert request. Simply press any key, and DOS will execute the FORMAT command, formatting the disk in drive B. When it has finished the formatting operation, DOS will cause your monitor to display the following message:

```
Formatting...Format complete
    362496 bytes total disk space
    362496 bytes available on disk
Format another (Y/N)?_
```

DOS is asking if you want to format another disk in drive B. If you wanted to do this, you could remove the newly formatted disk from drive B, insert another disk into drive B, and answer Y to the prompt; DOS would then begin formatting the newly inserted disk. For now, though, answer N to the Format another (Y/N)? prompt. This will terminate the FORMAT.COM program and return you to the DOS prompt.

It is a good idea to label any newly formatted disk so that you do not forget that it has already been formatted.

Backing up and Copying Files

Every computer user is responsible for maintaining and managing floppy disks and the files stored on floppy disks. Disks wear out. A pet or young child may grab a floppy disk that contains your most valuable files and chew it up. Horror stories abound, many of which could have been prevented through proper care, maintenance, and management of the floppy disks involved.

Backing up—the process of making duplicate copies of files by copying them on to another disk—is the primary method of protecting the valuable information in your disk's data files. The importance of backing up on a regular basis (such as once a week), and storing your back-up copies in a secure place cannot be stressed too much. You may use the DOS COPY command (which is automatically loaded into the memory chips of your computer when you turn the computer on) to back up a single file, a group of related files, or all files on a disk.

Backing up and Copying All Files on a Disk

Begin your practice with the COPY command by using it to back up the entire set of program files already on the DOS disk. Insert your DOS disk in drive A, if it is not there already, and insert a newly formatted disk in drive B. At the DOS prompt, enter the following COPY command:

```
A>COPY *.*  B:      <Return>
```

Watch the lights on disk drives A and B go on and off as all files are copied from the disk in drive A onto the disk in drive B. Be prepared to wait a while for the computer to complete copying the files.

The COPY command takes the following form:

```
COPY [from drive:filename] [to
drive:filename]
```

The asterisk (*) is a special DOS character. It signifies to DOS that any and all characters may be substituted for the asterisk wherever it appears in a file name or file name extension. When used (as in the preceding example) on both sides of the period (.) in place of the file name and file name extension, it tells DOS to apply the relevant command (here, COPY) to all files on the floppy disk. (The asterisk may also be used to copy a group of related files, as you will see in the next subsection.)

Now issue a DIR command for the disk in drive B, to see how the files in drive A have been copied:

```
A>DIR B:      <Return>
```

Notice that the files on the disk in drive B have been copied with exactly the same names and other directory information as the files on the disk in drive A.

Backing up and Copying a Group of Related Files

When only a few files have changed during a computing session, you can save time and disk space by copying only the changed files. For example, when you are using Lotus 1-2-3, generally the only files that get changed are those having the file name extension WK1. To copy just the files that have the file name extension WK1, you would enter the following COPY command (assuming that the floppy disk containing your original 1-2-3 data files is in drive A and that the back-up disk is in drive B):

```
A>COPY *.WK1 B:      <Return>
```

In this case, the asterisk tells DOS to copy every file having a file name extension of WK1 from the disk in drive A onto the disk in drive B. Here again the asterisk preceding the period is a wild card character that represents any and all valid characters possible in a file name. The WK1 file name extension following the period, however, limits the COPY command to copying only files that have this extension.

Now try copying a group of files from the DOS disk in drive A. Remove the disk from drive B, insert a new, formatted disk, and enter the following command in response to the DOS prompt:

```
A>COPY *.COM B:      <Return>
```

When the computer has finished copying, issue a DIR command for drive B. Notice that, as explained above, only files with the COM file name extension have been copied to the disk in drive B.

Copying a Single File

Sometimes you may just want to copy a single data file. To do this, simply enter the name of the file as the originating file in the COPY command:

```
A>COPY A:COMMAND.COM B:    <Return>
```

The only time a blank space is used, other than after the word COPY, is to separate the originating disk drive and file name from the receiving disk drive and file name. As the preceding examples have shown, it is not necessary to specify the receiving file by name if the name will remain the same after the file is copied to the receiving disk; it is only necessary to specify the letter of the receiving disk drive. If you wish to change the name of a file, however, you may do so by identifying a different file name as the receiving file:

```
A>COPY A:OLDNAME.WK1 B:NEWNAME.WK1
<Return>
```

This would cause DOS to copy the file called OLDNAME.WK1 from the disk in drive A onto the disk in drive B in a file with the name NEWNAME.WK1.

Care of Floppy Disks and Disk Drives

Even though floppy disks are referred to as permanent storage media, they are vulnerable to certain external forces that are capable of erasing or destroying the information on them. Precautions should be taken in light of the following dangers:

1. Magnetic and magnetizable items—such as paper clips, magnets, electric motors, loud speakers, and telephones—can erase information from a disk if they come into contact with or in close proximity to the disk.
2. Extreme temperatures, especially temperatures produced by direct sunlight through a window, can warp and destroy a disk.
3. Bending a disk can make it unusable.
4. Dust on a disk is like boulders on a highway, as far as the disk drive's read/write head is concerned. Dust (as well as smoke particles from cigarettes, cigars, and pipes) can damage both the disk and the read/write head.
5. Liquids and moisture can damage a disk permanently.
6. Greasy fingers can damage a disk. Do not touch the thin plastic surface of a disk with your fingers. The natural oils of your body contain acids capable of destroying the information on a disk.
7. Writing on the disk or on the disk envelope with a ball-point pen may damage a disk. Ball-point pens exert a pressure of many pounds per square inch and can destroy a disk even when applied very gently. Use felt-tip pens to mark floppy disk envelopes and labels.

Always insert the floppy disk into the disk drive properly—that is, with the large, oblong cutout in the diskette envelope facing the back of the disk drive and with the small write-protect notch on the edge of the envelope facing to your left. Inserting the disk improperly can damage the read/write head of the disk drive.

Finally, never forcibly open or close a disk drive door or handle. Many disk drives are designed in such a way that the disk drive door cannot be closed unless a disk has first been inserted into the drive. In addition, most disk drive doors are automatically and temporarily locked while data are being written onto or read from the disk inside. When a disk is being read from or written onto, the little red light on the disk drive is turned on. Never try to remove a disk when the red light is on.

Problems

1. **What computer components do you need in order to use Lotus 1-2-3?**
2. **Explain the difference between *memory* and *storage*.**
3. **Why is memory referred to as temporary storage?**
4. **Is storage really permanent? Explain why or why not.**
5. **How are memory and storage quantified in descriptions of how much information a disk or memory chips can hold?**

6. Is running out of memory equivalent to running out of disk space? Why or why not? What problems are created by each situation?

7. How can you check disk space to find out how much is still available?

8. What is DOS? What does DOS do?

9. What are some DOS programs and commands? Explain how and why they are used.

10. What are the rules for naming files?

11. Explain how the DOS COPY command is used. Explain the format of the COPY command.

12. How and when may the asterisk (*) be used in the COPY command?

13. How would you enter the COPY command to copy a file named SALESONE.WK1 to a file of a different name on the same disk? Assume that you want the receiving file to be named SALESTWO.WK1 and that the originating file is on the disk in drive A.

14. How would you enter the COPY command to copy a file named FILEONB.WK1 from the disk in drive B to the disk in drive A? Assume that the active drive is drive A and that you are entering the command in response to the DOS prompt **A>**.

15. What external forces can be harmful to floppy disks? What dangers do they pose?

2. Introduction to Lotus 1-2-3

The term *spreadsheet,* as used in this book, refers to a computer software version of the large green-and-white ruled paper worksheets that accountants use for recording, analyzing, and presenting accounting records. Before the advent of electronic spreadsheets, bookkeepers spent much of their time "putting numbers in little boxes" on paper forms of this kind.

The spreadsheets you will create using this book and Lotus 1-2-3 are sometimes referred to as *worksheets,* and their subdivided units resemble in layout the "little boxes" on a paper worksheet. Instead of being called *boxes,* however, these units are called *cells.* Lotus 1-2-3 spreadsheets are made up of thousands of cells patterned on a huge paper worksheet. In fact, looking at the portion of a Lotus spreadsheet that is visible on your computer screen at any given time is like viewing a very small part of a paper worksheet that is 1,500 feet long and 50 feet wide.

Using the Lotus 1-2-3 Manual

This book is not intended to replace the Lotus 1-2-3 manuals in describing the features of Lotus 1-2-3. Instead, you should use this chapter to supplement the material in the tutorial and introductory chapters of the Lotus 1-2-3 manual; use it as a review and a brief reference guide to basic spreadsheet terms and concepts.

Cells, Rows, Columns, and Cell Ranges

The Lotus 1-2-3 spreadsheet consists of cells identified by row and by column. Columns run vertically up and down the spreadsheet and are labeled with letters (beginning with the letter A), as illustrated in figure 2-1. There are 256 columns in a Lotus 1-2-3 spreadsheet, running from A to IV.

Rows run horizontally across the spreadsheet from left to right and are labeled with numbers (beginning with the number 1), as illustrated in figure 2-1. There are 8,192 rows in a Lotus 1-2-3 spreadsheet, running from 1 to 8192.

The place where a given row intersects a given column is called a *cell.* Each cell serves as a single box where data and formulas for the spreadsheet can be entered. A cell is referenced by the unique column letter and row number meeting at that intersection point. For example, cell B5 is the cell located where column B and row 5 intersect. A cell reference, such as B5, is also called the cell's *location* or *address.*

A *cell range* is a set of contiguous cells forming a square or rectangular group. A cell range is referenced by the cell address of the upper left-hand corner and the cell address of the lower right-hand corner of the cell range. Lotus syntax requires that you separate these two cell identifications with two periods (..) in order to signify that a cell range is being referenced. For example, Cell Range A1..B5 refers to all the cells from Cell A1 (in the upper left-hand corner) to Cell B5

2-1. Lotus 1-2-3 opening screen.

(in the lower right-hand corner), of the block of cells comprising cells A1, A2, A3, A4, A5, B1, B2, B3, B4, and B5. A cell range may be confined to a single row or column, as in the case of Cell Range A1..A15; and technically, Lotus even allows a single cell to be referenced as a cell range, as in the case of Cell Range C5..C5.

Allowable Cell Entries

The data you are allowed to enter into a cell can take different forms.

Text, labels, and headings are any combinations of alphanumeric (letter and numeral) characters and other keyboard characters that are stored by Lotus as text. You can not perform mathematical calculations with data that have been stored as text—no matter what the data look like. Labels are a specific variety of text used to identify row and column contents. On a typical spreadsheet, the labels might consist of calendar months across the top of the spreadsheet and general ledger account names down the side of the spreadsheet. Headings are the same as labels, except that they usually refer to text identifying column contents only.

Numbers are combinations of numeric characters upon which mathematical calculations are performed by formulas located in other spreadsheet cells.

Formulas and functions are mathematical expressions and statements that enable the computer to perform specific calculations using values and numbers in the formula and/or in other spreadsheet cells. Functions are special, frequently used formulas that are built into the Lotus 1-2-3 program and are accessed by means of special Lotus 1-2-3 codes. (These coded functions are not to be confused with function keys, to which Lotus assigns special commands.)

A *cell reference* is simply a shorthand way of copying the contents of one cell into another. For example, if the text *JANUARY* has been entered in Cell C6, and you enter the cell reference *+C6* in Cell Z125, the text *JANUARY* will appear in Cell Z125.

Starting Lotus 1-2-3

The instructions that follow assume you have a computer with two floppy disk drives. If your computer has a different disk drive configuration, you must install the Lotus 1-2-3 software according to the instructions in the Lotus manual for your specific disk drive and computer configuration. If you have not already done this, refer to your Lotus manual and do so now.

First, place your Lotus 1-2-3 program disk in drive A and a newly formatted disk in drive B. To start Lotus, you may enter either *LOTUS* or *123* at the DOS (A>) prompt:

A>LOTUS   <Return>

The newly formatted disk you inserted in disk drive B will be used to store data files only. In a configuration that uses two disk drives, the disk containing the program files is typically situated in drive A, and the disk for the data files is situated in disk drive B.

The first thing Lotus 1-2-3 displays on your screen is the Access Menu for selecting the program you want. Lotus 1-2-3 consists of several related software programs, including the 1-2-3 program (this is the spreadsheet program—the only program you will use with this book), the PrintGraph program (for printing graphs of spreadsheet data), the Install program (for changing the installation parameters of 1-2-3), and various utility programs (for manipulating files).

When the Access Menu is displayed, the choice 1-2-3 is already highlighted on the screen by the menu cursor. If you press the <Return> key, you will choose 1-2-3 from the menu as the program to access. If you wanted to choose a different program from the menu, you would simply move the menu cursor by pressing one of the arrow keys on your keyboard; but because you want to select the 1-2-3 program, press the <Return> key now.

The Lotus 1-2-3 Screen

Look at the Lotus 1-2-3 screen, and notice the area above the column border. This upper area of the screen is called the *control panel*. When you first encounter the Lotus screen, the only information given in the control panel is the current cell cursor location (in the upper left-hand corner of the panel) and the mode indicator (in the upper right-hand corner). The mode indicator is there to remind you of what you are performing at any given moment. Because you are not performing an operation now, the mode indicator should say READY, signifying that Lotus is ready and waiting for you to do something.

The three lines of the control panel are used for various operations and can display the following information (depending on the mode of operation):

1. *Cell contents* of the cell at which the cell pointer is located are displayed on the first line of the control panel.

2. *Command menus,* from which you may select any of various commands, are displayed on the second line of the control panel.
3. *Messages* that indicate actions you should take, describe what will happen if you do take a specific action, or prompt you to input information are also displayed on the third line of the control panel.
4. *Your input* is displayed on the second line of the control panel, before it is entered into a cell.
5. *Edit* of existing cell information is performed in the second line of the control panel when you instruct Lotus to place existing cell data there.

At the bottom of the screen, in the lower left-hand corner, is the date and time indicator.

Lotus 1-2-3's Cursors

Lotus uses three types of cursors to highlight data and mark positions on the screen.

The *cell cursor* is the bar of light that highlights the currently active cell on your monitor. You can enter data only in the currently active cell, so the cell cursor must be situated on the cell into which you want to enter data. The cell cursor is also called a *pointer* or *cell pointer;* to avoid confusion, the term *cell pointer* will be used throughout this book.

The *menu cursor* is the bar of light that highlights menu options in the control panel. Menu options may be selected either by positioning the menu cursor on the desired menu option and then pressing the <Return> key or by pressing the key matching the first letter in the name of the desired menu option. The menu cursor is also called a *menu pointer.*

The *edit/entry cursor* is the narrow underscore of light that marks your place on the edit/entry line (the second line) of the control panel when you are entering or editing cell data.

The Lotus 1-2-3 Keyboard

Figure 2-2 illustrates the special keys used by the 1-2-3 program. These keys are explained in tables 2-1 and 2-2.

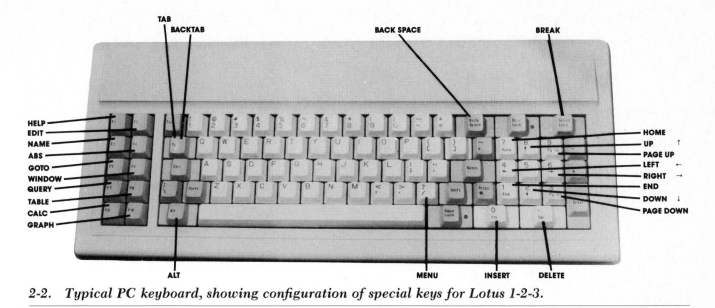

2-2. *Typical PC keyboard, showing configuration of special keys for Lotus 1-2-3.*

Combination Keys

Combination keys are keys that produce special actions when pressed either simultaneously (as <Ctrl> and <Alt> combination keys) or separately but sequentially (as <End> combination keys). Tables 2-3 and 2-4 describe the actions performed by various combination keys.

Entering Data into Cells

Before entering data into cells, always check to make sure that the mode indicator is in READY

mode and that the cell pointer is positioned on the cell you wish to receive your data entry. You may enter text, numbers, formulas, functions, or another cell reference into a cell. As you enter data into a cell, each character you enter will be echoed on the second line of the control panel so that you can see what you are typing. To complete entry of data into a cell, you must press one of the pointer movement arrow keys or the <Return> key. If you press any one of the arrow keys, your data entry will be entered in the cell, and the cell pointer will move one cell in the direction of the arrow key pressed. If you

TABLE 2-1. FUNCTION KEYS.

Key	Key Name	Action
<F1>	HELP	Displays context-sensitive help from wherever you are in 1-2-3.
<F2>	EDIT	Places contents of the currently active cell on the third line of the control panel for you to edit.
<F3>	NAME	Displays special name of named cells in response to 1-2-3 prompt to enter the name of a cell or cell range.
<F4>	ABS	Makes cell reference absolute when you are entering or editing formulas.
<F5>	GOTO	Moves cell pointer to a specific cell anywhere in the spreadsheet.
<F6>	WINDOW	Splits screen into one, two, or four different windows, for viewing different parts of the spreadsheet simultaneously.
<F7>	QUERY	Repeats last Data Query command entered.
<F8>	TABLE	Repeats last Data Table command entered.
<F9>	CALC	Forces recalculation of the spreadsheet when the spreadsheet is set for manual recalculation.
<F10>	GRAPH	Displays most recent graph developed for the current spreadsheet.

TABLE 2-2. CURSOR MOVEMENT AND EDITING KEYS.

(Please notice that numeric keys, where indicated, are found on the numeric keypad, not on the number keys located above the alphabet keys on the keyboard.)

Key	Key Name	Action
<Return>	RETURN	Enters data into a cell, indicates acceptance of command input, and initiates performance of command actions.
<Backspace>	BACKSPACE	Deletes one character to the left of the edit cursor.
<←>	LEFT ARROW	Moves edit cursor or cell pointer one space or cell to the left. (Also enters data into a cell.)
<→>	RIGHT ARROW	Moves edit cursor or cell pointer one space or cell to the right. (Also enters data into a cell.)
<↓>	DOWN ARROW	Moves cell pointer one cell down. (Also enters data into a cell.)
<↑>	UP ARROW	Moves cell pointer one cell up. (Also enters data into a cell.)
<7>	HOME	Moves cell pointer to Cell A1.
<9>	PAGE UP	Moves cell pointer up one screen (twenty rows).
<3>	PAGE DOWN	Moves cell pointer down one screen (twenty rows).
<Insert>	INSERT	Toggles between typeover mode and character insertion mode (during editing), allowing insertion of text between characters.
<Delete>	DELETE	Deletes character directly above the edit cursor (during editing).
<→ | >	TAB	Moves edit cursor five spaces to the right.
< | ←>	BACKTAB	Moves edit cursor five spaces to the left.

press the <Return> key, the cell pointer will remain on the cell that has just received your data entry.

Entering Text, Labels, and Headings

You enter text by typing your entry and then pressing the <Return> key. You may need to precede your text entry with a label alignment prefix that aligns or centers the entry. Your alignment options are as follows: left-justified (that is,

aligned to the left side of the cell); right-justified (aligned to the right side of the cell); or centered within the cell. The prefix symbols used to accomplish these three alignments are given in table 2-5.

The use of a text alignment prefix is required when you want to use a number character as the first character of a text entry. If the first character you enter into a cell is a number (0 to 9) or any one of the characters recognized by Lotus as a number character (., +, −, (, @, #, $), then Lotus assumes that character and every other succes-

TABLE 2-3. COMBINATION KEYS.

Keys	Key Name	Action
<Ctrl> + <←>	BIGLEFT	Moves cell pointer left one screen (72 characters).
<Ctrl> + <→>	BIGRIGHT	Moves cell pointer right one screen (72 characters).
<End> + <↓>	END DOWN	Moves cell pointer to the bottom of the spreadsheet.
<End> + <↑>	END UP	Moves cell pointer to the top of the spreadsheet.
<End> + <←>	END LEFT	Moves cell pointer to the far left of the spreadsheet.
<End> + <→>	END RIGHT	Moves cell pointer to the far right of the spreadsheet.
<End> + <Home>	END HOME	Moves cell pointer to the lower right-hand corner of the data entered into the spreadsheet.
<Alt> + <F1>	COMPOSE	Accesses international characters.
<Alt> + <F2>	STEP	Allows you to debug macros by single-stepping through each command.

TABLE 2-4. SPECIAL KEYS AND KEY
COMBINATIONS.

Key(s)	Key Name	Action
<Esc>	ESCAPE	Backtracks one command step or cancels current range or entry.
</>	MENU	Displays command menu.
<Alt> + <Letter>	ALT	Initiates macro.
<Ctrl> + <Break>	BREAK	Cancels current procedure.

sive character is a number, formula, or mathematical expression. For example, if you try to enter the column heading "100% TEST SCORES" into a cell, you must use a text alignment prefix to begin the heading; otherwise Lotus automatically recognizes an error in what it assumes to be a formula or numeric expression, beeps at you and puts you in the EDIT mode to correct the cell input. The solution is to enter a text alignment prefix as the first character or to rewrite the heading without a number as the first character.

Entering Numbers

You enter numbers just as you enter text—by typing your entry and then pressing the <Return> key. Acceptable characters that may be used in a numeric value entry include:

- Numbers from 0 to 9
- Decimal point (.)
- Plus (+) and minus (−) signs
- Dollar sign ($)
- Parentheses [( )]

Numbers are automatically aligned to the right side of a cell and cannot be aligned in any other way.

TABLE 2-5. LOTUS TEXT PREFIX SYMBOLS.

Text Prefix	Text Cell Justification
'	Aligns text to cell's left side.
"	Aligns text to cell's right side.
^	Centers text within cell.

Entering Formulas and Functions

You enter formulas by typing your entry and pressing the <Return> key. A formula must begin with a character that is acceptable in a number entry (as described previously) or with one of the following two characters:

1. @ (called the *at* symbol) signals a function name. Any of the many special 1-2-3 built-in functions beginning with @ may be used as part of a formula or as a formula by itself.
2. # (called the *pound* sign) denotes the special 1-2-3 logical functions AND, OR, and NOT, which may be used in formulas that return a true or false result.

A formula can use any of the mathematical operators listed in table 2-6.

Using the / (MENU) Key to Access the Lotus Command Menu

To display the 1-2-3 command menu in the control panel, press the slash (/) character on the keyboard. This is the same key that has the question mark (?) on it, and in 1-2-3 it is also known as the MENU command key. Press the / key now:

/

Having reached the command menu, you may choose a command from it in either of two ways: by moving the menu cursor to highlight the

TABLE 2-6. MATHEMATICAL OPERATORS USED BY LOTUS 1-2-3.

OPERATOR	Explanation of Operator
+	Addition
−	Subtraction
*	Multiplication
/	Division
^	Exponentiation
=	Equal to
<>	Not equal to
<	Less than
>	Greater than
>=	Greater than or equal to
<=	Less than or equal to

command of your choice and then pressing the <Return> key; or by pressing the first capital letter in the name of a command displayed on the command menu. Try to get used to the latter method (pressing the first letter in the name of a menu choice) because it is faster once you learn the commands.

What to Do if You Make a Mistake

One of the most frustrating situations to be in when you are learning a new software program occurs when you find yourself stuck in the middle of a program, not knowing how to get out; another occurs when you make a mistake and do not know how to recover. If you find yourself in either of these situations with Lotus 1-2-3, there are several potential recovery routes worth trying. Not every possible method of recovery from every possible mistake is presented here, but the suggestions that do appear should help you recover from or get out of many situations.

Using the <Esc> (ESCAPE Command) Key to Backtrack One Step at a Time

If you are looking at the command menu in the control panel right now (and you should be if you performed the last instruction to press the / [MENU command] key), press the <Esc> (ESCAPE command) key. This will return you to READY mode—demonstrating the most important feature of the <Esc> key, which is to allow you to backtrack one command step to wherever you were just before you got to where you are now. Thus, for example, if you are deep in the subcommand structure of a command, you can repeatedly press the <Esc> key to get from wherever you are all the way back to READY mode and the 1-2-3 spreadsheet.

Using the BREAK Command to Return to READY Mode

Simultaneously pressing the <Ctrl> and <Break> keys causes any ongoing procedure to cancel and returns you directly to READY mode. This is a

much quicker and more direct method of getting from wherever you are back to READY mode than is offered by repeated use of the <Esc> key. The <Break> key is identical to the <Scroll Lock> key.

Quitting 1-2-3 and Returning to the DOS Prompt

So far, we have discussed how to get from wherever you are in the program back to READY mode. But suppose you do not even want to be in READY mode—you just want to get out of Lotus 1-2-3 altogether. In this situation, first get back to READY mode; then press /, the MENU command key:

/

Then press Q, for the Quit command, or move the menu cursor to the Quit command and press the <Return> key. 1-2-3 will respond with a prompt that double-checks to see if you really want to quit or not. Answer by pressing the Y key for *yes* (if you want to quit) or the N key for *no* (if you change your mind). If you press Y, you will return to the Access Menu. At the Access Menu, press the E key for the Exit command that will take you completely out of Lotus 1-2-3 and return you to the DOS prompt.

Using the <F2> (EDIT Command) Key to Correct Mistakes in Cell Entries

The EDIT command key, <F2>, may be used to edit the contents of a cell. To edit the contents of a cell, place the cell pointer on the cell whose contents you want to edit, and then press <F2>, the EDIT command key. The contents of the cell will thereupon be placed on the second line of the control panel, where you may edit your entry. Move around the edit line by using the cursor movement keys and edit keys discussed on page 22.

Using the /Range Erase Command to Erase Cells and Cell Ranges

Suppose that you do not want to edit the contents of a cell or cell range, but instead want to blank them out completely. In this situation, you should use the /Range Erase command.

To use the /Range Erase command, first return the spreadsheet to READY mode, if you are not there already. Place the cell pointer on the cell you want to erase or on the cell in the upper left-hand corner of the cell range you want to erase. Then, press / the MENU command key:

/

Then press R, for the Range command:

R

Then press E, for the Erase command:

E

Then, if you are just erasing a single cell, simply press <Return>. If you are erasing a cell range, however, use the arrow keys on your keyboard to move the cell pointer to the cell in the lower right-hand corner of the cell range you want to erase; then press the <Return> key. Pressing the <Return> key executes the command.

The action of moving the cell pointer to indicate to Lotus 1-2-3 the cell or cell range to which a command (as described above) or a formula is to be applied is called *pointing*. This feature makes 1-2-3 extremely easy to use. You will be instructed throughout this book about when and where to use pointing to enter cell references in commands and formulas.

Using the /Worksheet Erase Command to Start Over

If you want to erase an entire spreadsheet and start over, or if you just want to erase what is on the screen and begin creating a completely new spreadsheet, use the /Worksheet Erase command. First return to READY mode, if you are not there already. Then press /, the MENU command key:

/

Then press W, for the Worksheet command:

W

Then press E, for the Erase command:

E

Then press <Return>. Pressing the <Return> key executes the command.

Using the /Range Format Command to Make Spreadsheets More Readable

Lotus 1-2-3 does not automatically format numbers with dollar signs or percentage signs unless you tell it to. The process of setting off cells and cell ranges with these and other character decorations is called *formatting* and is accomplished, in part, by using the /Range Format command. The purpose of formatting is to give the spreadsheet a neat, professional appearance and to make it easy to read; formatting is not crucial to achieving the strictly computational objectives of a spreadsheet.

One important use of formatting is to change the width of spreadsheet columns. The ability to widen columns to accommodate large numbers and long text/label strings and the ability to make columns narrow for small numbers and labels are both extremely valuable. Lotus 1-2-3 columns have a default column width of nine characters.

To change the width of a single spreadsheet column, you would use the /Worksheet Column Set-width command. To change the width of all spreadsheet columns, you would use the /Worksheet Global Column command. These are the first commands you will encounter in chapter 3.

The /Range Format command allows you to format cells and cell ranges so that they possess one or more of the following characteristics:

1. *Currency* format lets you display a dollar sign in front of numbers or values.
2. *Percent* format lets you display values with a percentage sign.
3. *Fixed* format lets you fix the number of digits to the right of a decimal point, from one to fifteen digits.
4. *Scientific* format lets you display numbers in scientific notation.
5. *Comma* format lets you display numbers greater than 999 with commas separating the thousands.

6. +/− (plus/minus) format lets you display a number as a horizontal bar graph composed of either + symbols or − symbols.
7. *Date* format lets you display a date entered in a cell in one of several different date formats.
8. *Time* format lets you display the time of day in a cell in one of several different time formats.
9. *Text* format lets you see the formulas entered in cells rather than the values resulting from calculation of the formulas.
10. *Hidden* format lets you hide the display of text, values, and formulas in cells so that they are not displayed on the screen.
11. *Reset* format lets you undo hidden formatting and reestablish the default (original) format of cells.

Spreadsheet Conventions and Assumptions Used in This Book

For the sake of brevity and clarity, several conventions are used throughout this book. Familiarize yourself with these conventions before beginning part II.

Symbols Used in This Book

This book uses the typographic symbols listed in table 2-7.

Lotus 1-2-3 Command Abbreviations

Lotus 1-2-3 commands are abbreviated in this book. The method used to abbreviate commands is to present the command exactly as you would enter it from the keyboard as a command string.

Most Lotus 1-2-3 commands require a series of several keystrokes to accomplish a complete command. Typically, each keystroke in the series makes a selection from one of a succession of menus offered by the 1-2-3 system. When you enter a command from the keyboard, you press the keyboard character that corresponds to the first capital letter of the command or that represents a built-in command (such as /, the MENU command). When struck in series, these individ-

TABLE 2-7. TYPOGRAPHIC SYMBOLS.

Symbol	Meaning
/Range	A capitalized word preceded by a slash (/) represents a Lotus 1-2-3 command.
@NOW	A word in all-capital letters or beginning with the symbol @ represents a Lotus 1-2-3 built-in function. In some situations, however, a word in all-capital letters represents a file name.
<Return>	A word, character, or combination of characters in angle brackets represents a key on your keyboard. <Return>, for example, represents the <Return> or <Enter> key on your keyboard. When used in connection with a command abbreviation, it instructs you to press the corresponding key on your keyboard.
A1..D2	Two periods between cell references indicate a cell range (that is, here, from Cell A1 to Cell D2).

ual characters form what is called a *command string*.

For example, to erase the contents of a single cell by means of the /Range Erase command, you must press four keys in succession on the keyboard: /key, the R key, the E key, and the <Return> key. The command string abbreviation for these keyboard characters is therefore:

/RE   <Return>

This example demonstrates the abbreviation method used in this book for the /Range Erase command and similar commands. The string abbreviation consists of each key (in consecutive order) that you are required to press in order to complete the command.

When you are requested to enter a command string abbreviation, begin by pressing the key associated with the first character in the command string; then continue from left to right, striking each successive key until you have completed the command. As you enter the command string, watch the screen to see how 1-2-3 responds to each keystroke.

Turning Automatic Recalculation Off

Lotus has a feature called *automatic recalculation* that allows it to recalculate all formulas entered in your spreadsheet's cells every time you enter data into a cell. Unfortunately, as your spreadsheet gets bigger and bigger, you must wait longer and longer for the entire spreadsheet to be recalculated every time you enter data into a subsequent cell. The way to avoid such lengthy and repeated delays is to turn off the automatic recalculation feature (which is active by default each time you begin using a spreadsheet).

This book assumes that you will turn off the automatic recalculation feature as your first act whenever you begin to create a new spreadsheet. To accomplish this, you must turn manual recalculation on. Begin by returning the spreadsheet to READY mode, if you are not already there. Then enter the following command string abbreviation (with the mode indicator in READY mode):

```
/WGRM
```

These characters constitute the 1-2-3 command sequence for /Worksheet Global Recalculation Manual, the command that turns manual recalculation on and automatic recalculation off.

Part II.
USING
LOTUS 1-2-3
SPREADSHEETS
IN
FOODSERVICE
OPERATIONS

3. Daily Purchases Register

TABLE 3-1. SUMMARY OF LOTUS COMMANDS USED IN THIS CHAPTER.

Commands Used

Command String Abbreviation	Command	Functions Used
/C	/Copy	@NOW
/FR	/File Retrieve	@SUM
/FS	/File Save	
/PP	/Print Printer	
/RE	/Range Erase	
/RL	/Range Label	
/RF	/Range Format	
/RNC	/Range Name Create	
/RU	/Range Unprotect	
/WCS	/Worksheet Column Set-width	
/WGE	/Worksheet Global Erase	
/WGP	/Worksheet Global Protect	
/WGR	/Worksheet Global Recalculation	

Purchasing in a foodservice operation encompasses many activities, beginning with preparing purchase specifications to ensure consistent food product quality and packaging. Other daily purchasing activities include requisitioning, purchasing, receiving, storing, issuing, and recording. The extent to which you separate these activities in your operation and the amount of paper work associated with each one depend on the size of your operation and on the level of control you want to maintain. In small operations, responsibility for many of these duties may be assigned to one person, and control may be informal. In large operations, each purchasing activity may be delegated to a different employee, who must then process and maintain the relevant paper control forms.

No matter what size your operation is, some level of purchasing control is necessary. The Daily Purchases Register is used by many foodservice operations to provide a record of daily purchases and to aid in purchasing control. Information for the Daily Purchases Register comes from delivery invoices accompanying the day's deliveries, from in-store purchase orders, from interstore transfer slips, and from credit memos sent by your suppliers. Typically, you, your manager, or your office assistant enters information from these documents at the end of each day. Information relating to each supplier is broken out and entered under the appropriate food or beverage category (see figure 3-1).

Using the Daily Purchases Register regularly gives you a readily accessible summary of many of the day's purchasing activities and provides an accurate record of purchases and deliveries from purveyors. The simple discipline of entering delivery and receiving information in the Daily Purchases Register every day keeps you in touch with fluctuating food prices, which in turn may alert you to reevaluate your recipes, your menu prices, or other factors influencing your food and beverage

| | | | MEAT/FISH | | | | | | | PAPER | ****TRANSFERS**** | | CREDITS | TOTAL BY |
SUPPLIER	GROCERY	BEVERAGE	POULTRY	FROZEN	DAIRY	PRODUCE	CHEESE	EGGS	GRAINS	PLASTIC	IN	OUT	RETURNS	SUPPLIER
ABC GROCERY SUPPLY	$249.53	$38.54	$9.55	$86.00					$16.88	$56.00			$15.25	$441.25
MOMS PRODUCE						$83.24								$83.24
BRISBANE DAIRY FARMS					$60.59									$60.59
MILPITAS EGG CO.								$125.00						$125.00
CHEESES OF ALBANY							$156.60							$156.60
DUBLIN MEAT CO.			$266.52											$266.52
LOFAT MEAT SUPPLY			$149.50											$149.50
FROM STORE 1											$18.63			$18.63
TO STORE 1												$36.99		($36.99)
KING FROZEN FOODS				$190.35										$190.35
DEEPSEA FISH CO.			$340.20											$340.20
KOOKLA COLA CO.		$46.46												$46.46
**TOTAL BY CATEGORY:	$249.53	$85.00	$765.77	$276.35	$60.59	$83.24	$156.60	$125.00	$16.88	$56.00	$18.63	$36.99	$15.25	$1,841.35
% OF TOT FOOD PURCH:	13.55%	4.62%	41.59%	15.01%	3.29%	4.52%	8.50%	6.79%	0.92%	3.04%	1.01%	2.01%	0.83%	100.00%

DAILY FOOD PURCHASES REGISTER
DATE: 03/01/86
DAY: SATURDAY
CLERK: J. Chaban

```
                    FOOD SUMMARY
                  --------------------
         BEVERAGE:         $85.00
           CHEESE:        $156.60
            DAIRY:         $60.59
             EGGS:        $125.00
           FROZEN:        $276.35
          GROCERY:        $249.53
           GRAINS:         $16.88
MEAT/FISH/POULTRY:        $765.77
          PRODUCE:         $83.24
    PAPER/PLASTIC:         $56.00
     TRANSFERS IN:         $18.63
    TRANSFERS OUT:        ($36.99)
  CREDITS/RETURNS:        ($15.25)
                  --------------------
                          $1,841.35
                  ====================
```

3-1. *Daily Purchases Register spreadsheet.*

costs. The register also allows you to review each day's receiving activity, to reconcile differences between what was ordered and what was received, and to audit your receiving clerk's performance on the basis of recording discrepancies.

Because it provides an accurate record of purchases and deliveries, the Daily Purchases Register can be used to reconcile bills and statements from suppliers at bill-paying time. It can be used as a historical reference for forecasting period purchases in budgeting and planning. Finally, it provides some of the data used in the spreadsheet in chapter 7, the Daily and Period-to-date Report, to calculate the cost of goods sold.

Before you begin creating this spreadsheet, look at figure 3-1. Notice that deliveries received from suppliers are listed and categorized in rows 9 through 20. Your own operation may receive more daily deliveries than does the operation represented in this example. If so, you will need to use more rows for suppliers in your spreadsheet than the twelve illustrated in figure 3-1. But because this book was written to serve as a tutorial and because the spreadsheet in chapter 7 relies on the information in the Daily Purchases Register spreadsheet in figure 3-1 being set down in your spreadsheet exactly as illustrated there, you should not make any modifications until you have completed working the exercises in this book and feel confident about any spreadsheet modifications you make.

Formatting, Headings, and Labels

Step 1. Reformat columns A through O from the normal Lotus default column width of nine characters to the widths indicated in table 3-2. Enter each command given in the far right-hand column of the table exactly as indicated there.

TABLE 3-2. STEP 1 FORMATTING COMMANDS.

Column	Width	Command to Enter	
A	20	/WCS20	<Return>
B through O	12	/WGC12	<Return>

The second command, /WGC12, globally sets the width of columns B through O (and all remaining columns in the spreadsheet, as well) to a width of twelve characters. The first command, /WCS20, sets the width of column A to twenty characters and ensures that column A will retain its setting when the second, global command is executed; it prevents column A from being reset to a width of twelve characters by the second, global command.

Step 2. Begin re-creating the example in figure 3-1 by entering the appropriate headings and labels into columns A through O, rows 1 through 42. Enter the headings exactly as given in table 3-3 into the corresponding cells. You may need to pad some of your cell entries with blank spaces to get your headings to look like those pictured in figure 3-1. Any heading beginning with one of the three Lotus label alignment prefixes (', ", and ^) signifies a label to be padded with blank spaces or to be given a special cell alignment. Remember (from chapter 2) that the prefix ' aligns text to the left margin of the cell, the prefix " aligns text to the right margin of the cell, and the prefix ^ centers text within the cell. Unless a label alignment prefix is indicated in table 3-3, do not use one of these prefixes to begin a label or heading.

Step 3. Enter dashed lines and double-dashed lines into the spreadsheet, as indicated in table 3-4. Use the backslash (\) key to begin each cell entry. The backslash is Lotus's command to repeat text. When used in conjunction with a dash (–) or any other single character, it will draw that character across the entire cell in which the REPEAT command character is entered.

To repeat a character across several individual cells, use Lotus's /Copy command, as indicated in table 3-4. The /Copy command copies the designated character from the beginning cell into each character space in the remaining cells of the

TABLE 3-3. STEP 2 HEADINGS.

Cell	Heading
A1	DAILY FOOD PURCHASES REGISTER
A2	''DATE:
A3	''DAY:
A4	''CLERK:
A7	SUPPLIER
A22	**TOTAL BY CATEGORY:
A23	% OF TOT FOOD PURCH:
B7	GROCERY
C7	BEVERAGE
D6	MEAT/FISH
D7	POULTRY
E7	FROZEN
F7	DAIRY
G7	PRODUCE
H7	CHEESE
I7	EGGS
J7	GRAINS
K6	PAPER
K7	PLASTIC
L6	' ****TRANSFERS****
L7	IN
M7	OUT
N6	CREDITS
N7	RETURNS
O6	TOTAL BY
O7	SUPPLIER
I25	FOOD SUMMARY
H27	'' BEVERAGE:
H28	'' CHEESE:
H29	'' DAIRY:
H30	'' EGGS:
H31	'' FROZEN:
H32	'' GROCERY:
H33	'' GRAINS:
H34	MEAT/FISH/POULTRY:
H35	'' PRODUCE:
H36	'' PAPER/PLASTIC:
H37	'' TRANSFERS IN:
H38	'' TRANSFERS OUT:
H39	'' CREDITS/RETURNS:

specified range across the spreadsheet, as is illustrated in figure 3-1 at rows 5, 8, 21, 24, 26, 40, and 42.

When using Lotus 1-2-3 to enter dashed or double-dashed lines, always position the cell pointer on the left-most cell of the row in which you want the first ruler line to begin (in this case, Cell A5), and enter the following command:

TABLE 3-4. STEP 3 REPEAT AND /COPY COMMANDS.

Cell	REPEAT Command to Enter	/Copy Command to Enter			
A5	\-	/CA5	<Return>	B5..O5	<Return>
A8	\-	/CA8	<Return>	B8..O8	<Return>
A21	\-	/CA21	<Return>	B21..O21	<Return>
A24	\=	/CA24	<Return>	B24..O24	<Return>
H26	\-	/CH26	<Return>	I26..J26	<Return>
H40	\-	/CH40	<Return>	I40..J40	<Return>
H42	\=	/CH42	<Return>	I42..J42	<Return>

\- <Return>

Next, because you want the first ruler line to extend from cells A5 to O5, you need to issue a /Copy command. To initiate the /Copy operation, place the cell pointer on Cell A5 and enter the following command:

/C   <Return>

As soon as you enter this command, Lotus prompts you to enter the cell range to copy FROM. By hitting <Return>, you indicate your acceptance of Cell A5 as the originating cell range. Lotus may show this as Cell Range A5..A5—which is the same as saying Cell A5.

Next Lotus prompts you to enter the cell range to copy TO. Lotus has a special feature that allows you to point to the cell (in this case, Cell B5 of Cell Range B5..O5) that begins the receiving cell range you want to copy the originating cell range to. Pointing is accomplished by moving the cell pointer by means of the arrow keys on your numeric keypad. Here, you point to Cell B5 by using your right arrow key to move the cell pointer to Cell B5.

Next, enter a period (.), to let Lotus know that you are ready to point to the last cell in the receiving cell range. Using the right arrow key,

move the cell pointer to Cell O5, the last cell in the receiving cell range. As you move the cell pointer, Lotus highlights the cell range. The cell range indicated in the second line of the control panel (in the upper left-hand corner of your screen) also changes as you point.

Hit the <Return> key to complete the /Copy command. Watch as Lotus copies the ruler line from Cell A5 to cells B5 through O5. The above steps may be written in the following abbreviated command form:

/C   <Return>   [point to cell B5].
[point to cell O5]   <Return>

Enter the ruler lines in rows 21, 26, and 40 and the double-dash lines (using the equal sign, =) into rows 24 and 42. Use the /Copy command and the pointing method just described to repeat these characters from one cell across a range of cells.

Step 4. Format the cells and cell ranges identified in table 3-5, as indicated there. Enter each command given in the far right-hand column of the table exactly as it appears by typing the characters shown and then hitting the <Return> key.

Some of the steps that follow contain instructions about making cells absolute when copying formulas and cell references. When a cell refer-

TABLE 3-5. STEP 4 /RANGE FORMAT COMMANDS.

Cell(s)	Format/Alignment	Command to Enter			
A6..O7	center	/RLCA6..O7	<Return>		
B2	date type 4	/RFD4	<Return>	<Return>	
B9..O22	currency	/RFC2	<Return>	B9..O22	<Return>
B23..O23	percent	/RFP2	<Return>	B23..O23	<Return>
J27..J41	currency	/RFC2	<Return>	J27..J41	<Return>

ence is made absolute in a formula, the cell reference will not change as the formula is copied; instead, it will remain exactly as you have specified in the formula. Any cell reference that you do not make absolute remains relative by default. A relative cell reference in a formula will change as the formula is copied, reflecting the formula's new cell location relative to the original cell containing the formula.

Step 5. Enter the following Lotus calendar function into Cell B2:

```
@NOW     <Return>
```

The @NOW function is one of Lotus's built-in calendar functions. If the target cell is formatted for date (as Cell B2 is), the @NOW function automatically obtains today's date from the system date you entered when you first turned on your computer—or from the date maintained by an automatic, battery-operated clock/calendar (if your computer has this feature). If the target cell is formatted for time, the time of day is returned when the @NOW function is entered.

Step 6. Enter the following formula into Cell O9:

```
@SUM(B9..L9)-(M9+N9)     <Return>
```

Rendered in English, this formula reads: "Sum the entries from cells B9 through L9 and subtract from this value the sum of cells M9 and N9." This formula totals the deliveries from each supplier. The total for each supplier should equal the total (before sales tax) on the supplier's delivery invoice.

Now copy the above formula from Cell O9 into cells O10 through O20 in column O, using the pointing method described in Step 3. When using the pointing method here, make sure that you have placed the cell pointer on cell O9 before entering the following command:

```
/C     <Return>     [point to cell O10].
[point to cell O20]     <Return>
```

When you become comfortable and familiar with pointing, you will find that it is easier than typing cell references manually. It also gives you visual confirmation of the receiving range that you are copying to and of the originating range that you are copying from.

Step 7. Enter the following formula into Cell B22:

```
@SUM(B8..B21)     <Return>
```

Rendered in English this formula reads: "Sum the entries from cells B8 through B21." This formula totals the purchases for the day for each food and beverage category.

Now copy the preceding formula from Cell B22 into cells C22 through O22 in row 22. From now on, this book will assume that you are using the pointing method in conjunction with the /Copy command and with other Lotus commands that utilize pointing. Place your cell pointer on Cell B22, and enter the following command:

```
/C     <Return>     [point to Cell C22].
[point to Cell O22]     <Return>
```

The ruler lines in rows 8 and 21 provide upper and lower limits, respectively, for summing each category. By including the ruler lines as limits in this formula and in the remaining formulas in row 22, you can insert (using the /Worksheet Insert command) or delete (using the /Worksheet Delete command) rows in the Daily Purchases Register without having to adjust these formulas or the formulas in the FOOD SUMMARY shown at the bottom of figure 3-1. The formulas in row 22 and in the FOOD SUMMARY will automatically be adjusted when new rows (which increase the range being summed) are inserted and when old rows (which decrease the range being summed) are deleted.

Step 8. Enter the following formula into Cell B23:

```
+B22/$O$22     <Return>
```

Rendered in English, this formula reads: "Divide the sum in Cell B22 by the sum in Cell O22." This formula calculates the percentage of total purchases expended in each food and beverage category.

Placing dollar signs in front of the column reference and in front of the row reference of Cell O22 makes the reference to Cell O22 absolute. This means that when the formula is subjected to a /Copy operation, the reference to Cell O22 will remain unchanged; in contrast, the reference to Cell B22 will change as it is copied.

Now use the /Copy command to copy the formula from Cell B23 into cells C23 through O23 in row 23. Place your cell pointer on Cell B23 and enter the following command:

```
/C    <Return>    [point to Cell C23].
[point to Cell O23]    <Return>
```

Because Cell O22 was designated as absolute, the reference to it will remain absolute in each formula that is copied. Examine each formula copied, and you will see that the reference to Cell O22 remains constant in each formula, while the reference to Cell B22 (which is relative) changes in response to each different column into which the formula is copied.

Lotus provides a special ABS (for *absolute*) function key, <F4>, for making a cell absolute. This feature relieves you of the tedium of having to type dollar signs in front of the column letter and the row number every time you want to make a cell reference absolute. More important, it makes editing a formula easier if you should happen to forget to make a cell reference absolute when entering the formula.

To use the ABS function key, <F4>, first place your cell pointer on Cell B23, where you entered the above formula. Then press the EDIT function key, <F2>. At this point, the formula in Cell B23 will appear on the second line of the control panel (in the upper left-hand corner of your screen), where you can edit it. Use the arrow keys, the <Backspace> key, the <Home> key, the <End> key, and the <Delete> key to move about and edit the formula.

Next, place the edit cursor under the reference to cell O22, and press the <F4> key. Notice how pressing this key changes the dollar signs in front of the reference to Cell O22. Press <F4> again, and again. The <F4> key simply changes the placement of dollar signs in front of the cell reference involved, stepping through the same dollar sign placements every four times you press it.

Hit the <Esc> key to cancel any editing you have done on the formula in Cell B22. Be sure you leave the formula exactly as it was when you originally entered it.

TABLE 3-6. STEP 9 CELL REFERENCES AND FORMULA.

Cell	Cell Reference/Formula
J27	+C22
J28	+H22
J29	+F22
J30	+I22
J31	+E22
J32	+B22
J33	+J22
J34	+D22
J35	+G22
J36	+K22
J37	+L22
J38	−M22
J39	−N22
J41	@SUM(J26..J40)

Step 9. Enter each formula or cell reference given in table 3-6 into each cell indicated in the left-hand column of the table.

Notice that the categories in the FOOD SUM-MARY are not laid out in the same order as the categories running across rows 6 and 7. The categories have been rearranged alphabetically in the FOOD SUMMARY for the sake of neatness and organization when they are transferred to the Daily and Period-to-date Report spreadsheet in chapter 7.

Notice, too, that the numeric value in a cell that is being referenced directly is transferred to the referencing cell. This method of referencing cells also works for cells that have text characters. Try directly referencing a cell that has a text heading or label, and see what happens.

Finally, notice that—if you preface a cell reference with a minus sign—the number in the cell being referenced becomes negative in the referencing cell if it was positive in the referenced cell, and becomes positive in the referencing cell if it was negative in the referenced cell. If you preface reference to a cell containing text with a minus sign, however, you get an ERR (error) message from Lotus.

Daily Operator Input

Step 10. Enter the specific data that appear in the shaded areas of figure 3-1. Input into this shaded portion of the screen is the only information you will have to enter on a daily basis. The remainder of the spreadsheet is calculated automatically. Daily operator input is described in table 3-7.

TABLE 3-7. DAILY INPUT INTO THE DAILY PURCHASES REGISTER SPREADSHEET.

Cell(s)	Input
B3	`DAY.` Enter the day of the week.
B4	`CLERK.` Enter the name of the employee filling in the spreadsheet.
A9..A20	`SUPPLIER.` Enter the names of suppliers, using the letterhead on your suppliers' delivery invoices. Use delivery invoices as a source of information for this report.
B9..N20	Food Supply Categories, `TRANSFERS`, and `CREDITS RETURNS`. Distribute the dollar amounts for each invoice by food or supply category, using the information from daily delivery invoices, credit memos, and interstore transfer forms. You can use Lotus's scratch pad feature to sum amounts for different categories when you need to distribute a single delivery invoice among several categories.

Step 11. Recalculate your spreadsheet by pressing <F9>, the CALC function key. As soon as you press this key, Lotus will automatically begin evaluating and calculating all expressions on your spreadsheet. Forcing a manual recalculation of your spreadsheet—as this procedure is called—may be performed whenever you change a value in a spreadsheet cell that is referenced by a formula. Of course, manual recalculation is only necessary when you have switched from automatic recalculation mode to manual recalculation mode (as discussed on page 27).

Protecting Your Spreadsheet

Step 12. It is important to protect the cells in the nonshaded areas of the spreadsheet from accidentally being filled (by you or by other spreadsheet users) with unwanted data. When a cell is protected, Lotus will not allow it to be altered unless it is first unprotected properly.

To protect cells in particular parts of the spreadsheet, you begin by protecting all cells in the spreadsheet. This involves entering the following command string:

`/WGPE`

This string is an abbreviated expression for the /Worksheet Global Protection Enable command, which protects every cell in the spreadsheet from entry and alteration. As an exercise in futility, now try to enter something in any cell you like.

The next step is to unprotect the cells in the shaded areas of the spreadsheet, by entering the /Range Unprotect commands indicated in table 3-8. Before entering each command, place your cell pointer on the first named cell of each cell range that you want to unprotect.

TABLE 3-8. STEP 12 /RANGE UNPROTECT COMMANDS.

Cells to Unprotect	Command to Enter	
B3..B4	`/RU [point to B4]`	<Return>
A9..N20	`/RU [point to N20]`	<Return>

Printing Your Spreadsheet

Step 13. Turn your printer on, align the paper in it, place your cell pointer on Cell A1 by pressing the <Home> key on your cursor/arrow keypad, and print your spreadsheet by issuing the following series of commands:

`/PPR.`   <End>   <Home>   <Return>   `AGPQ`

This is the abbreviated expression of the /Print Printer Go command, which in Lotus language means: "Print to the printer the spreadsheet range A1 through O42. The paper is aligned in the printer, so the spreadsheet should begin printing at the top of the page. Go and print the spreadsheet. Then page-eject the paper in the printer to the top of a new page, and quit the print commands."

The <End> and <Home> keys, when pressed consecutively, move the cell pointer to the end (that is, the lower right-hand corner) of your spreadsheet.

You may need to consult your Lotus 1-2-3 manual for information on how to adjust Lotus's printer settings for footers, margins, borders, page length, and special set-up strings. Because they vary so widely, printer configurations are beyond the scope of this book.

Because this spreadsheet will be used, erased, reused, and saved to the same file day after day, you should get in the habit of printing it every day so that you will have a permanent paper record of daily purchases. If you do not print the spreadsheet daily, the data on it will be erased from day to day as they are overwritten and replaced by new data about the following day's purchases.

If you would like to stop and take a break at this point, save the spreadsheet you are working on with Step 14. Otherwise, skip Step 14 and go on to Step 15.

Saving PURCHASE.WK1

Step 14. You can save the Daily Purchases Register spreadsheet you have created so far, by entering the following /File Save command:

`/FSB:PURCHASE    <Return>`

PURCHASE is the file name for the Daily Purchases Register spreadsheet and will be written onto the disk in drive B. If you have a hard disk or a single floppy drive system, save the PURCHASE spreadsheet to the appropriate drive and directory. When you save this file under the file name PURCHASE, Lotus will automatically add a period and the file name extension WK1 to the file name. When you look at a directory of files on drive B, you will see this file displayed as `PUR-CHASE WK1`. The WK1 extension identifies this file to you and to Lotus as a file in a spreadsheet format.

If you execute the /Quit and Exit commands to leave Lotus after saving your spreadsheet, you will need to retrieve the Daily Purchases Regis-

ter spreadsheet from disk before you can go on to Step 15. To retrieve the spreadsheet, enter the following /File Retrieve command:

`/FR [point to file name]    <Return>`

If only one file is listed on the third line of the control panel, you need not point to a file name; simply hit <Return> after entering `/FR`.

Naming Cells and Cell Ranges

Lotus has two shortcut features that enable you to enter commands and formulas in your spreadsheet without having to type cell ranges. Pointing, the first of these, has already been explained; by now, you should have some experience using the pointing method. The second feature is called *naming* cells and cell ranges, and it involves use of the /Range Name Create (`/RNC`) command.

Naming allows you to assign a descriptive name to a cell or cell range and thereafter to refer to the cell or cell range by that name in subsequent commands and formulas. For example, suppose you give Cell A5 in figure 3-1 (which contains a repeating line) the descriptive name *LINE*. Then, instead of copying A5 into B5 through O5 with the following command:

`/CA5    <Return>    B5..O5    <Return>`

you could write the following:

`/CLINE    <Return>    B5..O5    <Return>`

Similarly, you may give a complete cell range a name such as *SALES* or *EXPENSES* and thereafter refer to the cell range by that descriptive name in all commands and formulas you input into the spreadsheet. Lotus saves all the descriptive names you give to cells and cell ranges when you save your spreadsheet, retaining the relation between each cell or cell range and the name you create for it.

Step 15. You will find it very convenient to have a descriptive name for the range where you will be inputting data in the Daily Purchases Register spreadsheet every day. This area, Cell Range B9..N20 in figure 3-1, will be called INPUT_AREA. Later this name will be used in a command that erases the area to give you a clean slate on which to enter a new day's daily purchases.

To execute the /Range Name command to create the INPUT_AREA range name, first place your cell pointer on Cell B9 (the first cell of the range to be named); then enter the following command:

```
/RNCINPUT_AREA    <Return>    [point
to Cell N20]    <Return>
```

The first four characters, /RNC, represent Lotus's /Range Name Create command. They are followed by entry of the range name, INPUT_AREA. After pressing <Return> (which enters the name), you are prompted to point to the ending cell of the range you are naming (in this case, the ending cell is Cell N20). The final <Return> enters this cell range.

The obvious benefit of using descriptive names for cells and cell ranges is that you do not have to memorize (or repeatedly look up) the cell coordinates for various cells and cell ranges. Another important benefit of using names is that, when you insert or delete rows by means of the /Worksheet Global Insert or Delete command, the cell range defined for INPUT_AREA is automatically adjusted. For instance, if you were to insert a new row into the INPUT_AREA range, the INPUT_AREA range would automatically be redefined as Cell Range B9..N21. Without Lotus's /Range Name feature for cells and cell ranges, you would have to check the boundaries of the INPUT_AREA cell range each day (before you erased this area prior to entering a new day's daily purchases) to make sure you were not erasing something that should not be lost. In contrast, when you refer to this cell range by its descriptive name, INPUT_AREA, in a /Range Erase command, the INPUT_AREA cell range will have been adjusted automatically for any new added or deleted rows.

NOTE: A range name cannot be more than fourteen characters long.

Creating and Using Macros

The area where you or your manager enters the dollar amounts for daily purchases, Cell Range B9..N20, needs to be erased every day after you retrieve your Daily Purchases Register spreadsheet file. Erasing the area gives you a clean slate on which to enter the current day's delivered purchases.

Manually performing this action every day can be cumbersome, but there is an easy way to automate this procedure, using Lotus's macro capabilities. A *macro* (or *macroinstruction*) is a set of Lotus commands, consolidated into a single computer instruction. The commands involved are the same ones you have been entering up to this point—although, of course, Lotus possesses other commands that you have not encountered yet that may also be used to create a macro.

A macro is created by typing Lotus commands into a section of the Daily Purchases Register spreadsheet. The commands to be entered are those that you would normally need to enter from your keyboard to perform the action of erasing Cell Range B9..N20. You enter the macro command as you would a text label or heading, using the left-align prefix, '.

The advantage of a macro is that, once it has been created, all of the commands included in it can be executed automatically with a single instruction to Lotus.

When a macro is executed, each command in it is executed in succession. Look at the macro in the lower left-hand corner of the spreadsheet in figure 3-2. This macro has only one command, which is as follows:

```
/REINPUT_AREA~
```

This /Range Erase command erases the cell range associated with the range name INPUT_AREA. The ˜ character is called a tilde; it means the same thing to Lotus that <Return> or <Enter> means to you in this book—it instructs Lotus to perform the equivalent of pressing the <Return> key, which in the above command enters the /Range Erase command and terminates it. You will find the ˜ key next to the <Return> key on your keyboard.

SUPPLIER	GROCERY	BEVERAGE	MEAT/FISH POULTRY	FROZEN	DAIRY	PRODUCE	CHEESE	EGGS	GRAINS	PAPER PLASTIC	TRANSFERS IN	TRANSFERS OUT	CREDITS RETURNS	TOTAL BY SUPPLIER
DAILY FOOD PURCHASES REGISTER														
DATE: 03/01/86														
DAY: SATURDAY														
CLERK: J. Chaban														
ABC GROCERY SUPPLY	$249.53	$38.54	$9.55	$86.00					$16.88	$56.00			$15.25	$441.25
MOMS PRODUCE						$83.24								$83.24
BRISBANE DAIRY FARMS					$60.59									$60.59
MILPITAS EGG CO.								$125.00						$125.00
CHEESES OF ALBANY							$156.60							$156.60
DUBLIN MEAT CO.			$266.52											$266.52
LOFAT MEAT SUPPLY			$149.50											$149.50
FROM STORE 1											$18.63			$18.63
TO STORE 1												$36.99		($36.99)
KING FROZEN FOODS				$190.35										$190.35
DEEPSEA FISH CO.			$340.20											$340.20
KOOKLA COLA CO.		$46.46												$46.46
**TOTAL BY CATEGORY:	$249.53	$85.00	$765.77	$276.35	$60.59	$83.24	$156.60	$125.00	$16.88	$56.00	$18.63	$36.99	$15.25	$1,841.35
% OF TOT FOOD PURCH:	13.55%	4.62%	41.59%	15.01%	3.29%	4.52%	8.50%	6.79%	0.92%	3.04%	1.01%	2.01%	0.83%	100.00%

```
                   --------MACRO NAME-------    --------MACRO--------
                   :                                                 :
                   :            \E              /REINPUT_AREA~        :
                   :                                                 :
                   -----------------------------------------------------
                   Execute macro by pressing <alt>-<e> keys simultaneously.
```

FOOD SUMMARY

BEVERAGE:	$85.00
CHEESE:	$156.60
DAIRY:	$60.59
EGGS:	$125.00
FROZEN:	$276.35
GROCERY:	$249.53
GRAINS:	$16.88
MEAT/FISH/POULTRY:	$765.77
PRODUCE:	$83.24
PAPER/PLASTIC:	$56.00
TRANSFERS IN:	$18.63
TRANSFERS OUT:	($36.99)
CREDITS/RETURNS:	($15.25)
	$1,841.35

3-2. *Daily Purchases Register spreadsheet, showing the \E macro.*

Step 16. Enter the following macro command into Cell C29, as shown (beginning with a ' character, the left-align label prefix):

```
'/REINPUT__AREA~
```

Macro Rule #1. Always enter a macro command as a left-aligned text/label entry, using the left-align prefix character ' (a single apostrophe).

You have just created a macro. Obviously, creating a macro is rather easy. Now you need to set up this macro so that you can execute it automatically. All you need to do to set up a macro for automatic execution is to give it a name—just as you named the INPUT__AREA range earlier, but with one exception.

Macro Rule #2. A macro name can only be two characters long. The first character must be the backslash (\) character—not to be confused with the slash (/) character used to enter Lotus commands. The second character must be a letter in the alphabet, from A to Z.

Step 17. Name the macro you entered into Cell C29. Since this is an erase macro, you can name it \E. First place your cell pointer on Cell C29, if it is not there already, and enter the following command:

```
/RNC\E    <Return>    <Return>
```

The first three letters, /RNC, represent Lotus's /Range Name Create command; they are followed by the entry of the cell name, \E. After pressing <Return>, which enters the name, you are prompted to point to the ending cell of the range you are naming (again, Cell C29). There is no need to point this time, because you are naming the same cell that the cell pointer already is on. Hitting <Return> a second time enters this cell.

Step 18. Enter the following label into Cell B29:

```
'\E
```

Try to get in the habit of marking down the name you give each macro on your spreadsheet by entering the macro's name in the first cell to the left of the cell where the macro begins. This has nothing whatsoever to do with making the macro perform its commands; it is simply a way for you to avoid forgetting what you named the macro.

Now you are almost ready to try out your macro by executing it. But wait! When your macro executes its command instruction, it will erase the INPUT—AREA range of the Daily Purchases Register. Before that happens, you want to save your Daily Purchases Register spreadsheet with all the data in the INPUT—AREA range intact (as illustrated in figure 3-1) so that the Daily and Period-to-date Report spreadsheet in chapter 7 will work properly.

Remember that, after you issue a /File Retrieve command to bring up an existing spreadsheet from disk, you are working with it in memory only. It is not written back onto the disk until you perform a /File Save operation. This means that any changes you make in a spreadsheet while it is in memory—even if those changes are made using a macro—do not affect the original file stored on the disk. It is safe to play with a spreadsheet as long as the original version remains stored on disk and as long as you do not save your doctored-up version to the same file with the same file name and extension. If you do not like what you have done to the copy of the file you are playing with, you can always use the /Worksheet Erase command to zap the spreadsheet from your screen and memory and then issue a /File Retrieve command to recall the original version from disk.

Step 19. Save the Daily Purchases Register spreadsheet with the following command:

```
/FSB:PURCHASE    <Return>
```

If you already saved the Daily Purchases Register spreadsheet in Step 14, you will have to tell Lotus to overwrite the existing file PURCHASE.-WK1 on disk, replacing it with your latest version, as follows:

```
/FS [point to PURCHASE.WK1]
 <Return>    R
```

Step 20. Execute the macro by holding down the <Alt> key and the E key simultaneously.

Macro Rule #3. Always execute a macro by pressing the <Alt> key and pressing the letter (from A to Z) that you used in your macro name. Lotus recognizes a macro name because only macro names are allowed to begin with a backslash. Think of the backslash as representing the <Alt> key.

Notice that, as figure 3-3 illustrates, your macro command has erased the INPUT—AREA cell range and that the formulas in Row 23 say ERR. This is because Lotus cannot divide a number by zero, so it returns an error message in the cell.

Remember, do not save the Daily Purchases Register spreadsheet onto disk with the INPUT—AREA erased, or you will overwrite the intact PURCHASE.WK1 file. You have already saved your spreadsheet, with data intact, and will need it as originally saved in order for the spreadsheet in chapter 7 to work properly.

Macro Rule #4. When entering a macro that consists of more than one command, always place each subsequent command into a separate cell directly below the preceding command. Lotus always begins reading macro commands at the named macro cell and reads from left to right until all characters in the first cell have been read. When Lotus reaches the last character in the cell, it drops down to the next cell below. If there is another command in the cell below, Lotus resumes reading from left to right. If the next cell below is blank, the macro automatically terminates.

You may use as many commands in a macro as you can fit in a single spreadsheet column below the first, named cell. As long as Lotus does not encounter a blank cell, it will continue executing one command after another.

	SUPPLIER	GROCERY	BEVERAGE	MEAT/FISH POULTRY	FROZEN	DAIRY	PRODUCE	CHEESE	EGGS	GRAINS	PAPER PLASTIC	****TRANSFERS**** IN	OUT	CREDITS RETURNS	TOTAL BY SUPPLIER
1	DAILY FOOD PURCHASES REGISTER														
2	DATE: 03/01/86														
3	DAY: SATURDAY														
4	CLERK: J. Chaban														
9	ABC GROCERY SUPPLY														$0.00
10	MOMS PRODUCE														$0.00
11	BRISBANE DAIRY FARMS														$0.00
12	MILPITAS EGG CO.														$0.00
13	CHEESES OF ALBANY														$0.00
14	DUBLIN MEAT CO.														$0.00
15	LOFAT MEAT SUPPLY														$0.00
16	FROM STORE 1														$0.00
17	TO STORE 1														$0.00
18	KING FROZEN FOODS														$0.00
19	DEEPSEA FISH CO.														$0.00
20	KOOKLA COLA CO.														$0.00
22	**TOTAL BY CATEGORY:	$0.00	$0.00	$0.00	$0.00	$0.00	$0.00	$0.00	$0.00	$0.00	$0.00	$0.00	$0.00	$0.00	$0.00
23	% OF TOT FOOD PURCH:	ERR	ERR	ERR	ERR	ERR	ERR	ERR	ERR	ERR	ERR	ERR	ERR	ERR	ERR

```
                                                      FOOD SUMMARY
         --------MACRO NAME-------------  ---MACRO-------------
       :                                                    :         BEVERAGE:     $0.00
       :            \E            /REINPUT_AREA~             :           CHEESE:     $0.00
       :                                                    :            DAIRY:     $0.00
                                                                         EGGS:     $0.00
       Execute macro by pressing <alt>-<e> keys simultaneously.        FROZEN:     $0.00
                                                                      GROCERY:     $0.00
                                                                       GRAINS:     $0.00
                                                          MEAT/FISH/POULTRY:     $0.00
                                                                      PRODUCE:     $0.00
                                                                PAPER/PLASTIC:     $0.00
                                                                 TRANSFERS IN:     $0.00
                                                                TRANSFERS OUT:     $0.00
                                                              CREDITS/RETURNS:     $0.00

                                                                                   $0.00
```

   : DAILY PURCHASES REGISTER AFTER EXECUTING \E MACRO :

3-3. *Daily Purchases Register spreadsheet after execution of the \E macro.*

Macro Rule #5. Always leave a blank cell beneath the last command in a macro. This lets Lotus know that it has reached the end of the macro.

Macro Rule #6. Always begin creating a macro by manually executing the keystrokes you would need to enter to perform the action you wish to automate. On a piece of paper, write down each key you press as you manually execute the commands.

Macro Rule #7. Never enter a blank space (using your keyboard's space bar) into a macro unless you intend to create a blank space in a cell. Any time Lotus encounters blank spaces in the process of executing a macro, it enters the blank spaces into the current cell.

Macro Rule #8. Always put your macros in an out-of-the-way area of your spreadsheet so that, if you need to expand your spreadsheet, they will not get in the way. But be careful not to put a macro in a place where you might insert or delete rows. This sort of precarious placement can result in inadvertantly erased macro commands or in macros with gaping blank spaces that cause premature macro termination.

Using the Information in This Spreadsheet

Total by Supplier

The total by supplier (calculated by the spreadsheet) equals the sum of a supplier's category breakdown minus the transfers out and the credits/returns. Use this total when entering data into the Daily Purchases Register, to make sure you have entered all amounts from a delivery invoice. The total of a delivery invoice (not including sales tax) should equal the total by supplier figure. You should also use this total to reconcile bills and statements from your suppliers when you pay bills. Charges by suppliers for deliveries not recorded in the Daily Purchases Register suggest one of the following:

1. The employee who received the goods (your receiving clerk) lost the delivery invoice.
2. You are being charged for goods not received.
3. Employees are making unauthorized purchases.
4. The supplier's delivery person is stealing from you and from the supplier.

Total by Category

The total by category (calculated by the spreadsheet) equals the sum of all deliveries in a single food or beverage category. Use this total to track the dollar amount your operation spends daily on each food category. These totals can alert you to overspending in a single category and can serve as a warning signal for food cost/pilferage problems in your operation. The Daily and Period-to-date Report explained in chapter 7 keeps track of accumulated purchases in each category over whatever period you establish.

Percentage of Food Purchases

The percentage of food purchases (calculated by the spreadsheet) equals the category total divided by the total daily purchases. Use this percentage in conjunction with the dollar total by category to track your spending in any single category. You may want to adapt the Daily Purchases Register to accumulate dollar totals by category for a period of time and keep an accumulated calculation of the percentage of total food purchases. This additional information will assist you in developing a benchmark for how much (by percentage) each category total varies; significant variances may provide warning signals on food costs.

Problems

1. List five activities involved in the purchasing process.
2. Describe how the Daily Purchases Register can be used to help manage and control a food-service operation.
3. Explain what the TRANSFERS column in the Daily Purchases Register is used for.
4. Explain how to define a cell range by pointing. Use cell references in your explanation.
5. Describe Lotus's /Range Format command. In your description, include explanations of how the following format characteristics can be used to change the format of a cell:
   • currency
   • fixed
   • percent
   • date
   • , [comma]
   • general
6. Explain how a cell used in a formula may be relative.
7. Explain how a cell used in a formula may be absolute.
8. Define a *macro*. How are macros used in a spreadsheet?
9. Explain the /Range Name command. How are named cell ranges used in commands and formulas?
10. How does a name created by a /Range Name command for a macro differ from names created by the same command for nonmacro cells and cell ranges?
11. Make a list of ideas and procedures explained in this chapter which may be vague, ambiguous, or difficult for you to understand. Submit this list to your instructor for class discussion.

Cases

1. Insert a new row into your spreadsheet between row 8 and row 21, using the /Worksheet Insert Row command. You will need to disable the existing spreadsheet protection first, using the /Worksheet Global Protection Disable command.
   a. What happens to the formulas in column O when you insert the row? What happens to the cell range associated with the range name INPUT_AREA?

b. Use the /Copy command to copy the formula in column O into Cell O__ in the row you just inserted. (You must supply the row number!)

c. What happens to the formulas in row 23 labeled PERCENT OF TOTAL PURCHASES when you insert the row?

d. What happens to the formulas in row 22 labeled TOTAL BY CATEGORY when you insert the row?

2. Add the following delivery invoice in the row you just inserted:

Supplier	Meat/Fish/Poultry	Frozen
Bristol Meats	$100.00	$50.00

Recalculate the spreadsheet using the <F9> key. How do the totals change in column O? In rows 22 and 23?

3. Delete the row you just added, using the /Worksheet Delete Row command.

a. What happens to the formulas in column O when you delete the row? What happens to the cell range associated with the range name INPUT__AREA?

b. What happens to the formulas in row 23 labeled PERCENT OF TOTAL PUR- CHASES when you delete the row?

c. What happens to the formulas in row 22 labeled TOTAL BY CATEGORY when you delete the row?

4. There is a problem with the macro created for the Daily Purchases Register spreadsheet: when the INPUT__AREA range is erased, the formulas are not recalculated to show $0.00 (zero) totals (assuming that the /Worksheet Global Recalculation is set for manual recalculation). How can the macro be rewritten so that the spreadsheet turns automatic recalculation on before the INPUT__AREA range is erased but then resets the spreadsheet for manual recalculation after the INPUT__AREA range is erased?

4. Physical Inventory and Valuation

TABLE 4-1. SUMMARY OF LOTUS COMMANDS USED IN THIS CHAPTER.

Commands Used

Command String Abbreviation	Command Name	Functions Used
/C	/Copy	@SUM
/DS	/Data Sort	
/FR	/File Retrieve	
/FS	/File Save	
/PP	/Print Printer	
/RE	/Range Erase	
/RF	/Range Format	
/RNC	/Range Name Create	
/RU	/Range Unprotect	
/WGE	/Worksheet Global Erase	
/WGP	/Worksheet Global Protect	
/WGR	/Worksheet Global Recalculation	
/WI	/Worksheet Insert	

A physical inventory valuation provides the ending inventory value used in calculating the cost of goods sold for your profit-and-loss statement. The cost of goods sold is a necessary component in calculations of percentage food and beverage costs—costs that are used throughout the foodservice industry as a benchmark for food and beverage cost control. Accurate cost of goods sold and percentage food and beverage costs calculations depend on accurate physical inventorying.

A truism accepted by all foodservice operators is that accurate financial and managerial control over food costs cannot be achieved without taking an accurate physical inventory. Periodically taking a physical inventory is imperative in any foodservice business.

Some foodservice operators believe that the task of taking a physical inventory can be automated. Some individuals wish themselves into thinking that computers can eliminate the need to take a physical inventory; but no computer or software program has yet been designed that will physically count your inventory.

Computers can, however, provide some relief in the physical inventory process. The process of manually taking a physical inventory consists of the following steps:

1. *Print an inventory form.* This form lists all your inventory items, leaving blank spaces where you can enter the quantity on hand for each item and the count unit (for example, pounds, ounces, each, cases, or boxes).
2. *Take a physical inventory.* Count each inventory item and record the quantity on hand and the count unit on your printed form. It is a good idea to take inventory with a partner—one person counting and the other writing the information on the printed form.
3. *Price the inventory.* Go to the files where you keep delivery invoices and look up the latest

45

prices you have paid for goods. Use these invoices as your source of information for prices. Calculate the per-count-unit price.

4. *Extend and total the inventory.* Calculate the extended value of each inventory item by multiplying the per-unit price by the quantity on hand. Total the value of each inventory food and beverage category (meat, produce, dairy, and so on). Calculate the grand total value of the entire inventory. Have someone in your organization check your multiplication and addition.

The spreadsheet in this chapter provides some relief to taking a physical inventory by automating items 1 and 4 in the process described above.

The inventory spreadsheet shown in figures 4-1 and 4-2 functions in two ways: it provides a printed form for taking a physical inventory (see figure 4-1); and after you have input your inventory counts from the printed form into the computer spreadsheet, it automatically extends and totals the inventory values (see figure 4-2).

It is important that you regularly update the price per count unit before you value your inventory. A fundamental principle of inventory stock control in foodservice operations is to rotate the inventory so that the oldest items are used first. This principle forms the basis for valuing your inventory using the First In, First Out (FIFO) method of inventory control. Left on the shelf at inventory time should be the most recent items purchased, and these may be reflected on your inventory by the most recent prices paid.

Most computer inventory programs (including the spreadsheet illustrated in this chapter) require that a supplier's prices be continually updated by you or your data entry person; if current price information is not maintained, the inventory valuations will be inaccurate. One schedule for maintaining prices has already been described in item 3. This method assumes that you will wait until you take an inventory before updating prices on your inventory worksheet. Another schedule for maintaining prices involves updating the price per count unit (see figure 4-1) in the spreadsheet on a daily or weekly basis.

The spreadsheet in this chapter is built on the assumption that you take inventory in a regular sequence—that is, that you physically follow the order of your inventory in placing items on the shelf in your storeroom, walk-in, and so on. Before you begin using the spreadsheet presented here, go through your present inventory and arrange the inventory items on paper in order by their location and by the sequence in which you regularly take inventory. You will use this order to rearrange your electronic inventory spreadsheets every time you take a physical inventory.

Another assumption made in this chapter is that you group inventory items on your inventory forms by category (meat, produce, groceries, dairy, and so on). This way, you can see how much you are spending in each category for purposes of control and food cost analysis. The spreadsheet presented here uses this type of categorical arrangement. Inventory items will automatically be rearranged and grouped by category after the quantity-on-hand amount from a physical inventory has been entered on the spreadsheet.

You will need to create a numbering system for your inventory. Each inventory item on the spreadsheet is assigned an *item number* (see figure 4-1)—a code unique to that item. Notice that each category in figure 4-1 has been assigned a consecutive range of numbers. The BEVERAGES category, for example, ranges from item number 1000 to item number 1999; the GROCERIES category ranges from 3000 to 5999; and the PRODUCE category ranges from 6200 to 7499. You will need to design your actual numbering system so that each category has a sufficient range of numbers to allow new inventory items to be added to the category without any danger of running out of numbers.

Notice that the last number in each category is reserved, not for an inventory item, but for the category name. It is important that you use the last number in each category range for this purpose. Before creating your inventory spreadsheet, review your present inventory and then code each item according to its category.

This spreadsheet will be used to provide inventory and food cost data for the Daily and Period-to-date Report spreadsheet in chapter 7. It will also be used in chapter 10 to price menu

```
:A:: B :: C :: D    :: E:: F :: G :: H :: I :: J :: K :: L :
1  PHYSICAL INVENTORY AND VALUATION
2                         DATE: FEBRUARY 28, 1986
3                 COUNTER'S NAME: J. CHABAN
4                  WRITER'S NAME: M. DALTON
5  ------------------------------------------------------------------------
6          COUNT   ITEM                 COUNT QUANTITY PRICE PER        CATEGORY
7  LOC  SEQUENCE  NUMBER  DESCRIPTION   UNIT  ON HAND COUNT UNIT EXTENSION TOTALS
8
9  S1       1    1000 COFFEE           LB     25.00    $2.95    $73.75  _____
10 S1       3    1001 ORANGE PEKOE TEA BOX     6.00    $2.15    $12.90  _____
11 S2       6    1002 ROOT BEER        TANK    3.00   $15.00    $45.00  _____
12 S2       7    1003 APPLE JUICE      GAL     3.00    $5.25    $15.75  _____
13 ============ 1999 ==========================TOTAL BEVERAGES:        $147.40
14 F1       1    2000 MOZZERELLA       LB     15.00    $2.15    $32.25  _____
15 W1       1    2001 AMERICAN CHEESE  LB     20.00    $1.89    $37.80  _____
16 W1       2    2002 MOZZERELLA       LB     40.00    $2.15    $86.00  _____
17 W1       3    2003 WISCONSIN CHEDDAR LB    40.00    $3.25   $130.00  _____
18 ============ 2099 ===========================TOTAL CHEESES:         $286.05
19 W1       4    2100 HOMOGENIZED MILK 1/3PT   9.00    $0.27     $2.43  _____
20 W2       1    2101 HOMOGENIZED MILK 1/2GL   7.50    $0.94     $7.05  _____
21 W2       2    2102 COTTAGE CHEESE   LB     15.80    $1.10    $17.38  _____
22 W2       3    2103 SOLID BUTTER     LB     41.00    $1.47    $60.27  _____
23 ============ 2197 ============================TOTAL DAIRY:           $87.13
24 W2       4    2198 EGGS             DOZ    67.00    $0.90    $60.30  _____
25 ============ 2199 =============================TOTAL EGGS:           $60.30
26 F1       2    2200 CHOPPED SPINACH  BOX     2.00    $0.98     $1.96  _____
27 F1       3    2201 CABBAGE ROLLS    CASE   18.00   $11.50   $207.00  _____
28 F2       1    2202 RAVIOLIS         CASE    3.00   $10.00    $30.00  _____
29 F2       2    2203 LASAGNA          CASE    1.00   $12.00    $12.00  _____
30 ============ 2999 =====================TOTAL FROZEN FOODS:          $250.96
31 S1       4    3000 TUNA             CANS    5.00    $8.99    $44.95  _____
32 S1       5    3001 COTTONSEED OIL   TIN     0.75   $18.22    $13.67  _____
33 S2       8    3002 SUGAR PACKETS    CASE    3.33    $7.57    $25.21  _____
34 S2       9    3003 CATSUP - 33%     CAN     7.00    $4.89    $34.23  _____
35 ============ 5999 =========================TOTAL GROCERIES:         $118.05
36 S2       1    6000 WHITE RICE       LB     43.00    $1.23    $52.89  _____
37 S2       2    6001 LENTILS          LB     23.50    $1.10    $25.85  _____
38 S2      10    6002 SMALL WHITE BEANS LB    20.25    $1.56    $31.59  _____
39 S2      11    6003 BLACK BEANS      LB     61.67    $1.75   $107.92  _____
40 ============ 6199 ===========================TOTAL GRAINS:          $218.25
41 S2      12    6200 YELLOW ONIONS    LB      1.75    $0.15     $0.26  _____
42 W2       7    6201 ICEBERG LETTUCE  CASE    2.25    $9.89    $22.25  _____
43 W2       8    6202 TOMATOES         CASE    4.75   $17.65    $83.84  _____
44 W2       9    6203 BROCCOLI         LB     36.00    $0.98    $35.28  _____
45 ============ 7499 ==========================TOTAL PRODUCE:          $141.63
46 F2       3    7500 GROUND BEEF - BULK LB   52.40    $2.75   $144.10  _____
47 F2       4    7501 SAUSAGE LINKS    LB      8.50    $1.75    $14.88  _____
48 W2       5    7502 BACON            LB     11.00    $2.10    $23.10  _____
49 W2       6    7503 GROUND BEEF - BULK LB   10.50    $2.75    $28.88  _____
50 ============ 8999 =====================TOTAL MEAT/POULTRY:          $210.95
51 S1       2    9000 PAPER FOOD DIVIDERS BOX  9.00    $2.25    $20.25  _____
52 S2       3    9001 #6 BROWN BAGS    CASE    0.75   $25.00    $18.75  _____
53 S2       4    9002 12 OZ PAPER CUPS CASE    0.70   $48.99    $34.29  _____
54 S2       5    9003 STRAWS           BOX     5.00    $3.25    $16.25  _____
55 ============ 9999 ====================TOTAL PAPER/PLASTIC:          $89.54
56        9999999 _____                                             _____
57 _____ 9999999 _____                                            _____
58 _____ 9999999 _____                                            _____
59 _____ 9999999 _____                                            _____
60 ------------------------------------------------------------------------
61                                                       $1,610.27 $1,610.27
62 ========================================================================
63
64     INVENTORY SUMMARY:                                  LOCATION CODES:
65                        CATEGORY       RANGES FOR        S1 = STOREROOM #1
66             CATEGORY    TOTALS      ITEM NUMBERS:       S2 = STOREROOM #2
67     -----------------------------------------------    F1 = FREEZER #1
68          BEVERAGE:    $147.40      1000 TO 1999        F2 = FREEZER #2
69            CHEESE:    $286.05      2000 TO 2099        W1 = WALK-IN #1
70             DAIRY:     $87.13      2100 TO 2197        W2 = WALK-IN #2
71              EGGS:     $60.30      2198 TO 2199
72            FROZEN:    $250.96      2200 TO 2999
73           GROCERY:    $118.05      3000 TO 5999
74            GRAINS:    $218.25      6000 TO 6199
75           PRODUCE:    $141.63      6200 TO 7499
76  MEAT/FISH/POULTRY:   $210.95      7500 TO 8999
77      PAPER/PLASTIC:    $89.54      9000 TO 9999
78     -----------------------------------------------
79                      $1,610.27
80     =======================================
81
82     :  INVENTORY VALUATION AFTER EXECUTING \V MACRO  :
83     -----------------------------------------------
```

4-1. Physical Inventory and Valuation spreadsheet after execution of the \V macro.

```
: A::  B  ::  C  ::      D      :: E::   F   ::  G  ::  H  ::   I   :: J :: K :: L :
1   PHYSICAL INVENTORY AND VALUATION
2                            DATE: FEBRUARY 28, 1986
3                   COUNTER'S NAME: J. CHABAN
4                    WRITER'S NAME: M. DALTON
5   ----------------------------------------------------------------------------
6            COUNT    ITEM                     COUNT QUANTITY PRICE PER          PHYSICAL
7   LOC SEQUENCE  NUMBER   DESCRIPTION         UNIT  ON HAND COUNT UNIT EXTENSION  COUNT
8   ----------------------------------------------------------------------------
```

LOC	COUNT SEQUENCE	ITEM NUMBER	DESCRIPTION	COUNT UNIT	QUANTITY ON HAND	PRICE PER COUNT UNIT	EXTENSION	PHYSICAL COUNT
F1	1	2000	MOZZERELLA	LB	15.00	$2.15	$32.25	
F1	2	2200	CHOPPED SPINACH	BOX	2.00	$0.98	$1.96	
F1	3	2201	CABBAGE ROLLS	CASE	18.00	$11.50	$207.00	
F2	1	2202	RAVIOLIS	CASE	3.00	$10.00	$30.00	
F2	2	2203	LASAGNA	CASE	1.00	$12.00	$12.00	
F2	3	7500	GROUND BEEF - BULK	LB	52.40	$2.75	$144.10	
F2	4	7501	SAUSAGE LINKS	LB	8.50	$1.75	$14.88	
S1	1	1000	COFFEE	LB	25.00	$2.95	$73.75	
S1	2	9000	PAPER FOOD DIVIDERS	BOX	9.00	$2.25	$20.25	
S1	3	1001	ORANGE PEKOE TEA	BOX	6.00	$2.15	$12.90	
S1	4	3000	TUNA	CANS	5.00	$8.99	$44.95	
S1	5	3001	COTTONSEED OIL	TIN	0.75	$18.22	$13.67	
S2	1	6000	WHITE RICE	LB	43.00	$1.23	$52.89	
S2	2	6001	LENTILS	LB	23.50	$1.10	$25.85	
S2	3	9001	#6 BROWN BAGS	CASE	0.75	$25.00	$18.75	
S2	4	9002	12 OZ PAPER CUPS	CASE	0.70	$48.99	$34.29	
S2	5	9003	STRAWS	BOX	5.00	$3.25	$16.25	
S2	6	1002	ROOT BEER	TANK	3.00	$15.00	$45.00	
S2	7	1003	APPLE JUICE	GAL	3.00	$5.25	$15.75	
S2	8	3002	SUGAR PACKETS	CASE	3.33	$7.57	$25.21	
S2	9	3003	CATSUP - 33%	CAN	7.00	$4.89	$34.23	
S2	10	6002	SMALL WHITE BEANS	LB	20.25	$1.56	$31.59	
S2	11	6003	BLACK BEANS	LB	61.67	$1.75	$107.92	
S2	12	6200	YELLOW ONIONS	LB	1.75	$0.15	$0.26	
W1	1	2001	AMERICAN CHEESE	LB	20.00	$1.89	$37.80	
W1	2	2002	MOZZERELLA	LB	40.00	$2.15	$86.00	
W1	3	2003	WISCONSIN CHEDDAR	LB	40.00	$3.25	$130.00	
W1	4	2100	HOMOGENIZED MILK	1/3PT	9.00	$0.27	$2.43	
W2	1	2101	HOMOGENIZED MILK	1/2GL	7.50	$0.94	$7.05	
W2	2	2102	COTTAGE CHEESE	LB	15.80	$1.10	$17.38	
W2	3	2103	SOLID BUTTER	LB	41.00	$1.47	$60.27	
W2	4	2198	EGGS	DOZ	67.00	$0.90	$60.30	
W2	5	7502	BACON	LB	11.00	$2.10	$23.10	
W2	6	7503	GROUND BEEF - BULK	LB	10.50	$2.75	$28.88	
W2	7	6201	ICEBERG LETTUCE	CASE	2.25	$9.89	$22.25	
W2	8	6202	TOMATOES	CASE	4.75	$17.65	$83.84	
W2	9	6203	BROCCOLI	LB	36.00	$0.98	$35.28	

```
46  ============  1999 =================================TOTAL BEVERAGES:    $147.40
47  ============  7499 =================================TOTAL PRODUCE:      $141.63
48  ============  2199 =================================TOTAL EGGS:          $60.30
49  ============  2099 =================================TOTAL CHEESES:      $286.05
50  ============  9999 =================================TOTAL PAPER/PLASTIC: $89.54
51  ============  8999 ====================TOTAL MEAT/POULTRY:              $210.95
52  ============  2999 =================================TOTAL FROZEN FOODS: $250.96
53  ============  2197 =================================TOTAL DAIRY:         $87.13
54  ============  5999 =================================TOTAL GROCERIES:    $118.05
55  ============  6199 =================================TOTAL GRAINS:       $218.25
56  _____  9999999  _____                  _____
57  _____  9999999  _____                  _____
58  _____  9999999  _____                  _____
59  _____  9999999  _____                  _____
60  ----------------------------------------------------------------------------
61                                              $1,610.27 $1,610.27
62  ============================================================================
63
64         INVENTORY SUMMARY:                          LOCATION CODES:
65                          CATEGORY       RANGES FOR   S1 = STOREROOM #1
66              CATEGORY     TOTALS      ITEM NUMBERS:  S2 = STOREROOM #2
67         --------------------------------------      F1 = FREEZER #1
68             BEVERAGE:    $147.40      1000 TO 1999  F2 = FREEZER #2
69               CHEESE:    $286.05      2000 TO 2099  W1 = WALK-IN #1
70                DAIRY:     $87.13      2100 TO 2197  W2 = WALK-IN #2
71                 EGGS:     $60.30      2198 TO 2199
72               FROZEN:    $250.96      2200 TO 2999
73              GROCERY:    $118.05      3000 TO 5999
74               GRAINS:    $218.25      6000 TO 6199
75              PRODUCE:    $141.63      6200 TO 7499
76     MEAT/FISH/POULTRY:   $210.95      7500 TO 8999
77        PAPER/PLASTIC:     $89.54      9000 TO 9999
78         --------------------------------------
79                         $1,610.27
80         ============================================
81         --------------------------------------------
82         :  INVENTORY VALUATION AFTER EXECUTING \P MACRO  :
83         --------------------------------------------
```

4-2. Physical Inventory and Valuation spreadsheet after execution of the \P macro.

TABLE 4-2. STEP 1 FORMATTING COMMANDS.

Column	Width	Command to Enter	
A	4	/WCS4	<Return>
B	9	/WCS9	<Return>
C	9	/WCS9	<Return>
D	20	/WCS20	<Return>
E	6	/WCS6	<Return>
F through I	10	/WGC10	<Return>

entries and update inventory costs for items used in recipes.

Formatting, Headings, and Labels.

Step 1. Reformat columns A through I from the normal, Lotus default column width of nine characters to the widths indicated in table 4-2. Enter the command given in the far right-hand column of table 4-2 exactly as indicated there.

The last command, /WGC10, globally sets the width of columns F through I (and all remaining columns in the spreadsheet, as well) to a width of ten characters. The preceding commands, which individually set the widths for columns A through E, ensure that these columns will retain their settings when the global command is executed. Columns B and C are individually set to the existing default width, specifically to prevent their widths from being reset to ten characters by the final global command.

You may need to make the width of column H greater than ten characters in your actual spreadsheet if your total inventory valuation is $10,000 or more, in order to accommodate the extra digit. For the purpose of this exercise and tutorial, however, do not make any such changes.

Step 2. Begin re-creating the example shown in figure 4-1 by entering the appropriate headings and labels into columns A through L, rows 1 through 77, exactly as specified in table 4-3. You may need to pad some of your cell entries with blank spaces to get your headings to look like those pictured in figure 4-1. Any heading beginning with one of the three Lotus label alignment prefixes (', ", and ^) signifies a label to be padded with blank spaces or to be given a special cell alignment. Remember that the prefix ' aligns text

TABLE 4-3. STEP 2 HEADINGS.

Cell	Heading
A1	PHYSICAL INVENTORY AND VALUATION
D2	''DATE:
D3	''COUNTER'S NAME:
D4	''WRITER'S NAME:
A7	LOC
B6	''COUNT
B7	''SEQUENCE
C6	''ITEM
C7	''NUMBER
D7	^DESCRIPTION
E6	COUNT
E7	UNIT
F6	''QUANTITY
F7	''ON HAND
G6	'' PRICE PER
G7	''COUNT UNIT
H7	' EXTENSION
I6	^CATEGORY
I7	^TOTALS
C13	1999
G13	TOTAL BEVERAGES:
C18	2099
G18	TOTAL CHEESES:
C23	2197
G23	TOTAL DAIRY:
C25	2199
G25	TOTAL EGGS:
C30	2999
G30	TOTAL FROZEN FOODS:
C35	5999
G35	TOTAL GROCERIES:
C40	6199
G40	TOTAL GRAINS:
C45	7499
G45	TOTAL PRODUCE:
C50	8999
F50	TOTAL MEAT/FISH/POULTRY:
C55	9999
G55	TOTAL PAPER/PLASTIC:
D64	INVENTORY SUMMARY
D66	''CATEGORY
F65	CATEGORY
F66	TOTALS
H65	RANGES FOR
H66	ITEM NUMBERS:
D68	''BEVERAGE:
D69	''CHEESE:
D70	''DAIRY:

Continued

TABLE 4-3. CONTINUED.

Cell	Heading
D71	''EGGS:
D72	''FROZEN:
D73	''GROCERY:
D74	''GRAINS:
D75	''MEAT/FISH/POULTRY:
D76	''PRODUCE:
D77	''PAPER/PLASTIC:
H68	'1000 TO 1999
H69	'2000 TO 2099
H70	'2100 TO 2197
H71	'2198 TO 2199
H72	'3000 TO 5999
H73	'6000 TO 6199
H74	'6200 TO 7499
H75	'7500 TO 8999
H76	'9000 TO 9999
J64	LOCATION CODES:
K65	S1 = STOREROOM #1
K66	S2 = STOREROOM #2
K67	F1 = FREEZER #1
K68	F2 = FREEZER #2
K69	W1 = WALK-IN #1
K70	W2 = WALK-IN #2

to the left margin of the cell, the prefix " aligns text to the right margin of the cell, and the prefix ^ centers text within the cell. Unless a label alignment prefix is indicated in table 4-3, do not use one of these prefixes to begin a label or heading.

Step 3. Enter dashed lines and double-dashed lines into the spreadsheet, as indicated in table 4-4. Use the backslash (\) key to begin each cell entry. The backslash is Lotus's command to repeat text. When used in conjunction with a dash (–) or any other single character, it will draw that character across the entire cell in which the REPEAT command character is entered.

To repeat a character across several individual cells, use Lotus's /Copy command, as indicated in table 4-4. The /Copy command copies the designated character from the beginning cell into each character space in the remaining cells of the specified range across the spreadsheet, as is illustrated in figure 4-1 at (for example) rows 5, 8, 13, and 18. Use the pointing method described on page 34 to define the last cell of a cell range

when performing the /Copy operation. Remember to place the cell pointer on the originating cell (the cell being copied from) before you begin to enter each command listed in table 4-4.

Step 4. Format the cells and cell ranges identified in table 4-5, as indicated there. Enter each command given in the far right-hand column of the table exactly as it appears, by typing the characters shown and then hitting the <Return> key. When formatting a cell range, use the pointing method to define the last cell in each indicated cell range. Be sure to place the cell pointer on the first cell indicated in the far left-hand column of table 4-5 before entering the associated command.

Step 5. Before entering any formulas (steps 6 and 7), you should enter the specific data that appear in the shaded areas of figure 4-1. Input into this shaded portion of the screen is the only information you will normally have to enter. The remainder of the spreadsheet is calculated automatically. The only times you will need to input data into this spreadsheet are when you add new inventory items, change information on existing inventory items, or enter quantities on hand after having taken a physical inventory. Standard input is described in table 4-6.

A single inventory item may be located in several different storage places in your foodservice operation. In your actual inventory spreadsheet, be sure to list such an item more than once; multiple listings for an item ensure that none of its storage locations will be overlooked when an employee is taking inventory.

Formulas

Some of the steps that follow contain instructions about making cells absolute when copying formulas and cell references. The meaning of absolute and relative cells is discussed on pages 34–35 .

Step 6. Enter the following formula into Cell H9:

+F9*G9

Rendered in English, this formula reads: "Multiply the entry in Cell F9 (the quantity on hand) by the entry in cell G9 (the price per count unit)."

Now use the /Copy command and the pointing method to copy the formula from Cell H9 into the

TABLE 4-4. STEP 3 REPEAT AND / COPY COMMANDS.

Cell	REPEAT Command to Enter	/Copy Command to Enter			
A5	\‐	/CA5	\<Return\>	B5..I5	\<Return\>
A8	\‐	/CA8	\<Return\>	B8..I8	\<Return\>
A13	\=				
B13	\=				
D13	\=	/CD13	\<Return\>	E13..F13	\<Return\>
A18	\=				
B18	\=				
D18	\=	/CD18	\<Return\>	E18..F18	\<Return\>
A23	\=				
B23	\=				
D23	\=	/CD23	\<Return\>	E23..F23	\<Return\>
A25	\=				
B25	\=				
D25	\=	/CD25	\<Return\>	E25..F25	\<Return\>
A30	\=				
B30	\=				
D30	\=	/CD30	\<Return\>	E30..F30	\<Return\>
A35	\=				
B35	\=				
D35	\=	/CD35	\<Return\>	E35..F35	\<Return\>
A40	\=				
B40	\=				
D40	\=	/CD40	\<Return\>	E40..F40	\<Return\>
A45	\=				
B45	\=				
D45	\=	/CD45	\<Return\>	E45..F45	\<Return\>
A50	\=				
B50	\=				
D50	\=	/CD50	\<Return\>	E50..E50	\<Return\>
A55	\=				
B55	\=				
D55	\=	/CD55	\<Return\>	E55..F55	\<Return\>
A60	\‐	/CA60	\<Return\>	B60..I60	\<Return\>
A62	\=	/CA62	\<Return\>	B62..I62	\<Return\>
D67	\‐	/CD67	\<Return\>	E67..I67	\<Return\>
D78	\‐	/CD78	\<Return\>	E78..I78	\<Return\>
D80	\=	/CD80	\<Return\>	E80..F80	\<Return\>

cells and cell ranges indicated in table 4-7. When using the pointing method, place the cell pointer on the first cell indicated in the left-hand column of table 4-7 and then enter the associated command indicated in the right-hand column.

The blank lines at the bottom of the inventory spreadsheet in rows 56 through 59 are to be used for entering new inventory items, both on the printed form during a physical inventory and into the computer spreadsheet during input of information from your printed forms. When the inventory is sorted by item number, as explained in Step 16 of this chapter, new inventory items entered on these lines will automatically be inserted into their proper inventory category. Notice that these blank lines have been assigned the item number 9999999 to ensure that, when sorted, they will end up at the bottom of the spreadsheet.

TABLE 4-5. STEP 4 / RANGE FORMAT COMMANDS.

Cell(s)	Format/Alignment	Command to Enter				
F8..F60	Fixed—two decimal places	/RFF2	\<Return\>	F8..F60	\<Return\>	
G8..G60	currency	/RFC2	\<Return\>	G8..G60	\<Return\>	
H8..H62	currency	/RFC2	\<Return\>	H8..H62	\<Return\>	
I13	currency	/RFC2	\<Return\>	\<Return\>		
I18	currency	/RFC2	\<Return\>	\<Return\>		
I23	currency	/RFC2	\<Return\>	\<Return\>		
I25	currency	/RFC2	\<Return\>	\<Return\>		
I30	currency	/RFC2	\<Return\>	\<Return\>		
I35	currency	/RFC2	\<Return\>	\<Return\>		
I40	currency	/RFC2	\<Return\>	\<Return\>		
I45	currency	/RFC2	\<Return\>	\<Return\>		
I50	currency	/RFC2	\<Return\>	\<Return\>		
I55	currency	/RFC2	\<Return\>	\<Return\>		
I61	currency	/RFC2	\<Return\>	\<Return\>		
F68..F80	currency	/RFC2	\<Return\>	F68..F80	\<Return\>	

Step 7. Enter the formula or cell reference given in table 4-8 into each corresponding cell indicated in the left-hand column of the table.

When entering @SUM formulas, you may want to use the pointing method to define the beginning and ending cells of each cell range

TABLE 4-6. DATA INPUT INTO THE PHYSICAL INVENTORY AND VALUATION SPREADSHEET.

Cell	Input
E2	DATE. Enter the date of the physical inventory.
E3	COUNTER'S NAME. Enter the counter's name.
E4	WRITER'S NAME. Enter the writer's name.
A9..A59	LOC (Location Code). Enter the code identification for the storeroom, freezer, walk-in, refrigerator, or general location area of the inventory item.
B9..B59	COUNT SEQUENCE. Enter the sequence in which the inventory items are counted within each location. Usually this is the order in which you have placed the items on shelves.
C9..C59	ITEM NUMBER. Enter the inventory item number you have assigned to each inventory item.
D9..D59	DESCRIPTION. Enter the general description or name of each inventory item.
E9..E59	COUNT UNIT. Enter the unit you want to use to count each item for inventory purposes. This may or may not be the same as the delivery unit (the unit used by the supplier in packaging and delivering the item). Many inventory items, upon being received, are unpacked and broken down into smaller units for convenience of storage and counting.
F9..F59	QUANTITY ON HAND. Enter the quantity on hand for each inventory item in your physical inventory.
G9..G59	PRICE PER COUNT UNIT. Enter the current price being used to value each item in your inventory. In computing this price (if your count unit differs from your supplier's delivery unit), you will need to adjust the price by dividing the latest delivery unit price by the number of count units in a delivery unit.
I9..I59	CATEGORY TOTALS. Enter a ten-character-long underline from your keyboard as follows: "_____ This blank space is only used for entering your physical count by hand on the printed physical inventory form when taking an inventory. Otherwise, the underline is protected on your spreadsheet and is not used for data entry.

TABLE 4-7. STEP 6 / COPY COMMANDS.

Copy Cell H9 to Cells:	Command to Enter			
H10..H12	/CH9	\<Return\>	H10..H12	\<Return\>
H14..H17	/CH9	\<Return\>	H14..H17	\<Return\>
H19..H22	/CH9	\<Return\>	H19..H22	\<Return\>
H24	/CH9	\<Return\>	H24..H24	\<Return\>
H26..H29	/CH9	\<Return\>	H26..H29	\<Return\>
H31..H34	/CH9	\<Return\>	H31..H34	\<Return\>
H36..H39	/CH9	\<Return\>	H36..H39	\<Return\>
H41..H44	/CH9	\<Return\>	H41..H44	\<Return\>
H46..H49	/CH9	\<Return\>	H46..H49	\<Return\>
H51..H54	/CH9	\<Return\>	H51..H54	\<Return\>

to be summed. The following steps are involved:

1. Place the cell pointer on the cell into which you will be entering the @SUM formula.
2. Type the beginning of the formula (the characters preceding the cell range), as follows:

@SUM(

TABLE 4-8. STEP 7 FORMULAS AND CELL REFERENCES.

Cell	Cell Reference/Formula
I13	@SUM(H9..H13)
I18	@SUM(H14..H18)
I23	@SUM(H19..H23)
I25	@SUM(H24..H25)
I30	@SUM(H26..H30)
I35	@SUM(H31..H35)
I40	@SUM(H36..H40)
I45	@SUM(H41..H45)
I50	@SUM(H46..H50)
I55	@SUM(H51..H55)
H61	@SUM(H8..H60)
I61	@SUM(I8..I60)
F68	I13
F69	I18
F70	I23
F71	I25
F72	I30
F73	I35
F74	I40
F75	I45
F76	I50
F77	I55
F79	@SUM(F67..F78)

3. Point to the first cell of the cell range that is to be summed, using the arrow keys on your keyboard.
4. Enter a single period (.) from your keyboard.
5. Point to the last cell of the cell range that is to be summed.
6. Enter the closing parenthesis,), from your keyboard.
7. Press the \<Return\> key, and the formula will be entered in the cell.

Step 8. Recalculate your spreadsheet by pressing the CALC function key, \<F9\>. As soon as you press this key, Lotus will automatically begin evaluating and calculating all expressions on your spreadsheet. See page 37 for more information about forcing a manual recalculation of your spreadsheet.

Protecting Your Spreadsheet

Step 9. Use the /Worksheet Global Protection Enable command, followed by Unprotect commands for the shaded areas only, to protect the cells in the nonshaded areas of the spreadsheet from accidentally being filled (by you or by other spreadsheet users) with unwanted data. Begin by entering the following command string:

/WGPE

This string is an abbreviated expression for the /Worksheet Global Protection Enable command, which protects every cell in the spreadsheet from entry and alteration.

The next step is to unprotect the cells in the shaded areas of the spreadsheet, by entering the /Range Unprotect commands indicated in table 4-9. Before entering each command, place your cell pointer on the first named cell of each cell range that you want to unprotect.

Cells E3 and E4 are to be used for entering the names of the two people who take the physical inventory—the person who counts the inventory and the person who writes the quantity on hand onto the inventory forms. Spaces are provided for both people's names, even though you may not be using this team inventory method in your operation. Be careful not to protect these two cells.

Printing Your Spreadsheet

Step 10. Turn your printer on, align the paper in it, place your cell pointer on Cell A1 by pressing the <Home> key on your cursor/arrow keypad, and print your spreadsheet by issuing the following series of commands:

    /PPR.   <End> <Home> <Return>   AGPQ

This abbreviated command language means: "Print to the printer the spreadsheet range A1 through L80. The paper is aligned in the printer, so the spreadsheet should begin printing at the top of the page. Go and print the spreadsheet. Then page-eject the paper in the printer to the top of a new page, and quit the print commands."

For more information on the <End> and <Home> keys and on Lotus's printer settings, see page 38.

Saving INVENTRY.WK1

If you would like to stop and take a break at this point, save the spreadsheet you are working on with Step 11. Otherwise, skip Step 11 and go to Step 12.

Step 11. You can save the Physical Inventory and Valuation spreadsheet you have created so far, by entering the following /File Save command:

    /FSB:INVENTRY   <Return>

INVENTRY is the file name for the Physical Inventory and Valuation spreadsheet and will be written onto the disk in drive B. If you have a hard disk or a single floppy drive system, save the INVENTRY spreadsheet onto the appropriate drive and directory. When you save this file under the file name INVENTRY, Lotus will automatically add a period and the file name extension WK1 to the file name. When you look at a directory of files on drive B, you will see this file displayed as INVENTRY WK1. The WK1 extension identifies this file to you and to Lotus as a file in a spreadsheet format.

If you execute the /Quit and Exit commands to leave Lotus after saving your spreadsheet, you will need to retrieve the Physical Inventory and

TABLE 4-9. STEP 9 / RANGE UNPROTECT COMMANDS.

Cells to Unprotect	Command to Enter
E2..E4	/RU [point to E4] <Return>
A9..G12	/RU [point to G12] <Return>
A14..G17	/RU [point to G17] <Return>
A19..G22	/RU [point to G22] <Return>
A24..G24	/RU <Return>
A26..G29	/RU [point to G29] <Return>
A31..G34	/RU [point to G34] <Return>
A36..G39	/RU [point to G39] <Return>
A41..G44	/RU [point to G44] <Return>
A46..G49	/RU [point to G49] <Return>
A51..G54	/RU [point to G54] <Return>
A56..G59	/RU [point to G59] <Return>

Valuation spreadsheet from disk before you are able to go on to Step 12. To retrieve the spreadsheet, enter the following /File Retrieve command:

```
/FR [ point to file name]   <Return>
```

If only one file is listed on the third line of the control panel, you need not point to a file name; simply hit <Return> after entering **/FR**.

Creating and Using Macros

To prepare the spreadsheet each time you take a physical inventory, you will need to sort the inventory items by their location, in the sequence in which you take inventory. After you take your physical inventory and enter the quantities on hand in the computer spreadsheet, you will need to re-sort the inventory spreadsheet by item number and then extend and total the spreadsheet.

Since performing these steps manually may be cumbersome, it is advisable to create a macro to do this work for you. As discussed on page 39, a macro is a set of instructions to Lotus consisting of a succession of Lotus commands, all of which, when the macro is executed, are automatically performed.

The macro created in chapter 3 contained only one command. The two macros that will be created in this chapter, in contrast, will be composed of several commands each. The two macros will perform different specific functions.

One macro will be named \P (for *physical inventory form*). This macro will automatically sort the inventory items in the spreadsheet by their location in your workplace and by the count sequence for each location. The resulting spreadsheet may then be printed and used as a form for taking a physical inventory.

The second macro will be named \V (for *valuation*). This macro will automatically re-sort the inventory items by item number after you have entered your physical inventory count in the computer spreadsheet, and then it will automatically extend and total the spreadsheet's physical inventory data.

Before creating the first macro, it is necessary to name the area of the spreadsheet that will be sorted by the two macros—namely Cell Range A9..I59. This area of the spreadsheet will be called SORT-AREA.

Step 12. To execute the /Range Name command to create the SORT-AREA range name, first place your cell pointer on cell A9 (the first cell of the range to be named); then enter the following command:

```
/RNCSORT-AREA    <Return>    [point to
Cell I59]    <Return>
```

The first four characters **/RNC**, represent Lotus's /Range Name Create command. They are followed by entry of the range name, SORT-AREA. After pressing <Return> (which enters the name), you are prompted by Lotus to point to the ending cell of the range you are naming (in this case, the ending cell is Cell I59). The final <Return> enters this cell range.

Step 13. Begin creating the \P macro (see figures 4-1 and 4-3) by entering each macro command in the appropriate cell, as indicated in table 4-10. The command explanation in the far right-hand column of the table documents the action initiated by the corresponding command; each explanation should be entered in column E, opposite the command to which it refers.

Macro Rule #9. Never put more than one complete Lotus command in a single cell in a macro. This rule makes Macro Rule #10 easier to follow.

Macro Rule #10. Always document each macro command in the column to the right of the macro command. Documenting each command is important because, if you ever need to change an undocumented macro at a future date, you may have a very difficult time figuring it out—especially if it is a large, complex macro.

Two of the commands listed in table 4-10 require some explanation: the {GOTO} command in cells B90 and B93; and the lengthy /Data Sort command in Cell B96.

The {GOTO} command in curly brackets ({}) is one of Lotus's many curly-bracket commands, all of which are reserved especially for macros. The {GOTO} command moves the cell pointer to the cell identified next in the command. The tilde (˜) following the characters {GOTO} acts as a <Return> key, instructing Lotus to perform the

```
      : A:: B  :: C ::        D      :: E:: F  :: G ::  H  ::  I  :: J  :: K  :: L  :
84  M
85  A N
86  C A
87  R M
88  O E MACRO COMMANDS                    COMMAND EXPLANATION
89  === ================================  ========================================
90  \P  {GOTO}I6~                         * Go to Cell I6.
91      /RU~                              * Unprotect Cell I6.
92      ^PHYSICAL~                        * Enter the label "PHYSICAL" in Cell I6.
93      {GOTO}I7~                         * Go to Cell I7.
94      /RU~                              * Unprotect Cell I7.
95      ^COUNT~                           * Enter the label "COUNT" in Cell I7.
96      /DSRDSORT-AREA~PA9~A~SB9~A~G      * Sort inventory for taking a physical inventory.
97      {GOTO}A1~                         * Go to Cell A1.
98
99  \V  {GOTO}I6~                         * Go to Cell I6.
100     /RU~                              * Unprotect Cell I6.
101     ^CATEGORY~                        * Enter the label "PHYSICAL" in Cell I6.
102     /RP~                              * Protect Cell I6.
103     {GOTO}I7~                         * Go to Cell I7.
104     /RU~                              * Unprotect Cell I7.
105     ^TOTALS~                          * Enter the label "COUNT" in Cell I7.
106     /RP~                              * Protect Cell I7.
107     /DSRDSORT-AREA~PC9~A~G            * Sort inventory for extending and totaling.
108     {CALC}                            * Recalculate the spreadsheet.
109     {GOTO}A1~                         * Go to Cell A1.
110
```

4-3. **\P and \V *macros.***

action of the command. Thus the command performs the same sequence of actions that you would perform manually from the keyboard by pressing the GOTO function key, <F5>, entering the name of the cell you want the pointer to go to, and then pressing <Return> to execute the command. Tables of other curly-bracket commands are given on pages 59–60.

To understand the /Data Sort command, it is best to consider the command section by section. You can get a better idea of how the command works by manually entering each portion of the command as it is brought up for consideration.

The first three characters of the command, /DS, initiate the /Data Sort command.

The next character, R, resets and clears any previous settings for the sort data range (in this case, SORT-AREA) and the primary and secondary sort columns. Lotus does not automatically clear command settings for the /Data Sort command and several other commands such as /Print. It stores the settings with your spreadsheet when you save the file. Therefore, you must make sure that all previous settings have been cleared before performing a data sort; otherwise, you risk ruining your spreadsheet with erroneous sort settings.

The next command character, D, calls forth the Lotus prompt for the data range to sort. The data range is the complete cell range you want to sort, which you indicate by specifying a range name or the upper left-hand and lower right-hand cells in the range. The \P macro automatically supplies the range name, SORT-AREA, in response to the

TABLE 4-10. STEP 13 MACRO COMMANDS AND COMMAND EXPLANATIONS.

Cell	Command	Command Explanation
B90	{GOTO}I6~	* Go to Cell I6.
B91	'/RU~	* Unprotect Cell I6.
B92	^PHYSICAL~	* Enter the label ''PHYSICAL'' in Cell I6.
B93	{GOTO}I7~	* Go to Cell I7.
B94	'/RU~	* Unprotect Cell I7.
B95	^COUNT~	* Enter the label ''COUNT'' in Cell I7.
B96	'/DSRDSORT-AREA~PA9~A~SB9~A~G	* Sort inventory.
B97	{GOTO}A1~	* Go to Cell A1.

TABLE 4-11. STEP 16 MACRO COMMANDS AND COMMAND EXPLANATIONS.

Cell	Command	Command Explanation
B99	{GOTO}I6~	* Go to Cell I6.
B100	'/RU~	* Unprotect Cell I6.
B101	^CATEGORY~	* Enter the label ''CATEGORY'' in Cell I6.
B102	'/RP~	* Protect Cell I6.
B103	{GOTO}I7~	* Go to Cell I7.
B104	'/RU~	* Unprotect Cell I7.
B105	^TOTALS~	* Enter the label ''TOTALS'' in Cell I7.
B106	'RP~	* Protect Cell I7.
B107	'/DSRDSORT-AREA~PC9~A~G	* Sort inventory.
B108	{CALC}	* Recalculate the spreadsheet.
B109	{GOTO}A1~	* Go to Cell A1.

Lotus prompt, and the tilde (<Return> equivalent) following the range name in the command enters this name.

The next command characters, PA9~A~, specify the column in the sort range that will be used as the primary column on which the data will be sorted. Only a single cell from the primary sort column is needed to specify the primary sort column. The macro here specifies Cell A9, indicating to Lotus to sort the data range (either alphabetically or numerically) on the basis of the labels or values in column A. The data range, SORT-AREA, of the Physical Inventory and Valuation spreadsheet will automatically be sorted in alphabetic order because the entries in column A are labels, not values. Figure 4-1 shows the SORT-AREA data range alphabetized by column A, the location code. The tilde following A9 tells Lotus to accept Cell A9 as the primary sort column indicator, at which point Lotus responds with a prompt to enter an A or a D to indicate whether it should perform the sort in ascending or descending order. The macro specifies A, for ascending order—from A to Z or from 1 to infinity. Had it specified D, the SORT-AREA data in figure 4-1 would have been sorted from location code W2 to location code F1 instead of vice versa. The tilde following the A (for *ascending*) indicates to Lotus to accept ascending order as your choice.

The next command characters, SB9~A~, specify a secondary sort. The SORT-AREA data in figure 4-1 are sorted not only by location code but (within each inventory location) by count se-

quence in column B. Together, the two sorts arrange every inventory item on the physical inventory form by storage location and, within each location, by order of shelf arrangement. As is the case with the primary sort, a single cell from the secondary sort column suffices to specify the secondary sort column to Lotus. The \P macro here specifies Cell B9, indicating to Lotus to perform a secondary sort within the primary sort (either alphabetically or numerically) on the basis of the labels or values in column B.

The final character in the /Data Sort command of the \P macro is G, which stands for *go*—the instruction to Lotus to begin sorting the SORT-AREA data range.

Step 14. Name the macro you have just created (we have already been calling it \P), by placing the cell pointer on cell B90 (the first cell of the macro) and entering the following /Range Name command:

/RNC\P   <Return>   <Return>

Step 15. Enter the following label into Cell A90:

\P

This label is only to help you remember the name of the macro; it serves no other purpose.

Step 16. Begin creating the \V macro (see figures 4-2 and 4-3) by entering each macro command into the appropriate cell, as indicated in table 4-11. The command explanation in the far right-hand column of the table documents the action initiated by the corresponding command; each explanation should be entered into column E, (opposite the command to which it refers.)

Notice that the /Data Sort command in Cell B107, which sorts the data range SORT-AREA in numeric order according to item number (in column C), does not use or require a secondary sort. The /Data Sort command automatically resets the data range and clears the secondary sort that was set by the first macro (see Step 13).

Step 17. Name the \V macro you have just created, by placing the cell pointer on cell B99 (the first cell of the macro) and entering the following /Range Name command:

```
/RNC\V    <Return>    <Return>
```

Step 18. Enter the following label into Cell A99:

```
'\V
```

This label, like the one created in Step 15, is only to help you remember the name of the macro.

Step 19. Save the Physical Inventory and Valuation spreadsheet (including your newly created macros) by entering the following command:

```
/FSB:INVENTRY    <Return>
```

If you already saved the Physical Inventory and Valuation spreadsheet in Step 11, you will have to tell Lotus to overwrite the existing INVENTRY.WK 1 file that is on disk, replacing it with your latest version, as follows:

```
/FS[point to INVENTRY.WK1]
<Return>    R
```

Step 20. Execute the first macro, \P, by pressing the <Alt> key and the P key simultaneously. Notice how the macro sorts your spreadsheet.

Step 21. Execute the second macro, \V, by pressing the <Alt> key and the V key simultaneously. Notice how the macro re-sorts your spreadsheet. By alternating between Step 20 and Step 21, you can watch your spreadsheet sort and re-sort itself. Whenever the \P macro is executed, it will change the heading at the top of column I from CATEGORY TOTALS to PHYSICAL COUNT, sort inventory items by

location and count sequence, and return you to Cell A1. Whenever the \V macro is executed, it will change the heading at the top of column I from PHYSICAL COUNT to CATEGORY TOTALS, protect the new CATEGORY TOTALS heading for column I, resort inventory items by item number, recalculate the spreadsheet after it has been sorted, and return you to Cell A1.

At this point, if you were executing the \P macro to take an actual inventory, you would print the spreadsheet so that you could use it as the printed form for taking a physical inventory.

Try entering new quantities on hand (into column F, under QUANTITY ON HAND for each inventory item. You may have to make up these quantities as you go along; for the purpose of this exercise, it is not necessary to use real inventory quantities.

When you have finished entering the new quantities on hand, run the \V macro. As soon as the \V macro finishes running, you will see that the Physical Inventory and Valuation spreadsheet has been re-sorted by item number and recalculated. And once again the heading at the top of column I is CATEGORY TOTALS. Had you taken an actual inventory, you would now print the extended spreadsheet as a record of the physical inventory and its valuation.

Using the Information in This Spreadsheet

Taking a Physical Inventory

When using this spreadsheet for taking a physical inventory, perform the following steps:

1. Use the /File Retrieve command to bring the INVENTRY.WK1 up from disk.
2. Enter the date, the counter's name, and the writer's name on the spreadsheet.
3. Execute the \P macro.
4. Issue a /Print command to your printer, to print the form for taking a physical inventory.
5. Use the /File Save command to save the spreadsheet to the INVENTRY.WK1 file, in

the \P macro sorted order, overwriting the existing file. You want to save the spreadsheet sorted in the \P format because, when you transfer new quantity-on-hand information (after taking a physical inventory) from your manual forms to your computer spreadsheet, the new information will already be laid out in the same order as the old information on your spreadsheet was. This will facilitate data entry of your physical inventory.

6. Take a physical inventory by counting each inventory item and writing your count on the physical inventory form.
7. Retrieve INVENTRY.WK1 from disk, using the /File Retrieve command, in order to record the new quantity-on-hand data.
8. Input your physical inventory data from the paper form into your computer spreadsheet.
9. Execute the \V macro.
10. Print INVENTRY.WK1, by issuing a /Print command to your printer. Keep the printed output as your historical record of your physical inventory and its valuation.
11. Save INVENTRY.WK1 with the latest physical inventory and valuation, using the /File Save command.

Use the physical inventory data to calculate the cost of goods sold in your profit-and-loss statement and to calculate periodic food costs as a percentage of food sales.

Information from the Physical Inventory and Valuation spreadsheet is used in chapter 7 for determining cost of goods sold and in chapter 10 for costing recipes. In both cases, the information in the Physical Inventory and Valuation spreadsheet is transferred automatically by means of macros that are explained in the relevant chapters.

Adding New Inventory Items

There are two ways to add new inventory items. One method involves using the /Worksheet Insert command to add a new, blank row in the proper food category for the new item. Then you enter the information into each column, from column A to column G, for the new inventory item. When you get to columns H and I, you use the /Copy command to copy the formula in column H and the underscore line in column I into the new row you have inserted. This is a more cumbersome and less practical way of adding a new inventory item than the second method.

The second method involves creating a macro that automatically adds a new row, copies the necessary formula into column H and the necessary underscore line into column I, and prompts you to enter the new inventory information. Use the {?} curly-bracket command to force the macro to pause, prompt, and wait for you to enter information in the current cell. The macro will not continue until you press the <Return> key to place your entry into the current cell. An example of a macro command that goes to a specified cell and then pauses while you make an entry in the cell is as follows:

```
{GOTO}A32~{?}~
```

TABLE 4-12. CURLY-BRACKET COMMANDS PERFORMING FUNCTION KEY ACTIONS.

Macro Command	Key	Command Explanation
{EDIT}	<F2>	Enables user to edit the contents of a cell.
{NAME}	<F3>	Enables user to select a range name.
{ABS}	<F4>	Makes a cell reference absolute.
{GOTO}	<F5>	Moves cell pointer to a specific cell.
{WINDOW}	<F6>	Moves cell pointer from one window to another.
{QUERY}	<F7>	Enables user to query a database.
{TABLE}	<F8>	Recalculates a data table.
{CALC}	<F9>	Recalculates an entire spreadsheet.
{GRAPH}	<F10>	Enables user to view the current graph.

TABLE 4-13. CURLY-BRACKET COMMANDS PERFORMING POINTER MOVEMENT ACTIONS.

Macro Command	Key	Command Explanation
{UP}	< ↑ >	Moves cell pointer up one cell.
{DOWN}	< ↓ >	Moves cell pointer down one cell.
{LEFT}	<←>	Moves cell pointer left one cell.
{RIGHT}	<→>	Moves cell pointer right one cell.
{PGUP}	<9>	Moves cell pointer up one page.
{PGDN}	<3>	Moves cell pointer down one page.
{HOME}	<7>	Moves cell pointer to Cell A1.
{END}	<2>	(With {UP}, {DOWN}, {LEFT}, {RIGHT}, and {HOME}) Moves cell pointer to the corners of the spreadsheet.

NOTE: These cursor movement commands can also be used to perform actions in any situation where edit/entry cursor movement keys can be used, such as when editing a cell.

TABLE 4-14. CURLY-BRACKET COMMANDS PERFORMING SPECIAL KEY ACTIONS.

Macro Command	Key	Command Explanation
{ESC}	<Esc>	Cancels command.
{BS}	<Backspace>	Deletes character one space to the left.
{DEL}	<Delete>	Deletes character directly above the edit cursor (during editing).
{BIGLEFT}	<Ctrl>+<←>	Moves cell pointer one screen to the left.
{BIGRIGHT}	<Ctrl>+<→>	Moves cell pointer one screen to the right.
{?}		Pauses for user input.

The final tilde after the {?} characters is necessary to force the macro to continue its execution once you hit the <Return> key.

The remaining commands needed to create this macro should already be in your repertoire of commands from chapters 3 and 4.

Curly-bracket Commands

The curly-bracket commands in table 4-12 perform function key actions; those in table 4-13 perform pointer movement actions; and those in table 4-14 perform special key actions.

Problems

1. Define the following:
   a. *physical inventory*
   b. *physical inventory valuation*
2. Describe the steps involved in taking a physical inventory.

3. Why is it important to take a physical inventory? What financial calculations rely on a physical inventory valuation?
4. Explain how the /Data Sort command is used in the Physical Inventory and Valuation spreadsheet. Describe the effect on the spreadsheet before and after the command is used.
5. Explain the difference between a primary sort and a secondary sort. (You may need to experiment with the /Data Sort command to answer.)
6. Can you specify a secondary sort without specifying a primary sort? Why or why not? (You may need to experiment with the /Data Sort command to answer.)
7. What are curly-bracket commands? Which of the ones mentioned in this chapter are associated with keys on your keyboard, and which are not?
8. Explain how the ITEM NUMBER column (column D) in figure 4-1 is used to categorize inventory items.
9. Why is it important to document and explain

macro commands and to save those explanations with your spreadsheet?

10. Why is it important that each complete command in a macro occupy a separate cell?

Cases

1. The Physical Inventory and Valuation spreadsheet described in this chapter has a shortcoming. Look at the column headed PRICE PER COUNT UNIT in figure 4-1. When entering prices from delivery invoices into this column, you must calculate the price per count unit in your head or on a piece of paper if the delivery unit differs from the count unit. For example, suppose that canned tuna is delivered and priced by the case, but that you count it by the can for inventory purposes. If there are six cans of tuna in a case, you must divide 6 into the price per case of the tuna to get the price per count unit. This forces you to stop and perform a manual calculation that could be automated in your spreadsheet.

Solve this problem by changing the inventory spreadsheet you have created so that it automatically calculates the price per count unit, based on the price per delivery unit and on the number of count units per delivery unit. (*Hint:* You will need to use the /Worksheet Insert command to insert a minimum of two additional columns.)

2. Create a macro that will allow you to enter new inventory items automatically. This macro must perform the following steps:
   a. It must insert a new row after prompting you for the row number to insert. Use the /Worksheet Insert command to insert a new row.
   b. It must copy the formula in column H and the underscore line in column I into the new row.
   c. It must prompt you to enter the following data for the new inventory item:
      • The location code
      • The new item's count sequence
      • The item number for the new item
      • The description of the new item
      • The count unit for the new item
      • The quantity on hand of the new item
      • The price per count unit of the new item

   You will have to use the {?} curly-bracket command to cause the macro to pause to accept user input at the appropriate time. It and all other commands you will need for this macro have been discussed at various places in chapters 3 and 4.

5. Daily Labor Report

TABLE 5-1. SUMMARY OF LOTUS COMMANDS USED IN THIS CHAPTER.

Commands Used

Command String Abbreviation	Command Name	Functions Used
/C	/Copy	@AVG
/DS	/Data Sort	@CHOOSE
/FR	/File Retrieve	@DATE
/FS	/File Save	@DAY
/PP	/Print Printer	@IF
/RE	/Range Erase	@INT
/RF	/Range Format	@MAX
/RNC	/Range Name Create	@MIN
/RP	/Range Protect	@MOD
/RU	/Range Unprotect	@MONTH
/WGE	/Worksheet Global Erase	@NOW
/WGP	/Worksheet Global Protect	@ROUND
/WGR	/Worksheet Global Recalculation	@SUM
/WI	/Worksheet Insert	@VLOOKUP @YEAR #AND#

The Daily Labor Report spreadsheet described in this chapter exemplifies how computer spreadsheets can facilitate restaurant management and control. The Daily Labor Report spreadsheet, which can be maintained daily by a single man-ager, provides labor data at a level of detail that would be too time-consuming and burdensome for most managers to attempt to maintain manually.

The shaded area of figure 5-1 holds the required daily input of information for the Daily Labor Report spreadsheet. For each employee, you are required to enter the following items of information:

- The employee's number
- The employee's shift—A.M. or P.M.
- The hour and minute when the employee punched in (which comes from the employee's time card)
- The hour and minute when the employee punched out (which also comes from the employee's time card)
- The length (in minutes) of the unpaid meal period taken by the employee

The remainder of the spreadsheet is computed automatically and provides information for analyzing daily labor in your operation. It is designed to be used daily and to be printed and saved for historical reference.

Timely awareness and control of daily labor are important in producing a profit for your foodservice operation. Many foodservice operators rely on month-old labor information from their accountants; and by the time this information is received, it is too old to be of much use. The Daily Labor Report spreadsheet offers daily as-

DAILY LABOR REPORT

DATE: 03/01/86
DAY: SATURDAY
CLERK: J. CHABAN

EMP NO	SHIFT	(-IN-) HR MIN	(-OUT-) HR MIN	[In Min]	EMPLOYEE NAME	DEPT	HOURLY WAGE	TOTAL TIME	REGULAR TIME	OVER TIME	REGULAR PAY	OVERTIME PAY	GROSS PAY	AM OFFICE	PM OFFICE	AM BAR	PM BAR	AM D.R.	PM D.R.	AM KITCHEN	PM KITCHEN	AM JANITOR	PM JANITOR
3.20	AM	10 1	6 15	30	KIT CARSON	BAR	$5.00	7.7	7.7	0.00	$38.67	$0.00	$38.67	$0.00	$0.00	$38.67	$0.00	$0.00	$0.00	$0.00	$0.00	$0.00	$0.00
6.30	AM	3 15	12 15	45	MAY KAY	DINING ROOM	$4.25	8.3	8.0	0.25	$34.00	$1.59	$35.59	$0.00	$0.00	$0.00	$0.00	$35.59	$0.00	$0.00	$0.00	$0.00	$0.00
8.50	AM	5 30	1 32	48	BOB SHIFT	JANITORIAL	$4.50	7.2	7.2	0.00	$32.55	$0.00	$32.55	$0.00	$0.00	$0.00	$0.00	$0.00	$0.00	$0.00	$0.00	$32.55	$0.00
10.40	AM	9 10	6 45	59	JEFF BARRY	KITCHEN	$6.25	8.6	8.0	0.60	$50.00	$5.62	$55.63	$0.00	$0.00	$0.00	$0.00	$0.00	$0.00	$55.63	$0.00	$0.00	$0.00
1.10	AM	3 5	11 35	48	IDA SMITH	OFFICE	$8.00	7.7	7.7	0.00	$61.60	$0.00	$61.60	$61.60	$0.00	$0.00	$0.00	$0.00	$0.00	$0.00	$0.00	$0.00	$0.00
5.20	PM	8 30	5 15	33	CANDY DOWDY	BAR	$5.25	8.2	8.0	0.20	$42.00	$1.57	$43.58	$0.00	$0.00	$0.00	$43.58	$0.00	$0.00	$0.00	$0.00	$0.00	$0.00
4.20	PM	6 30	2 30	55	STEVE BLUE	BAR	$6.50	7.1	7.1	0.00	$46.04	$0.00	$46.04	$0.00	$0.00	$0.00	$46.04	$0.00	$0.00	$0.00	$0.00	$0.00	$0.00
7.30	PM	3 45	11 45	56	CINDY KLASS	DINING ROOM	$4.50	7.1	7.1	0.00	$31.80	$0.00	$31.80	$0.00	$0.00	$0.00	$0.00	$31.80	$0.00	$0.00	$0.00	$0.00	$0.00
9.50	PM	9 45	6 45	15	JOEL CHABAN	JANITORIAL	$3.35	8.8	8.0	0.75	$26.80	$3.77	$30.57	$0.00	$0.00	$0.00	$0.00	$0.00	$0.00	$0.00	$0.00	$0.00	$30.57
11.40	PM	6 15	3 45	58	ANN HERRON	KITCHEN	$8.50	8.5	8.0	0.53	$68.00	$6.80	$74.80	$0.00	$0.00	$0.00	$0.00	$0.00	$0.00	$0.00	$74.80	$0.00	$0.00
2.10	PM	9 1	5 25	57	ANDREA SELIG	OFFICE	$6.35	7.5	7.5	0.00	$47.31	$0.00	$47.31	$0.00	$47.31	$0.00	$0.00	$0.00	$0.00	$0.00	$0.00	$0.00	$0.00

<> Average Time Taken for Lunch: 45.82 Mins.   <> Avg.Hrly Wage = $5.68   86.6   84.3   2.3 $478.77 $19.36 $498.13 $61.60 $47.31 $38.67 $89.62 $35.59 $31.80 $55.63 $74.80 $32.55 $30.57
<> Labor Cost Per Hour = $5.75

**** PERCENT OF GROSS PAY: 12.37%   9.50%   7.76%   17.99%   7.15%   6.38%   11.17%   15.02%   6.53%   6.14%

		TABLE 1	**TABLE 2**		*****TABLE 3*****	
	EMPNO	EMPLOYEE NAME	WAGE		DEPTNO	JOB
LOOK-UP	1	IDA SMITH	$8.00		0.10	OFFICE
	2	ANDREA SELIG	$6.35		0.20	BAR
TABLES	3	KIT CARSON	$5.00		0.30	DINING ROOM
	4	STEVE BLUE	$6.50		0.40	KITCHEN
	5	CANDY DOWDY	$5.25		0.50	JANITORIAL
	6	MAY KAY	$4.25			
	7	CINDY KLASS	$4.50			
	8	BOB SHIFT	$4.50			
	9	JOEL CHABAN	$3.35			
	10	JEFF BARRY	$6.25			
	11	ANN HERRON	$8.50			

TABLE 1 **TABLE 2**   *****TABLE 3*****

5-1. Daily Labor Report spreadsheet.

sessments of what is going on, so you can take control of problems almost immediately.

In using this spreadsheet every day, you can begin to extrapolate and set your own wage-and-hour standards and standard variances/deviations. For example, you may set wage-and-hour standards that define the allowable minimum and maximum deviation from standard dollar department wages and from standard percentage of gross pay for:

- Office wages
- Bar wages
- Kitchen wages
- Dining room wages
- Janitorial wages

Setting standards for each department allows you to notice and pinpoint problems when they occur.

Data in the PERCENT OF GROSS PAY category (see figure 5-1, row 22) should fall into a recognizable pattern over time, from which you can develop a standard percentage of gross pay. Each department will vary from the standard, but the point at which each department's pay varies too much above or below your standard pay must be defined by you. Once you have defined allowable variances, the Daily Labor Report spreadsheet will provide you with immediate feedback on variances from the standard. For instance, you may find that AM KITCHEN labor usually accounts for 10 percent of gross pay and that it may vary from this standard day-to-day by as much as 1 percent. This means that, if the daily figure for AM KITCHEN labor is between 9 percent and 11 percent of gross pay, nothing is wrong. If it falls below 9 percent or exceeds 11 percent, however, the kitchen may be experiencing labor problems. If the percentage of gross pay for a department is too low, the quality of food and the speed of service may suffer. If it is too high, your profits may suffer.

In chapter 7, you will see how to construct a spreadsheet that compares daily department labor costs to daily sales.

TABLE 5-2. STEP 1 FORMATTING COMMANDS.

Column	Width	Command to Enter	
A	6	/WCS6	\<Return\>
C	4	/WCS4	\<Return\>
D	4	/WCS4	\<Return\>
E	6	/WCS6	\<Return\>
F	4	/WCS4	\<Return\>
G	6	/WCS6	\<Return\>
H	15	/WCS15	\<Return\>
I	11	/WCS11	\<Return\>

The discipline of entering the labor information from time cards keeps you or your manager in touch with your operation, giving you an opportunity to review each employee's time card for tardiness, overtime, overly long meal periods, and failure to punch in or punch out.

By regularly saving your Daily Labor Report printouts, you will accumulate a historical record that can be used for scheduling your employees. Daily Labor Report records can be used to project your daily, weekly, and monthly labor schedules more effectively and efficiently. Using these records can improve your scheduling skills and result in optimized labor schedules. Because the Daily Labor Report spreadsheet calculates regular time, overtime, regular pay, and overtime pay for each employee, you can use this information to pinpoint overtime problems and then plan your weekly labor schedule around these problem areas.

In the Daily Labor Report spreadsheet, time is expressed in terms of the standard 12-hour clock. If your operation uses a 24-hour clock, you will need to revise the formulas used to calculate **TOTAL TIME** in column K of figure 5-1.

Formatting, Headings, Labels, and Look-up Tables

Step 1. Reformat columns A through I from the normal, Lotus default column width of nine characters to the widths indicated in table 5-2.

Step 2. Begin re-creating the spreadsheet example shown in figure 5-1 by entering the appropriate headings and labels into columns A through Z, rows 1 through 39, exactly as specified in table 5-3. You may need to pad some of your cell entries with blank spaces to get your headings to look like those pictured in figure 5-1. Any heading beginning with one of the three Lotus label alignment prefixes (', ", and ^) signifies a label to be padded with blank spaces or to be given a special cell alignment. Remember that the prefix ' aligns text to the left margin of the cell, the prefix " aligns text to be right margin of the cell, and the prefix ^ centers text within the cell. Unless a label alignment prefix is indicated in table 5-3, do not use one of these prefixes to begin a label or heading.

Step 3. Enter dashed lines and double-dashed lines into the spreadsheet as indicated in table 5-4. Use the backslash (\) key at the beginning of each cell entry to signal to Lotus that the character immediately following it is to be repeated across the cell from end to end.

To repeat a character across several individual cells, use Lotus's /Copy command, as indicated in table 5-4. Use the pointing method described on page 34 to define the last cell of a cell range when performing the /Copy operation. Remember to place the cell pointer on the originating cell (the cell being copied from) before you begin to enter each command listed in table 5-4.

Step 4. Format the cells and cell ranges identified in table 5-5, as indicated there. Enter each command given in the far right-hand column of the table exactly as it appears, by typing the characters shown and then hitting the \<Return\> key. When formatting a cell range, use the pointing method to define the last cell in each indicated cell range. Be sure to place the cell pointer on the first cell indicated in the far left-hand column of table 5-5 before entering the associated command.

Step 5. Begin entering look-up tables 1, 2, and 3 (see tables 5-6, 5-7, and 5-8).

As a prerequisite for using the Daily Labor Report spreadsheet you must assign a unique employee number (from 1 to 999) to each of your employees. Notice that the employee numbers in column A (the column headed **EMP NO**) use a decimal point. This decimal point separates the employee number (on the left) from the employ-

TABLE 5-3. STEP 2 HEADINGS.

Cell	Heading		Cell	Heading
A1	Daily Labor Report		S7	^BAR
H2	''Date:		T7	^BAR
H3	''DAY:		U7	^D.R.
H4	''CLERK:		V7	^D.R.
C5	'-<<<		W7	^KITCHEN
E5	'TIME--		X7	^KITCHEN
F5	'->>>		Y7	^JANITOR
G5	'-<MEAL		Z7	^JANITOR
H5	'>-------------		G8	'-<TIME
A6	^EMP		H8	'>--------------
C6	' <-IN->		A21	'<> Average Time Taken for Lunch:
E6	' <-OUT->		H21	Mins. <> Avg. Hrly Wage =
G6	' [IN		H22	' <> Labor Cost Per Hour =
H6	^EMPLOYEE		N22	'**** PERCENT OF GROSS PAY:
J6	^HOURLY		H24	'***TABLE 1***
K6	^TOTAL		I24	'**TABLE 2**
L6	^REGULAR		L24	'*****TABLE 3*****
M6	^OVER		G25	''EMPNO
N6	^REGULAR		H25	''EMPLOYEE NAME
O6	^OVERTIME		I25	''WAGE
P6	^GROSS		L25	''DEPTNO
Q6	^AM		M25	^JOB
R6	^PM		H39	' ***TABLE 1***
S6	^AM		I39	'**TABLE 2**
T6	^PM		L39	'*****TABLE 3*****
U6	^AM			
V6	^PM			
W6	^AM			
X6	^PM			
Y6	^AM			
Z6	^PM			
A7	^NO			
B7	^SHIFT			
C7	''HR			
D7	'MIN			
E7	''HR			
F7	' MIN			
G7	' MIN]			
H7	^NAME			
I7	^DEPT			
J7	^WAGE			
K7	^TIME			
L7	^TIME			
M7	^TIME			
N7	^PAY			
O7	^PAY			
P7	^PAY			
Q7	^OFFICE			
R7	^OFFICE			

ee's job classification or department number (on the right).

Look-up Table 1 is used by Lotus to look up the employee number (EMP NO) entered in column A, and then to transfer the associated employee name in Look-up Table 1 automatically to the corresponding cell in column H under EMPLOYEE NAME. The formulas under EMPLOYEE NAME use Lotus's look-up function to perform the transfer.

Look-up Table 2 is accessed by the formulas in column J under HOURLY WAGE, which look up each employee's employee number in column A. Look-up Table 2 then returns each employee's hourly wage rate.

Look-up Table 3 is used to look up the employee's department number (the number to the right of the decimal point in the column A employee number) and to return the employee's job classification automatically to the cor-

TABLE 5-4. STEP 3 REPEAT AND /COPY COMMANDS.

Cell	REPEAT Command to Enter	/Copy Command to Enter			
A5	\−				
B5	\−				
D5	\−				
I5	\−	/CI5	\<Return>	J5..Z5	\<Return>
A8	\−	/CA5	\<Return>	B5..F5	\<Return>
I8	\−	/CI5	\<Return>	J5..Z5	\<Return>
A20	\−	/CA20	\<Return>	B20..Z20	\<Return>
A23	\=	/CA23	\<Return>	B23..Z23	\<Return>
G26	\−	/CG26	\<Return>	H26..I26	\<Return>
L26	\−				
M26	\−				

responding cell in column I. In our example the job classifications include OFFICE, BAR, DINING ROOM, KITCHEN, and JANITORIAL.

Notice that the look-up tables used in the Daily Labor Report run vertically (top-to-bottom), rather than horizontally (left-to-right). This becomes significant when you use one of Lotus's two look-up table functions that allow you to look up a value in a table and that return the number or text appearing in the cell adjacent to the value being look up. If the reference table is arranged vertically, as the ones in this spreadsheet are, you use the @VLOOKUP function; if it runs horizontally across the spreadsheet, you use the @HLOOKUP function. Use of the look-

up table functions is discussed at Step 10 of this chapter.

Daily Operator Input

Step 6. Enter the specific data that appear in the shaded areas of figure 5-1 (these shaded areas are shown enlarged in figure 5-2). Table 5-9 describes the standard input for this portion of the spreadsheet. This information is all that you will have to enter daily; the remainder of the spreadsheet is calculated automatically.

You must maintain Look-up Table 1 and Look-up Table 2 on a regular (though not daily) basis. Names and hourly wages for new employee's must

TABLE 5-5. STEP 4 /RANGE FORMAT COMMANDS.

Cell(s)	Format/Alignment	Command to Enter			
I2	date type 4	/RFD4	\<Return>		
A9..A19	fixed—two decimal places	/RFF2	\<Return>	A9..A19	\<Return>
C9..G9	fixed—zero decimal places	/RFF0	\<Return>	C9..G9	\<Return>
J9..J20	currency	/RFC2	\<Return>	J9..J20	\<Return>
K9..L19	fixed—one decimal place	/RFF1	\<Return>	K9..L19	\<Return>
M9..M19	fixed—two decimal places	/RFF2	\<Return>	M9..M19	\<Return>
N9..Z19	currency	/RFC2	\<Return>	N9..Z19	\<Return>
G21	fixed—two decimal places	/RFF2	\<Return>	\<Return>	
J21..J22	currency	/RFC2	\<Return>	J21..J22	\<Return>
K21..M21	fixed—one decimal place	/RFF1	\<Return>	K21..M21	\<Return>
N21..Z21	currency	/RFC2	\<Return>	N21..Z21	\<Return>
Q22..Z22	percent	/RFP2	\<Return>	Q22..Z22	\<Return>
I27..I39	currency	/RFC2	\<Return>	I27..I39	\<Return>
L27..L39	fixed—two decimal places	/RFF2	\<Return>	L27..L39	\<Return>

be added to these tables, and the names and hourly wages of terminated employees must be removed.

Formulas

Some of the steps that follow contain instructions about making cells absolute when copying formu-

TABLE 5-6. DATA TO ENTER FOR LOOK-UP TABLE 1.

Cell	Entry
G27	1
G28	2
G29	3
G30	4
G31	5
G32	6
G33	7
G34	8
G35	9
G36	10
G37	11
H27	''IDA SMITH
H28	''ANDREA SELIG
H29	''KIT CARSON
H30	''STEVE BLUE
H31	''CANDY DOWDY
H32	''MAY KAY
H33	''CINDY KLASS
H34	''BOB SHIFT
H35	''JOEL CHABAN
H36	''JEFF BARRY
H37	''ANN HERON

TABLE 5-7. DATA TO ENTER FOR LOOK-UP TABLE 2.

Cell	Entry
I27	8.00
I28	6.35
I29	5.00
I30	6.50
I31	5.25
I32	4.25
I33	4.50
I34	4.50
I35	3.35
I36	6.25
I37	8.50

TABLE 5-8. DATA TO ENTER FOR LOOK-UP TABLE 3.

Cell	Entry
L27	.1
L28	.2
L29	.3
L30	.4
L31	.5
M27	^OFFICE
M28	^BAR
M29	^DINING ROOM
M30	^KITCHEN
M31	^JANITORIAL

las and cell references. The meaning of absolute and relative cells is discussed on pages 34–35.

Step 7. Enter the following Lotus calendar function into cell I2:

```
@NOW
```

If the target cell is formatted for date (as Cell I2 is), the @NOW function automatically gets today's date from the system date you entered when you first turned on your computer or from the date maintained by an automatic, battery-operated clock/calendar (if your computer has this feature). If the target cell is formatted for time, the time of day is returned when the @NOW function is entered.

Step 8. Enter the following formula into Cell I3 (this is a long formula, so take your time to prevent entry errors):

```
@CHOOSE(@MOD(@DATE(@YEAR(@NOW),
@MONTH(@NOW),@DAY(@NOW)),7),''
SATURDAY'',''SUNDAY'',''MONDAY'',
''TUESDAY'',''WEDNESDAY'',
''THURSDAY'',''FRIDAY'')
```

Although the formula is reproduced here on five lines, it should be typed into your computer without any break, as though it were a single long word. This formula automatically determines the day of the week (Sunday through Saturday) by means of seven different Lotus functions, five of which are Lotus calendar functions. As you can see from this formula, Lotus allows you to use functions within functions. This powerful feature

TABLE 5-9. DAILY INPUT INTO THE DAILY LABOR REPORT SPREADSHEET.

Cell	Input
I4	CLERK. Enter the name of the employee who is filling in the Daily Labor Report spreadsheet.
A9..A19	EMP NO. Enter each employee's employee number and department code.
B9..B19	SHIFT. Enter each employee's shift—A.M. or P.M.
C9..C19	HOUR IN. From each employee's time card, enter the *hour* punched in. If an employee punches in at 10:01 A.M., for example, enter 10 for the hour; do not enter the minutes.
D9..D19	MINUTE IN. From each employee's time card, enter the minutes past the hour punched in. If an employee punches in at 10:01 A.M., for example, enter 1 for the minutes past the hour. Do not precede single-digit entries (from 1 to 9) with a 0, as in 01.
E9..E19	HOUR OUT. From each employee's time card, enter the hour punched out. If an employee punches out at 6:15 (P.M.), for example, enter 6 for the hour; do not enter the minutes in this column.
F9..F19	MINUTE OUT. From employee's time card, enter the minutes past the hour punched out. If an employee punches out at 6:15 P.M., for example, enter 15 for the minutes. Do not precede single-digit entries (from 1 to 9) with a 0, as in 08.
G9..G19	MEAL TIME. Enter the length of each employee's meal break, in minutes. You may need to do this computation in your head, on a piece of paper, or with the help of Lotus's scratch pad feature. If an employee punches out for lunch at 11:45 A.M. and punches back in to work at 12:15 P.M., you would compute in your head that the meal break was 30 minutes long.

allows you to automate processes such as this one that determines the day of the week.

An *argument* to a function is an item listed in parentheses after the function name. Some functions (such as the @SUM function) need only one argument in parentheses. The only argument the @SUM function requires is the cell range being summed—such as @SUM(B7..B17). Other functions (such as the @CHOOSE function) require more than one argument in parentheses; in these functions, the arguments are separated by commas. An argument may be a single number (such as 7), a cell range (such as B7..B17), a label (such as ''SUNDAY''), or an expression (such as B7 + @AVG(B7..B17)). Sometimes Lotus specifies the exact form that the argument must take. Generally, however, if Lotus says you may use a number as an argument in a function, you may, in place of the number, use an expression that Lotus evaluates as a single number.

To understand how the formula given at the beginning of Step 8 works, consider first the

```
    : A ::   B   :: C:: D:: E :: F:: G ::      H      ::    I
1   DAILY LABOR REPORT
2
3
4                                          CLERK: J. Chaban
5   ----------------<<<---TIME--->>>-<MEAL>------------
6     EMP          <-IN->  <-OUT-> [In   EMPLOYEE
7      NO   SHIFT  HR MIN   HR MIN  Min]   NAME
8   -------------------------------------<TIME>----------
9   3.20    AM     10  1    6  15    30
10  6.30    AM     3  15   12  15    45
11  8.50    AM     5  30    1  32    48
12  10.40   AM     9  10    6  45    59
13  1.10    AM     3   5   11  35    48
14  5.20    PM     8  30    5  15    33
15  4.20    PM     6  30    2  30    55
16  7.30    PM     3  45   11  45    56
17  9.50    PM     9  45    6  45    15
18  11.40   PM     6  30    3  45    58
19  2.10    PM     9   1    5  25    57
20  --------------------------------------------------
```

5-2. *Enlarged view of shaded areas of the Daily Labor Report spreadsheet.*

@CHOOSE function by itself. If the @MOD function and its arguments are removed from the formula, the following terms remain:

```
@CHOOSE( [number or expression],
''SATURDAY'',''SUNDAY'',''MONDAY'',
''TUESDAY'',''WEDNESDAY'',
''THURSDAY'',''FRIDAY'')
```

The @CHOOSE function is used to enable Lotus to choose from a list of arguments—in this case, a list of the days of the week. The particular day of the week that ends up being displayed in Cell I3 is determined by the [number or expression] portion of the formula (shown above as the first argument of the @CHOOSE function). If the expression evaluates to 5, THURSDAY will be displayed in Cell I3. The @CHOOSE function automatically numbers the items in the @CHOOSE list, starting with ''SATURDAY'' (0), ''SUNDAY'' (1), and so on. The last item in the list, ''FRIDAY'', is thus assigned the number 6.

The @CHOOSE function allows you to use numbers as well as labels in a list; the only restriction is that the characters in the list may not add up to more than 240 characters. In typing the list, remember to separate each item with commas and to put double quotes (") around the labels, as illustrated in the preceding formula.

Now consider the portion of the formula that causes the appropriate number from 0 to 6 to be selected as the day of the week from the @CHOOSE list. If we remove the @CHOOSE expression from the formula, the following expression remains:

```
@MOD(@DATE(@YEAR(@NOW),
@MONTH(@NOW),@DAY(@NOW)),7)
```

The @MOD function is used to calculate the indivisible remainder that is left when one number is divided by another. If 7 is divided by 2, for example, the integer quotient is 3 and the remainder is 1. Lotus's @MOD function takes two arguments: the number to be divided (the *dividend*); and the number to divide by (the *divisor*). The form this function takes is as follows:

```
@MOD( [dividend], [divisor] )
```

The divisor in the above formula is 7 because there are seven items on the @CHOOSE list, representing the seven days of the week.

The dividend is a serial number, more commonly referred to as a Julian calendar number, representing the number of days that have passed since a specific date. Lotus uses January 1, 1900, as the starting date from which to begin calculating the number of days that will be used as the dividend. January 1, 1900, is built into Lotus as serial number 1 for exclusive use by Lotus's calendar functions; it is not entered by the user.

It is important that you understand how the number from 0 to 6—that is, the number representing the correct day of the week—is calculated. Even though the number of days in a year may be either 364 or 365, the number of days in the week remains constant. As it happens, January 1, 1900, was a Sunday. Therefore, given that January 1, 1900, is assigned serial number 1, Lotus can calculate the correct day of the week (from 0 to 6) on the basis of its running count of dates, simply by dividing the date's serial number by 7 and recognizing the remainder of the quotient as the number of the day of the week. For example, the serial number 1 divided by 7 leaves a remainder of 1—which, according to the @CHOOSE list, is a Sunday. Hence, to find the day of the week for the date with serial number 1,000, Lotus would divide 1,000 by 7 and use the remainder of that division (namely, 6) to identify the corresponding day of the week (namely, Friday). If a division leaves no remainder, the remainder is expressed as 0, which is the @CHOOSE list's identifying number for Saturday.

The dividend—the number of days from January 1, 1900, to today's date (the @NOW date)—is calculated by the following series of Lotus calendar functions:

```
@DATE(@YEAR(@NOW),@MONTH(@NOW),
@DAY(@NOW))
```

The @DATE function calculates the number of days from January 1, 1900, when given a year, a month, and a day as arguments. The @DATE function may be expressed as follows:

```
@DATE( [year], [month], [day] )
```

In this formulation, [year], [month], and [day] are numbers, and [year] is expressed using the last two digits of the year.

The secret to automating the formula in Cell I3 is to use the @NOW function. This function automatically returns today's date from the system date you entered when you first turned on your computer or from the date maintained by an automatic, battery-operated clock/calendar (if your computer has this feature). Used in combination with three other Lotus calendar functions—@YEAR, @MONTH, and @DAY—the @NOW function supplies the numbers needed for the [year], [month], and [day] entries in the @DATE function. The @YEAR function calculates the year number from the Julian calendar number returned by the @NOW function; similarly, the @MONTH and @DAY functions return the month and day numbers, respectively, from the Julian calendar number returned by the @NOW function.

Step 9. Use the /Range Name command to create names for look-up tables 1, 2, and 3. The range comprising look-up tables 1 and 2 will be named EMP_DATA after the employee data in these tables. The range around Look-up Table 3 will be named DEPT_DATA, after the department data continued there. Notice that these ranges allow you extra space, for adding new table data.

To create the range name EMP_DATA, place your cell pointer on Cell G27 (the first cell of the range you want to name), and enter the following command:

```
/RNCEMP_DATA    <Return>    [point to
Cell I39]    <Return>
```

To create the range name DEPT_DATA, place your cell pointer on Cell L27 (the first cell of the range you want to name), and enter the following command:

```
/RNCDEPT_DATA    <Return>    [point to
Cell M39]    <Return>
```

Step 10. Enter the following formula into Cell H9:

```
@VLOOKUP(@INT(A9),$EMP_DATA,1)
```

Rendered in English, this formula reads: "Look up the integer of the number in Cell A9 in the EMP_DATA look-up tables, which range from Cells G27 to Cell I39, and return with the appropriate label or value from Look-up Table 1—namely, the contents of the first cell to the right of the number being looked up."

An *integer*, as understood by Lotus when it receives the @INT function, is the number or numbers appearing to the left of a decimal point in a named cell. The number in Cell A9 is 3.20. The number to the left of the decimal point is 3, and this is the integer of Cell A9—or, as expressed in the above formula, @INT(A9). If you examine Look-up Table 1, you will see that the label opposite the number 3 is KIT CARSON. The @VLOOKUP function always searches for the last value in the range of numbers that is less than or equal to the search value given, and it returns the adjacent value to the right of the search column.

Now copy the preceding formula from Cell H9 into cells H10 through H19, using the following /Copy command:

```
/CH9    <Return>    H10..H19    <Return>
```

Because the EMP_DATA range was designated as absolute (by preceding its name with a dollar sign), the reference to it will remain absolute in each formula that is copied. If you examine each formula copied, you will see that the EMP_DATA range reference remains constant, while the reference to Cell A9 changes in each cell into which the formula is copied.

Step 11. Enter the following formula into Cell I9:

```
@VLOOKUP(@ROUND(A9-@INT(A9),2),
$DEPT_DATA,1)
```

This formula first instructs Lotus to subtract the integer of A9 (3) from the full contents of A9 (3.20):

$$3.20 - 3 = .20$$

The remainder of .20 is then rounded to two decimal places, in accordance with the formula's

@ROUND function.* Next, Lotus looks up the value .20 in the DEPT_DATA range (the range containing Look-up Table 3) and returns the value BAR, which lies opposite the search value .20.

Now copy this formula from Cell I9 into cells I10 through I19, using the following /Copy command:

```
/CI9    <Return>   I10..I19   <Return>
```

Because the DEPT_DATA range was designated as absolute (by preceding its name with a dollar sign), the reference to it will remain the same in each cell containing the copied formula. If you examine each formula copied, you will see that the reference to the DEPT_DATA range remains constant, while the reference to Cell A9 changes in each cell containing the copied formula.

Step 12. Enter the following formula into Cell J9:

```
@VLOOKUP(@INT(A9),$EMP_DATA,2)
```

Rendered in English, this formula reads: "Look up the integer of the number in Cell A9 in the EMP_DATA Look-up tables, which range from Cell G27 to Cell I39, and return with the appropriate value from the second column to the right (in Look-up) Table 2."

Now copy this formula from Cell J9 into cells J10 through J19, using the following /Copy command:

```
/CJ9    <Return>   J10..J19   <Return>
```

Once again designating the EMP_DATA range as absolute by preceding it with a dollar sign causes the reference to EMP_DATA to remain the same in each formula that is copied.

---

*This calculation is rounded to adjust for an anomoly in Lotus. When the @INT function is used in the calculation illustrated in this example, the resulting difference should be .20. To Lotus, however, the result is .199999 or some such value less than .20. Unless this calculation is rounded, the look-up table will either return the wrong value or no value at all. The @VLOOKUP function always searches for the last value in the range of numbers that is less than or equal to the search value given and will return the adjacent value (to the right of the search column). When Lotus searches for .199999, it will return the value adjacent to .10, not the one adjacent to .20

Step 13. Enter the following formula into Cell K9 (this is a long formula, so take your time to prevent entry errors):

```
@IF(E9>C9,((E9-C9)+((F9/60)
-(D9/60))-G9/60),((12-C9)+E9)+
((((60-D9)/60)-1)+(F9/60))-G9/60)
```

This formula calculates an employee's total work time, based on your input into columns C through G for time punched in, time punched out, and uncompensated meal time. The formula makes the following basic assumptions:

1. No hourly employee works over 12 hours per day.
2. Only hourly employees are analyzed in this Daily Labor Report—not salaried employees.
3. Each employee's total work time is computed to the nearest tenth of an hour.
4. Your employees punch in and out when they take their meal break, and they are not paid during this break.
5. Your employees are paid for time spent on coffee break.

If any of your hourly employees works more than 12 hours per day, or if any of the other assumptions does not apply to the way your operation is run, the formula for total work time used in this Daily Labor Report may be inapplicable to your operation or may inaccurately reflect worktime in the operation.

The formula is complex, in part, because the standard 12-hour clock (on which the Daily Labor Report is based) divides the day into two 12-hour periods—and this creates some confusion. If employee A works from 11 A.M. to 6 P.M. and if employee B works from 1 P.M. to 9 P.M., the formula for computing the total number of hours worked in each employee's case is different. Employee B's total time can be computed simply by subtracting the punched-in time (1 P.M.) from the punch-out time (9 P.M.) to get the total work time of 8 hours.

Employee A's total time is a little more complicated to calculate. First you must subtract the punch-in time (11 A.M.) from 12 noon, which comes out to 1 hour. Then you must add this remainder (1 hour) to the punch-out time (6 P.M.

= 6 hours) to get the total worktime of 7 hours. To complicate things even further, employees rarely punch in or out exactly on the hour, so you must account for minutes as well as for hours in the formula for computing total time. In the formula given at the beginning of this step, minutes are converted to a decimal fraction of an hour by dividing all numbers representing minutes by 60.

The formula can be separated into three major sections to make it a little easier to analyze. The first section of the formula tests for the condition described earlier in the cases of employee A and employee B. This test is expressed in the formula as:

```
@IF(E9>C9,
```

Rendered in English, this expression reads: "If the hour punched in (at Cell E9) is greater than the hour punched out (at Cell C9), the second major section of the formula will be applied, and the result of the expression in the second major section of the formula will be returned (in cell K9) as the total time worked." The second major section of the formula is as follows:

```
((E9-C9)+((F9/60)-(D9/60))-G9/60),
```

The solution to this expression represents the simple calculation of employee B's total time (described previously).

If it is not true that E9 is greater than C9, the third major section of the formula will be applied. That section is as follows:

```
((12-C9)+E9)+((((60-D9)/60)-1)
+(F9/60))-G9/60)
```

The result of the expression in this third major section of the formula will then be returned (in cell K9) as the total time worked. This solution represents the more complex calculation of employee A's total time (described previously).

Now copy the preceding formula from Cell K9 into cells K10 through K19, by placing the cell pointer on Cell K9 and entering the following /Copy command:

```
/C    <Return>    [point to Cell K10].
[point to Cell K19]    <Return>
```

Expressions containing the @IF command (such as the formula in this step) are defined as follows:

```
IF( [expression 1 is true], [then
expression 2], [otherwise expression
3]
```

In other words, if the first argument/expression is true, the result of the second argument/expression will be returned; but if the first argument/expression is false, the result of the third argument/expression will be returned.

Step 14. Enter the following formula into Cell L9:

```
@MIN(K9,8)
```

Rendered in English, this formula reads: "Return to Cell L9 the Minimum (that is, the lesser) of the numerical value in Cell K9 and the value 8." The formula and the spreadsheet assume that regular time for a single day is 8 hours or less. The value returned to Cell L9 by this formula will be either 8 (hours) or the numerical value in Cell K9, if that value is less than 8.

Now copy this formula from Cell L9 into cells L10 through L19, by entering the following /Copy command:

```
/CL9    <Return>    L10..L19    <Return>
```

Step 15. Enter the following formula into Cell M9:

```
@MAX(K9-L9,0)
```

Rendered in English, this formula reads: "Return to Cell M9 the maximum (that is, the greater) of [on the one hand] total time (in Cell K9) minus regular time (in Cell L9) and [on the other] 0. If total time is greater than regular time, the difference is overtime, and that difference will be returned in Cell M9.

Using Lotus's @MAX function prevents a negative number from being displayed in Cell M9. If the total time registered in Cell K9 is equal to or less than the specified regular time in Cell L9 (8 hours), there will be no overtime. The result of K9-L9 by itself could be a negative number, but the @MAX alternative in this case ensures that the lowest possible value that can be returned is a 0.

Now copy the preceding formula from Cell M9 into cells M10 through M19, by entering the following /Copy command:

```
/CM9    <Return>    M10..M19    <Return>
```

Step 16. Enter the following formula into Cell N9:

```
+J9*L9
```

Rendered in English, this expression reads: "Multiply the hourly wage in Cell J9 by the regular time in Cell L9, and return the result to this cell." The result returned in Cell N9 will be the dollar amount of regular pay.

Now copy this formula from Cell N9 into cells N10 through N19, by entering the following /Copy command:

```
/CN9    <Return>    N10..N19    <Return>
```

Step 17. Enter the following formula into Cell O9:

```
+J9*M9*1.5
```

Rendered in English, this expression reads: "Multiply the hourly wage in Cell J9 by the overtime in Cell M9, multiply this result by 1.5, and return the final result to this cell." It is assumed in the spreadsheet that overtime for your employees is one-and-a-half (1.5) times their regular hourly wage rate. If your operation uses a wage-rate differential other than 1.5 for overtime, simply replace 1.5 with the correct multiplier.

Now copy this formula from Cell O9 into cells O10 through O19, by entering the following /Copy command:

```
/CO9    <Return>    O10..O19    <Return>
```

Step 18. Enter the following formula into Cell P9:

```
+N9+O9
```

Rendered in English, this formula reads: "Add the regular pay in Cell N9 to the overtime pay in

Cell O9, and return the result to Cell P9." This number represents gross pay.

Now copy this formula from Cell P9 into cells P10 through P19, by entering the following /Copy command:

```
/CP9    <Return>    P10..P19    <Return>
```

Step 19. The remaining columns of the spreadsheet allocate each employee's gross pay to the appropriate job classification, by shift (A.M. or P.M.). This breakdown provides you with day-to-day department and shift totals for comparison, enabling you to pinpoint where labor costs are increasing or decreasing and giving you a greater handle on controlling labor costs.

Enter the following formula into Cell Q9:

```
@IF(B9=''AM''#AND#I9=
''OFFICE'',P9,0)
```

Rendered in English, this formula reads: "If the shift identified in Cell B9 is AM and the department identified in Cell I9 is OFFICE, return the gross pay value from Cell P9 to Cell Q9; otherwise, return 0 to Cell Q9.

The #AND# term is called a *logical operator*. It mandates that the conditions on either side of it must be true as a prerequisite for having the value of the second argument returned. If either or both conditions are false, the value of the third argument is returned.

Now copy the preceding formula from Cell Q9 into cells Q10 through Q19, by entering the following /Copy command:

```
/CQ9    <Return>    Q10..Q19    <Return>
```

Step 20. Using the same general instructions given in Step 19, enter the formulas specified in table 5-10 into columns R through Z, and copy each formula into the corresponding cells in rows 10 through 19.

Step 21. Enter the following formula into Cell K21:

```
@SUM(K8..K20)
```

Rendered in English, this formula reads: "Sum the entries from cells K8 through K20, and return

TABLE 5-10. STEP 20 CELL FORMULAS.

Cell	Formula
R9	@IF(B9=''PM''#AND#I9=''OFFICE'',P9,0)
S9	@IF(B9=''AM''#AND#I9=''BAR'',P9,0)
T9	@IF(B9=''PM''#AND#I9=''BAR'',P9,0)
U9	@IF(B9=''AM''#AND#I9=''DINING ROOM'',P9,0)
V9	@IF(B9=''PM''#AND#I9=''DINING ROOM'',P9,0)
W9	@IF(B9=''AM''#AND#I9=''KITCHEN'',P9,0)
X9	@IF(B9=''PM''#AND#I9=''KITCHEN'',P9,0)
Y9	@IF(B9=''AM''#AND#I9=''JANITORIAL'',P9,0)
Z9	@IF(B9=''PM''#AND#I9=''JANITORIAL'',P9,0)

the total in Cell K21." This formula computes the total worktime put in by all employees for the day of record.

Now copy the formula from Cell K21 into cells L21 through Z21, by entering the following /Copy command:

```
/CK21    <Return>    L21..Z21    <Return>
```

Averages and Percentages

Step 22. Enter the following formula into Cell G21:

```
@AVG(G9..G19)
```

The @AVG function in Lotus automatically sums the range of cells indicated in parentheses, counts the number of items in that range, and divides the sum by the number of items, returning a mean average. In the present example, the time taken for lunch by employees is totaled and then divided by the number of employees, to yield an average time taken for lunch. This average may be used to develop a standard benchmark of time taken for meal periods and to establish maximum allowable deviations from the standard, for purposes of management and control.

Step 23. Enter the following formula into Cell J21:

```
@AVG(J9..J19)
```

This formula, in which the hourly wages of all employees are totaled and then divided by the total number of employes, calculates the mean average hourly wage of your employees. How much and how often this average increases or decreases may indicate your manager's performance in controlling labor costs, labor scheduling, wage increases, turnover, and hiring.

Step 24. Enter the following formula into Cell J22:

```
+P21/K21
```

This formula calculates labor cost per hour, by dividing the gross pay total in Cell P21 by the total worktime figure in Cell K21. This per-hour ratio indicates the effect of overtime on the average hourly wage calculated in Cell J21.

Step 25. Enter the following formula into Cell Q22:

```
+Q21/$P$21
```

This formula calculates the total wages paid to workers in the **AM OFFICE** category (in Cell Q21) as a percentage of the total gross pay for the day (in Cell P21). This percentage may be used to establish benchmark standards, to indicate the efficiency of daily labor scheduling, to project future labor schedules, and to indicate the relative productivity of each department.

Now copy this formula from Cell Q22 into cells R22 through Z22, by entering the following command:

```
/CQ22    <Return>    R22..Z22    <Return>
```

Designating Cell P21 as absolute, by preceding the row and column designations with a

```
: A :: B  :: C:: D:: E :: F:: G ::    H     ::  I  ::  J  :: K  :: L  ::  M   ::  N   :: O ::  P  :: Q  ::  R  ::  S  ::  T  ::  U  ::  V  ::  W  ::  X  ::  Y  :: Z  :
DAILY LABOR REPORT
                                   DATE:   03/01/86
                                   DAY:  SATURDAY
                                   CLERK:  J. CHABAN
-------------(((----TIME--->>>-(MEAL)-----
EMP         <-IN->  <-OUT->  [In   EMPLOYEE                 HOURLY  TOTAL  REGULAR  OVER   REGULAR  OVERIME  GROSS    AM      PM      AM      PM      AM      PM      AM       PM       AM       PM
NO   SHIFT  HR MIN  HR MIN   Min]  NAME       DEPT          WAGE    TIME   TIME     TIME   PAY      PAY      PAY      OFFICE  OFFICE  BAR     BAR     D.R.    D.R.    KITCHEN  KITCHEN  JANITOR  JANITOR
                              -----(TIME)-----
```

EMP NO	SHIFT	IN HR MIN	OUT HR MIN	[In Min]	EMPLOYEE NAME	DEPT	HOURLY WAGE	TOTAL TIME	REGULAR TIME	OVER TIME	REGULAR PAY	OVERIME PAY	GROSS PAY	AM OFFICE	PM OFFICE	AM BAR	PM BAR	AM D.R.	PM D.R.	AM KITCHEN	PM KITCHEN	AM JANITOR	PM JANITOR
3.20	AM	10 1	6 15	30	KIT CARSON	BAR	$5.00	7.7	7.7	0.00	$38.67	$0.00	$38.67	$0.00	$0.00	$38.67	$0.00	$0.00	$0.00	$0.00	$0.00	$0.00	$0.00
6.30	AM	3 15	12 15	45	MAY KAY	DINING ROOM	$4.25	8.3	8.0	0.25	$34.00	$1.59	$35.59	$0.00	$0.00	$0.00	$0.00	$35.59	$0.00	$0.00	$0.00	$0.00	$0.00
8.50	AM	5 30	1 32	48	BOB SHIFT	JANITORIAL	$4.50	7.2	7.2	0.00	$32.55	$0.00	$32.55	$0.00	$0.00	$0.00	$0.00	$0.00	$0.00	$0.00	$0.00	$32.55	$0.00
10.40	AM	9 10	6 45	59	JEFF BARRY	KITCHEN	$6.25	8.6	8.0	0.60	$50.00	$5.62	$55.63	$0.00	$0.00	$0.00	$0.00	$0.00	$0.00	$55.63	$0.00	$0.00	$0.00
1.10	AM	3 5	11 35	48	IDA SMITH	OFFICE	$8.00	7.7	7.7	0.00	$61.60	$0.00	$61.60	$61.60	$0.00	$0.00	$0.00	$0.00	$0.00	$0.00	$0.00	$0.00	$0.00
5.20	PM	8 30	5 15	33	CANDY DOWDY	BAR	$5.25	8.2	8.0	0.20	$42.00	$1.57	$43.58	$0.00	$0.00	$0.00	$43.58	$0.00	$0.00	$0.00	$0.00	$0.00	$0.00
4.20	PM	6 30	2 30	55	STEVE BLUE	BAR	$6.50	7.1	7.1	0.00	$46.04	$0.00	$46.04	$0.00	$0.00	$0.00	$46.04	$0.00	$0.00	$0.00	$0.00	$0.00	$0.00
7.30	PM	3 45	11 45	56	CINDY KLASS	DINING ROOM	$4.50	7.1	7.1	0.00	$31.80	$0.00	$31.80	$0.00	$0.00	$0.00	$0.00	$0.00	$31.80	$0.00	$0.00	$0.00	$0.00
9.50	PM	9 45	6 45	15	JOEL CHABAN	JANITORIAL	$3.35	8.8	8.0	0.75	$26.80	$3.77	$30.57	$0.00	$0.00	$0.00	$0.00	$0.00	$0.00	$0.00	$0.00	$0.00	$30.57
11.40	PM	6 15	3 45	58	ANN HERRON	KITCHEN	$8.50	8.5	8.0	0.53	$68.00	$6.80	$74.80	$0.00	$0.00	$0.00	$0.00	$0.00	$0.00	$0.00	$74.80	$0.00	$0.00
2.10	PM	9 1	5 25	57	ANDREA SELIG	OFFICE	$6.35	7.5	7.5	0.00	$47.31	$0.00	$47.31	$0.00	$47.31	$0.00	$0.00	$0.00	$0.00	$0.00	$0.00	$0.00	$0.00

```
<> Average Time Taken for Lunch: 45.82 Mins.  <> Avg.Hrly Wage =  $5.68   86.6   84.3   2.3  $478.77  $19.36  $498.13  $61.60  $47.31  $38.67  $89.62  $35.59  $31.80  $55.63  $74.80  $32.55  $30.57
                                     <> Labor Cost Per Hour =  $5.75           **** PERCENT OF GROSS PAY:  12.37%  9.50%  7.76%  17.99%  7.15%  6.38%  11.17%  15.02%  6.53%  6.14%
```

	TABLE 1	**TABLE 2**		*****TABLE 3*****	
LOOKUP	EMPNO	EMPLOYEE NAME	WAGE	DEPTNO	JOB
TABLES	1	IDA SMITH	$8.00	0.10	OFFICE
	2	ANDREA SELIG	$6.35	0.20	BAR
	3	KIT CARSON	$5.00	0.30	DINING ROOM
	4	STEVE BLUE	$6.50	0.40	KITCHEN
	5	CANDY DOWDY	$5.25	0.50	JANITORIAL
	6	MAY KAY	$4.25		
	7	CINDY KLASS	$4.50		
	8	BOB SHIFT	$4.50		
	9	JOEL CHABAN	$3.35		
	10	JEFF BARRY	$6.25		
	11	ANN HERRON	$8.50		

MACRO NAME	MACRO COMMAND	COMMAND EXPLANATION
\S	/DSRDSORT-AREA~PB9~A~SI9~A~G	* Sort employees by SHIFT and DEPARTMENT

```
                         ***TABLE 1***  **TABLE 2**        *****TABLE 3*****
```

5-3. Daily Labor Report spreadsheet, showing the \S macro.

dollar sign, causes the reference to that cell to remain the same in each cell containing the copied formula. Thus, the reference to Cell P21 remains constant, while the Cell Q21 reference changes in each cell into which the formula is copied.

Using a Macro to Sort Rows

Before creating the sort macro that will be used with this spreadsheet, you have to name the area of the spreadsheet that will be sorted—namely Cell Range A9..Z19. This area of the spreadsheet will be called SORT-AREA.

Step 26. To execute the /Range Name command to create the SORT-AREA range name, first place your cell pointer on cell A9 (the first cell of the range that is to be named); then enter the following command:

```
/RNCSORT-AREA    <Return>    [point to
Cell Z19]    <Return>
```

The first four characters, /RNC, represent Lotus's /Range name Create command. They are followed by entry of the range name, SORT-AREA. After pressing <Return> (which enters the name), you are prompted by Lotus to point to the ending cell of the range you are naming (in this case, the ending cell is Cell Z19). The final <Return> enters this cell range.

Step 27. Begin creating the \S macro (see figure 5-3) by entering the following command into Cell R30:

```
'/DSRDSORT-AREA~PB9~A~SI9~A~G
```

This command sorts and groups all employees, first by shift and then by job department.

Next, enter the following command explanation into Cell V30:

```
* Sort employees by SHIFT and
DEPARTMENT.
```

The sorting done by the \S macro allows you to see employees grouped by shift—so that you can more easily review your operation's labor performance in each work period—as well as by department within each shift. For a more detailed explanation of the /Data Sort command, see page 56.

Step 28. Name the macro you have just created (we have already been calling it \S) by placing the cell pointer on cell R30 (the first cell of the macro) and entering the following /Range Name command:

```
/RNC\S    <Return>    <Return>
```

Step 29. Enter the following label into Cell Q30

```
^\S
```

Step 30. Recalculate your spreadsheet by pressing the CALC function key, <F9>. As soon as you press this key, Lotus will automatically begin evaluating and calculating all expressions on your spreadsheet. See page 37 for more information about forcing a manual recalculation of your spreadsheet.

Protecting Your Spreadsheet

Step 31. Use the /Worksheet Global Protection Enable command sequence, followed by Unprotect commands for the shaded areas of the spreadsheet, to protect the cells in the nonshaded areas of the spreadsheet from accidentally being filled (by you or by other spreadsheet users) with unwanted data. Begin by entering the following command string:

```
/WGPE
```

This string is an abbreviated expression for the /Worksheet Global Protection Enable command, which protects every cell in the spreadsheet from entry and alteration.

The next step is to unprotect the cells in the shaded areas of the spreadsheet by entering the /Range Unprotect commands indicated in table 5-11. Before entering each command, place your cell pointer on the first named cell of each cell or cell range that you want to unprotect.

TABLE 5-11. STEP 31 /RANGE UNPROTECT COMMANDS.

Cell(s) to Unprotect	Command to Enter		
I4	/RU	<Return>	
A9..G19	/RU [point to G9]		<Return>

Printing Your Spreadsheet

Step 32. Turn your printer on, align the paper in it, place your cell pointer on Cell A1 by pressing the <Home> key on your cursor/arrow keypad, and print your spreadsheet by issuing the following series of commands:

```
/PPR.    <End>    <Home>
<Return>    AGPQ
```

This abbreviated command language means: "Print to the printer the spreadsheet range A1 through Z39. The paper is aligned in the printer, so the spreadsheet should begin printing at the top of the page. Go and print the spreadsheet. Then page-eject the paper in the printer to the top of a new page, and quit the print commands."

For more information on the <End> and <Home> keys and on Lotus's printer settings, see page 38.

Saving LABOR.WK1

Step 33. To save the Daily Labor Report spreadsheet you have created, enter the following /File Save command:

```
/FSB:LABOR    <Return>
```

LABOR is the file name for the Daily Labor Report spreadsheet and will be written onto the disk in drive B. If you have a hard disk or a single floppy drive system, save the LABOR spreadsheet onto the appropriate drive and directory. When you save this file under the name LABOR, Lotus will automatically add a period and the file name extension WK1 to the file name. LABOR. When you look at a directory of files on disk drive B, you will see this file displayed as LABOR

WK1. The WK1 extension identifies this file to you and to Lotus as a file in a spreadsheet format.

Using the Information in This Spreadsheet

"What If" Labor Analysis

Your Daily Labor Report spreadsheet easily allows you to change and manipulate the following variables:

- Employee number (EMP NO)
- A.M. or P.M. shift (SHIFT)
- Time punched in and time punched out
- Time taken for meal break
- Employee's wage
- Employee's department
- Number of employees

By doing so, you can check to see what effect that one or several changes have on the following categories (for each employee or for all employees):

- Total time
- Regular time
- Overtime
- Regular pay
- Overtime pay
- Gross pay
- A.M./P.M. department expense
- Average hourly wage
- Each department's labor as a percentage of gross pay

Feel free to experiment with and adjust these variables until you are satisfied that your Daily Labor Report spreadsheet meets your labor requirements both operationally and financially.

Individual Employee Totals for Total Time, Regular Time, Overtime, Gross Pay, and Department Totals

Use these breakdown totals (calculated by the spreadsheet) to review each employee's adher-

ence to your operation's overtime rules and policies and to your weekly labor schedule. These totals can also be used to evaluate employees' tardiness, failure to punch in or out, and exceeding of time allowed for the meal-period break.

Totals for Total Time, Regular Time, Overtime, Gross Pay, and Department Totals

These totals (calculated by the spreadsheet) are produced by summing the individual labor breakdowns of all employees. Use these totals (in row 21) to develop daily labor standards and maximum allowable deviations for total time, regular time, and overtime. Use paper records of past Daily Labor Reports, along with your budget and planning tools, to set minimum and maximum time and dollar amounts allowable for total time, regular time, overtime, regular pay, overtime pay, and gross pay. Set similar standards for each department. Treat deviations below the minimum and above the maximum allowable amounts as indicators of problems.

Use these derived standards and deviations to spot problems in conjunction with similar standards and deviations set for percentage of gross pay in row 22.

Percentage of Gross Pay

The percentage of gross pay (calculated by the spreadsheet) equals department total pay divided by gross pay. Use these percentages (in row 22) to develop daily labor standards and maximum allowable deviations from the standard for percentage of gross pay. Use paper records of past Daily Labor Reports, along with your budget and planning tools to set minimum and maximum allowable percentages for each department's total pay. Set similar standards for each department. Treat deviations below the minimum and above the maximum percentages as indicators of problems.

Use these derived standards and deviations to spot problems in conjunction with standards and deviations for total time, regular time, and overtime in row 21.

Average Time Taken for Lunch

The average time taken for lunch (calculated by the spreadsheet) equals the total time taken for meal period breaks by all employees, divided by the number of employees. Use this average as a standard in scanning to see if rules for allowable meal-period time are being abused.

Average Hourly Wage

The average hourly wage (calculated by the spreadsheet) equals the total of all hourly wages divided by the number of employees. Use this average as a standard for quick review of how the average hourly wage fluctuates. Compare this average with the figure for labor cost per hour to see the per-hour effect of overtime on hourly wages. If the average hourly wage increases, you should immediately recognize that labor costs are rising and that immediate action needs to be taken to remedy the situation. Direct action—such as cutting back employees, reducing hours on the weekly labor schedule, retraining employees to be more productive, or delaying wage raises—may need to be taken. Indirect action—such as increasing menu prices—may be another solution.

Labor Cost Per Hour

Labor cost per hour (calculated by the spreadsheet) equals total gross pay divided by total time. Use this ratio in conjunction with the average hourly wage to measure the effect of overtime on average hourly wages. Any difference between the average hourly wage and the figure for labor cost per hour is the result of overtime incurred in your operation.

Problems

1. How can the Daily Labor Report help you manage and control labor in a foodservice operation?

2. What is the difference between wages and salaries? Why are salaries not included in the Daily Labor Report?

3. How can the Daily Labor Report help you to produce an optimized labor schedule for your employees?

4. Explain how to use the Daily Labor Report to set standards and maximum allowable variances for labor control.

5. Explain how Lotus's @INT function is used in the Daily Labor Report. Describe the @INT function's effect on a number.

6. Explain how Lotus's @AVG function is used in the Daily Labor Report. How does this function calculate an average?

7. Define the following ideas/terms, and explain how Lotus uses them:
   • *Serial/Julian calendar number*
   • *Argument*
   • *Function within a function*

8. Explain how the following Lotus calendar functions may be used, discussing the arguments for each function and stating what each function may return (a number, a serial/Julian calendar number, or a label) as a result of its evaluation:
   • @NOW
   • @DATE
   • @YEAR
   • @MONTH
   • @DAY
   • @MOD

9. Explain how Lotus's @CHOOSE function is used in the Daily Labor Report spreadsheet. What arguments does the @CHOOSE function take, and how are these arguments used?

10. Explain how and why Lotus's /Data Sort command is used to sort the Daily Labor Report.

11. The \S macro in Step 27 performs a primary sort and secondary sort of rows 9 through 19 in one command. Trying to perform this sort in two commands might result in the following commands;

    Command 1 (this command sorts rows 9 through 19 by SHIFT:

    ```
    /DSRDSORT-AREA~PB9~A~G
    ```

    Command 2 (this command sorts rows 9 through 19 by DEPT:

```
/DSRDSORT-AREA~PI¶~A~G
```

Enter these two commands, using the Daily Labor Report spreadsheet you have created. Explain the difference between the \S macro command used in Step 27 and the preceding two commands in terms of their effect on the spreadsheet.

Cases

1. Assume that your foodservice operation uses a time clock based on 24-hour (military) time. Rewrite the formula for total time in column K, to enable your spreadsheet to work with a 24-hour time clock. (*Hint:* You will not need to use the A.M. and P.M. shift designations to calculate total time if you use a 24-hour clock.)
2. Assume the following percentage-of-gross-pay standards and variances have been set for each department:

Department	Allowable Variance	Standard Percentage of Gross Pay
AM OFFICE	1%	10%
PM OFFICE	1%	10%
AM BAR	2%	10%
PM BAR	2%	15%
AM DINING ROOM	1%	10%
PM DINING ROOM	1%	10%
AM KITCHEN	2%	10%
PM KITCHEN	2%	15%
AM JANITORIAL	2%	5%
PM JANITORIAL	2%	5%

Adapt the Daily Labor Report spreadsheet to compare these standards to percentage of gross pay for each department and to flag (indicate with an asterisk or other noticeable symbol) any department whose percentage of gross pay falls below or exceeds the allowable variance.

6. Daily Sales/Cash Report

TABLE 6-1. SUMMARY OF LOTUS COMMANDS USED IN THIS CHAPTER.

Commands Used

Command String Abbreviation	Command Name	Functions Used
/C	/Copy	@IF
/FR	/File Retrieve	@SUM
/FS	/File Save	
/PP	/Print Printer	
/RE	/Range Erase	
/RF	/Range Format	
/RI	/Range Input	
/RNC	/Range Name Create	
/RU	/Range Unprotect	
/WGP	/Worksheet Global Protect	
/WGR	/Worksheet Global Recalculation	
{MENUBRANCH cell}	Menu Macro	
{BRANCH cell}	Branch Macro	

Cash control is in the mind of every foodservice operator. No wonder the most universally generated report for foodservice control is the Daily Sales/Cash Report. Unfortunately, this report is also one of the business's most time-consuming manual paperwork tasks.

The main purpose of the Daily Sales/Cash Report is to reconcile cash payments and vouchers from customers with total dollar sales reported by your electronic cash register (ECR) or point-of-sale (POS) system. The result of this reconciliation is a net cash overage, shortage, or balance. Many former foodservice employees have experienced the wrath of a foodservice owner/manager whose Daily Sales/Cash Report showed a shortage of cash at the end of the day.

Anyone who has ever used a Daily Cash Report to reconcile the cash in a cash register with what the cash register journal tape reports knows how frustrating it can be to balance. The Daily Sales/Cash Report spreadsheet described in this chapter alleviates many of those frustrations by doing automatic error checking to locate out-of-balance problems.

Cash registers and cash systems vary from operation to operation. Your foodservice operation may require a Daily Cash Report that is more specialized than the one presented here; this one is certainly not capable of meeting every operation's needs. The general outlines of the report, however, can be modified to suit your own cash reporting requirements.

Data on tangible cash and credit card slips, listed under PAYMENTS/VOUCHERS (see figure 6-1, columns E through G) represent one side of the Daily Sales/Cash Report. When counted, these must balance with the data listed under SALES DATA (columns A through C)—the record of sales entered into and reported by your cash register. Source information for payments and vouchers may originate from the following

```
    :    A    ::B:!  C  ::D::     E    ::F:: G ::H::    I    ::J:: K ::L:: M ::N::      O      :
 1  DAILY SALES/CASH REPORT
 2
 3           DATE:    03/01/86
 4            DAY:    SATURDAY
 5           NAME:    J. CHABAN
 6        WEATHER:    SUNNY
 7  SALES TAX RATE:   6.5%
 8  CUSTOMER COUNT:   200
 9  ==========================================================================================
10  SALES DATA (from journal tape) ::  PAYMENTS/VOUCHERS (manual count) ::   ERROR      :  ERROR   : ERROR    :   CORRECTIVE
11  DESCRIPTION        AMOUNT    ::  DESCRIPTION         AMOUNT    ::  TEST FOR:      :  AMOUNT  : INDICATOR :     ACTION
12  ==========================================================================================
13  *** DEPARTMENT SALES ***   ::    ****** CASH ******    :: CASH COUNT        :   $22.78 : <--ERROR! : RECOUNT CASH !!!!
14     APPETIZERS  :   $204.95  ::       PENNIES  :   $0.27 :: CREDIT CARD COUNT :  ($2.00) : <--ERROR! : RECOUNT CR.CARD VCHRS!
15        ENTREES  :   $591.80  ::       NICKELS  :   $2.65 :: OVERRING COUNT    :    $0.00 : O.K.     : NONE...GO HOME !!
16       DESSERTS  :    $75.85  ::         DIMES  :   $7.50 :: CHG TIP ALLOCATION:    6.6%  : <--ERROR! : REPORTED TIPS TOO LOW !
17           WINE  :   $195.00  ::      QUARTERS  :  $17.75 :: CHARGED TIPS COUNT:  ($1.00) : <--ERROR! : RECOUNT CHG.TIP VCHRS !
18           BEER  :    $50.00  ::  HALF DOLLARS  :   $1.50 :: PROMO SALES COUNT :    $0.00 : O.K.     : NONE...GO HOME !!
19  PROMOTIONAL SALES :  $36.75 :: SILVER DOLLARS :   $3.00 :: SALES TAX         :    $0.00 : O.K.     : NONE...GO HOME !!
20  ------------------------   ::        $1 BILLS  :  $67.00 :: CASH OVER/(SHORT) :   $20.78 : <--ERROR! : CHECK ALL ERRORS !
21  TOTAL SALES BY DEPT : $1,154.35 ::    $2 BILLS  :   $4.00 ::                   :         :          :
22  ==========================::        $5 BILLS  : $165.00 ::                   :         :          :
23  *** SALES BY TAX STATUS *** ::     $10 BILLS  : $140.00 ::                   :         :          :
24  TOTAL TAXABLE SALES : $1,106.60 ::   $20 BILLS  : $220.00 :: ==================================================
25  TOTAL NON-TAX SALES :  $47.75  ::    $50 BILLS  :  $50.00 ::
26  ------------------------   ::      $100 BILLS  : $100.00 :: ****************************************
27  TOTAL SALES BY TAX : $1,154.35 ::  $1000 BILLS  :   $0.00 :: ****************************************
28  ==========================:: PERSONAL CHECKS  :  $11.25 ::   CASH DEPOSIT:     $1,209.31
29  *** SALES BY TENDER ***    :: TRAVELERS CHECKS :  $20.00 ::
30          CASH  :   $789.64  :: ----------------------------- ::   TRUE SALES:     $1,134.88
31   CREDIT CARD  :   $396.39  ::    TOTAL CASH  : $809.92 :: ****************************************
32  --------------------------::                             :: ****************************************
33  TOTAL BY TENDER : $1,186.03 ::  **** CREDIT CARDS ****    ::
34  ==========================::  BANKAMERICARD  : $161.08 ::
35  *** MISCELLANEOUS ***      ::          VISA  :  $89.00 ::
36                             ::    MASTERCARD  : $120.00 ::
37      PAID-OUTS  :    $2.50  :: CREDIT CARD TIPS :  $24.31 ::
38   MISC. INCOME  :    $5.00  :: ----------------------------- ::
39      OVERRINGS  :    $3.50  :: TOTAL CREDIT CARDS : $394.39 ::
40      SALES TAX  :   $71.93  :: =============================::
41                             ::  *** VOUCHERS & MISC. ***    ::
42                             ::       OVERRINGS  :   $3.50 ::
43                             :: CR.CARD TIPS PAIDOUT : $25.31 ::
44                             :: PROMOTIONAL SALES :  $36.75 ::
45                             ::       PAID-OUTS  :   $2.50 ::
46                             ::     MISC.INCOME  :   $5.00 ::
47                             ::       SALES TAX  :  $71.93 ::
```

6-1. Daily Sales/Cash Report spreadsheet.

items received from customers or generated from daily business activity:

From Customers

- Cash
- Personal checks
- Traveler's checks
- Credit cards
- House accounts
- Promotional coupons/vouchers
- Tips/gratuities

From Business Activity

- Over-ring/under-ring vouchers (documentation for mistakes made by employees who accidentally ring up a value on the cash register that is more or less than the menu price)
- Paid-out vouchers (documentation for cash that has been taken from the cash register to pay for goods and services during the day or during the shift)
- Miscellaneous income (income not derived directly from food and beverage sales)

Each foodservice operation has its own policies regarding how customers may pay a bill. Many operations will not accept personal checks from customers. Some have house accounts that allow a customer to charge meals and then receive a cumulative bill at the end of the month. Most restaurants today accept at least one brand of credit card, but the particular credit cards accepted and refused vary from one operation to the next.

Customer payments and vouchers are counted manually from cash and vouchers in the cash register drawer.

Sales data originate from your cash register journal tape or ECR/POS system cash report. The journal tape or system cash report maintains a record of all transactions entered in the system. The SALES DATA categories you will list in the Daily Sales/Cash Report spreadsheet depend on how your sales/cash system is organized and on how your cash register or ECR/POS system is designed. Some machines are configured with department keys that register each sale rung in the cash register by menu category. Other, more sophisticated POS systems are computer-programmed to register each sale according to menu item, using preset keys on the POS keyboard that represent each menu item and its menu price. Depending on your cash register and system, sales data may be organized by:

- Sales by menu item
- Sales by food and beverage category
- Taxable sales
- Nontaxable sales
- Sales by tender (that is, by payment type):
  – Cash
  – Credit card
  – House account
  – Promotional sales
- Miscellaneous income and contrasales activity:
  – Amounts paid out
  – Miscellaneous income
  – Over-rings

In order to simplify the Daily Sales/Cash Report spreadsheet in this chapter, certain assumptions have been made. First, it is assumed that the cash register in use is a simple electronic cash register without preset or price look-up keys. In other words, the hypothetical register has the following keys: numeric keys for entering the price; seven department keys for separate entry of appetizers, entrées, desserts, wine, beer, promotional sale items, and nontaxable sales items; two settlement keys for separate entry of cash tendered and credit cards tendered; and several miscellaneous keys for amounts paid out, miscellaneous income, over-rings, and sales tax.

A second assumption made here is that charged tips are paid to servers from the cash drawer at the end of each server's shift. A third assumption is that the cash register is "Z'd" out every day. (This practice of resetting all cash register department totals and other sales totals to zero at the end of each business day is neither advocated nor condoned by the author; it is merely used to simplify the example in this book.) Remember that the example presented here is not intended to match your specific situation precisely, but rather to serve as a sample reference on the basis of which you design your own Daily Cash Report spreadsheet.

Formatting, Headings, and Labels

Step 1. Reformat columns A through O from the normal, default Lotus column width of nine characters to the widths indicated in table 6-2.

Step 2. Begin re-creating the spreadsheet example shown in figure 6-1 by entering the appropriate headings and labels into columns A through O, rows 1 through 47, exactly as specified in table 6-3.

You may need to pad some of your cell entries with blank spaces to get your headings to look like those pictured in figure 6-1. Any heading beginning with one of the three Lotus label alignment prefixes (', '', and ^) signifies a label to be padded with blank spaces or to be given a

TABLE 6-2. STEP 1 FORMATTING COMMANDS.

Column	Width	Command to Enter	
A	20	/WCS20	<Return>
B	3	/WCS3	<Return>
C	12	/WCS12	<Return>
D	3	/WCS3	<Return>
E	20	/WCS20	<Return>
F	3	/WCS3	<Return>
G	12	/WCS12	<Return>
H	3	/WCS3	<Return>
I	18	/WCS18	<Return>
J	3	/WCS3	<Return>
K	12	/WCS12	<Return>
L	3	/WCS3	<Return>
M	10	/WCS10	<Return>
N	3	/WCS3	<Return>
O	23	/WCS23	<Return>

TABLE 6-3. STEP 2 HEADINGS.

Cell	Heading
A1	DAILY SALES/CASH REPORT
A3	''DATE:
A4	''DAY:
A5	''NAME:
A6	''WEATHER:
A7	''SALES TAX RATE:
A8	''CUSTOMER COUNT:
A10	' SALES DATA (from journal tape)
A11	^DESCRIPTION
A13	' *** DEPARTMENT SALES ***
A14	''APPETIZERS
A15	''ENTREES
A16	''DESSERTS
A17	''WINE
A18	''BEER
A19	''PROMOTIONAL SALES
A21	''TOTAL SALES BY DEPT
A23	' *** SALES BY TAX STATUS ***
A24	''TOTAL TAXABLE SALES
A25	''TOTAL NONTAXABLE SALES
A27	''TOTAL SALES BY TAX
A29	' *** SALES BY TENDER ***
A30	''CASH
A31	''CREDIT CARD
A33	''TOTAL BY TENDER
A35	' *** MISCELLANEOUS ***
A37	''PAID-OUTS
A38	''MISC. INCOME
A39	''OVER-RINGS
A40	''SALES TAX
C11	^AMOUNT
E10	' PAYMENTS/VOUCHERS (manual count)
E11	^DESCRIPTION
E13	' ****** CASH ******
E14	''PENNIES
E15	''NICKELS
E16	''DIMES
E17	''QUARTERS
E18	''HALF DOLLARS
E19	''SILVER DOLLARS
E20	''$1.00 BILLS
E21	''$2.00 BILLS
E22	''$5.00 BILLS
E23	''$10.00 BILLS
E24	''$20.00 BILLS
E25	''$50.00 BILLS
E26	''$100.00 BILLS
E27	''$1000.00 BILLS
E28	''PERSONAL CHECKS
E29	''TRAVELER'S CHECKS
E31	''TOTAL CASH
E33	' **** CREDIT CARDS ****
E34	''BANKAMERICARD
E35	''VISA
E36	''MASTERCARD
E37	''CREDIT CARD TIPS
E39	''TOTAL CREDIT CARDS
E41	' *** VOUCHERS MISC. ***
E42	''OVER-RINGS
E43	''CR.CARD TIPS PAIDOUT
E44	''PROMOTIONAL SALES
E45	''PAID-OUTS
E46	''MISC. INCOME
E47	''SALES TAX
G11	^AMOUNT
I10	^ERROR
I11	^TEST FOR:
I13	CASH COUNT
I14	CREDIT CARD COUNT
I15	OVER-RING COUNT
I16	CHG TIP ALLOCATION
I17	CHARGED TIPS COUNT
I18	PROMO SALES COUNT
I19	SALES TAX
I20	CASH OVER/(SHORT)
I28	''CASH DEPOSIT:
I30	''TRUE SALES:
K10	^ERROR
K11	^AMOUNT
M10	^ERROR
M11	^INDICATOR
O10	^CORRECTIVE
O11	^ACTION

special cell alignment. Remember that the prefix ' aligns text to the left margin of the cell, the prefix " aligns text to the right margin of the cell, and the prefix ^ centers text within the cell. Unless a label alignment prefix is indicated in table 6-3, do not use one of these prefixes to begin a label or heading.

Step 3. Enter dashed lines and double-dashed lines into the spreadsheet, as indicated in table 6-4. Use the backslash (\) key at the beginning of each cell entry to signal to Lotus that the charac-

TABLE 6-4. STEP 3 REPEAT AND /COPY COMMANDS.

Cell	Repeat Command to Enter	/Copy Command to Enter			
A9	\=	/CA9	\<Return\>	B9..O9	\<Return\>
A12	\=	/CA12	\<Return\>	B12..O12	\<Return\>
A20	\-	/CA20	\<Return\>	B20..C20	\<Return\>
A22	\=	/CA22	\<Return\>	B22..C22	\<Return\>
A26	\-	/CA26	\<Return\>	B26..C26	\<Return\>
A28	\=	/CA28	\<Return\>	B28..C28	\<Return\>
A32	\-	/CA32	\<Return\>	B32..C32	\<Return\>
A34	\=	/CA34	\<Return\>	B34..C34	\<Return\>
E30	\-	/CE30	\<Return\>	F30..G30	\<Return\>
E32	\=	/CE32	\<Return\>	F32..G32	\<Return\>
E38	\-	/CE38	\<Return\>	F38..G38	\<Return\>
E40	\=	/CE40	\<Return\>	F40..G40	\<Return\>
I24	\=	/CI24	\<Return\>	J24..O24	\<Return\>
I26	*	/CI26	\<Return\>	J26..L26	\<Return\>
I27	*	/CI27	\<Return\>	J27..L27	\<Return\>
I31	*	/CI31	\<Return\>	J31..L31	\<Return\>
I32	*	/CI32	\<Return\>	J32..L32	\<Return\>

ter immediately following it is to be repeated across the cell from end to end.

To repeat a character across several individual cells, use Lotus's /Copy command, as indicated in table 6-4. Use the pointing method described on page 34 to define the last cell of a cell range when performing the /Copy operation. Remember to place the cell pointer on the originating cell (the cell being copied from) before you begin to enter each command listed in table 6-4.

Step 4. Enter the colons (:) and uprights (|) into columns B, D, F, H, J, L, and N, as they appear in figure 6-1. Use two uprights (||) for the double uprights in columns D and H. In any case where you need to repeat colons or double uprights throughout a column, use the /Copy command. For instance, to copy the double uprights from Cell D13 into cells D14 through D50, first enter

the double uprights in Cell D13, using the right-align prefix:

```
"||
```

Then enter the following /Copy command to copy the double uprights:

```
/C    <Return>    [point to D14] .
[point to D50]    <Return>
```

The double uprights will thereupon be copied from Cell D13 into cells D14 through D50.

Step 5. Format the cells and cell ranges identified in table 6-5, as indicated there. Enter each command given in the far right-hand column of the table exactly as it appears, by typing the characters shown and then hitting the \<Return\> key.

TABLE 6-5. STEP 5 /RANGE FORMAT COMMANDS.

Cell(s)	Format/Alignment	Command to Enter			
C3	date type 4	/RFD4	\<Return\>		
C7	percent	/RFP1	\<Return\>	C7..C7	\<Return\>
C12..C40	currency	/RFC2	\<Return\>	C12..C40	\<Return\>
G12..G47	currency	/RFC2	\<Return\>	G12..G47	\<Return\>
K14..K24	currency	/RFC2	\<Return\>	K14..K24	\<Return\>
K16	percent	/RFP1	\<Return\>	K16..K16	\<Return\>
K28..K30	currency	/RFC2	\<Return\>	K28..K30	\<Return\>

TABLE 6-6. DAILY INPUT INTO THE DAILY SALES/CASH REPORT SPREADSHEET.

Cell(s)	Input
C5	NAME. Enter the name of the employee who is filling in the Daily Cash Report.
C6	WEATHER. Enter the day's weather conditions.
C7	SALES TAX RATE. Enter your state/local sales tax rate.
C8	CUSTOMER COUNT. Enter the day's customer count.
C14..C19	DEPARTMENT SALES. Enter the department key totals from your journal/report tape.
C24..C25	SALES BY TAX STATUS. Enter the totals of taxable and nontaxable sales from your journal/report tape.
C30..C31	SALES BY TENDER. Enter the settlement keys totals (indicating how customers paid for food and beverages in your establishment) from your journal/report tape.
C37..C40	MISCELLANEOUS. Enter the totals of any miscellaneous cash register keys from your journal/report tape.
G14..G29	CASH. Enter your manual count of cash, by type of coin or bill.
G34..G37	CREDIT CARDS. Enter your manual counts of food and beverage credit card sales for each kind of credit card (not including credit card tips). Count credit card tips separately from food and beverage sales on credit card vouchers, and enter your total for credit card tips in Cell G37.
G42..G47	VOUCHERS MISC. Enter your manual count of vouchers and miscellaneous income including over-ring vouchers, vouchers for cash paid out as credit card tips to service employees, promotional sale coupons/vouchers, records of other amounts paid out, and miscellaneous income. Do not enter sales tax figures; this tax is calculated using the spreadsheet formula explained in step 10.

When formatting a cell range, use the pointing method to define the last cell in each indicated cell range. Be sure to place the cell pointer on the first cell indicated in the far left-hand column of table 6-5 before entering the associated command.

Daily Operator Input

Step 6. Enter the specific data that appear in the shaded areas of figure 6-1. Table 6-6 describes the standard input for this portion of the spreadsheet. This is the only information you normally have to enter daily; the remainder of the spreadsheet is calculated automatically.

Formulas

Step 7. Enter the following Lotus calendar function into Cell C3:

```
@NOW
```

If the target cell is formatted for date (as Cell C3 is), the @NOW function automatically gets to-

day's date from the system date you entered when you first turned on your computer or from the date maintained by an automatic, battery-operated clock/calendar (if your computer has this feature). If the target cell is formatted for time, the time of day is returned when the @NOW function is entered.

Step 8. Enter the following formula into Cell C4 (this is a long formula, so take your time to prevent entry errors):

```
@CHOOSE(@MOD(@DATE(@YEAR(@NOW),
@MONTH(@NOW),@DAY(@NOW)),7),
''SATURDAY'',''SUNDAY'',''MONDAY'',
''TUESDAY'',''WEDNESDAY'',
''THURSDAY'',''FRIDAY'')
```

Although the formula is reproduced here on five lines, it should be typed into your computer without any break, as though it were a single long word. This formula automatically determines the day of the week (Sunday through Saturday). For a more detailed explanation of how this lengthy formula works, see pages 67–70.

TABLE 6-7. STEP 9 FORMULAS.

Cell	Formula
C21	@SUM(C12..C20)
C27	@SUM(C22..C26)
C33	@SUM(C28..C32)
G31	@SUM(G12..G30)
G39	@SUM(G32..G38)

Step 9. Enter each formula given in table 6-7 into the corresponding cell. These formulas sum SALES DATA categories to produce totals for DEPARTMENT SALES, SALES BY TAX STATUS, and SALES BY TENDER. They sum PAYMENTS/VOUCHERS categories to produce totals for CASH and CREDIT CARDS.

Step 10. Enter the following formula into Cell G47:

+C24*C7

This formula multiplies the sales tax rate in Cell C7 by the total taxable sales in Cell C24, returning sales tax in Cell G47.

Step 11. Enter the following formula into Cell K13:

+G31-(C30-C37)

This formula subtracts the net cash reported by your cash register journal/report tape (Cell C30 − Cell C37) from your manual count of cash (Cell G31). It subtracts cash paid out (Cell C37) from cash received (Cell C30) because it assumes that the cash register used in our illustrated spreadsheet does not automatically give you a net cash balance. Theoretically, the net cash according to the cash register and the net cash according to your manual count should be equal. If there is a difference, the spreadsheet advises in Cell O13 that you re-count the cash to double-check for an error in your manual count.

Step 12. Enter the following formula into Cell K14:

+G39-C31

This formula subtracts the dollar total of credit card receipts reported by your cash register (Cell C31) from your manual computation of the same total by addition of credit card vouchers (Cell G39). If there is a difference, the spreadsheet advises in Cell O14 that you re-count your credit card vouchers.

Step 13. Enter the following formula into Cell K15:

+G42-C39

This formula subtracts over-rings reported by your cash register (Cell C39) from your manual count of over-ring vouchers (Cell G42). If there is a difference, the spreadsheet advises in Cell O15 that you re-count your over-ring vouchers.

Step 14. Enter the following formula into Cell K16:

+G37/(G34+G35+G36)

This formula divides your manual count of tips charged on credit cards (Cell G37) by total credit card sales (Cell G34 + Cell G35 + G36), returning the percentage of charged tips in Cell K16. If this percentage is less than the 8 percent defined by the Internal Revenue Service's tip allocation factor, the spreadsheet advises in Cell O16 that the charged tips are too low.

Step 15. Enter the following formula into Cell K17:

+G37-G43

This formula subtracts your manual addition of tip vouchers documenting cash paid to servers for charged tips that they have earned (Cell G43) from your manual addition of credit card tips on credit card vouchers (Cell G37). These vouchers for credit card tips paid out should equal the amount of tips charged on credit cards. If there is a difference, the spreadsheet advises in Cell O17 that you re-count the charged tips on credit card vouchers and/or the vouchers for charged tips paid out.

Step 16. Enter the following formula into Cell K18:

+G44-C19

This formula subtracts promotional sales reported by your cash register journal/report tape

(Cell C19) from your manual count of vouchers/coupons for promotional sales (Cell G44). If there is a difference, the spreadsheet advises in Cell O18 that you re-count the promotional sales vouchers.

Step 17. Enter the following formula into Cell K19:

```
@ROUND(+G47-C40,2)
```

This formula subtracts the sales tax reported by your cash register journal/report tape (Cell C40) from the spreadsheet calculation of sales tax (Cell G47). If there is a difference, the spreadsheet advises in Cell O19 that you reprogram the tax rate in your cash register.

Step 18. Enter the following formula into Cell K20:

```
(G31+G39+G46)-(C27+C40-C37-C39
-C19+C38)
```

This formula subtracts cash/deposit data reported by your cash register journal/report tape from your manual count of cash and deposit items. The cash register journal report tape data consists of the following totals (by cell and category):

```
C27 = TOTAL SALES BY TAX
C40 = SALES TAX
C37 = PAID-OUTS
C39 = OVER-RINGS
C19 = PROMOTIONAL SALES
C38 = MISCELLANEOUS INCOME
```

The manual count data consists of the following totals (by cell and category):

```
G31 = TOTAL CASH
G39 = TOTAL CREDIT CARDS
G46 = MISCELLANEOUS INCOME
```

The preceding formula attempts to reconcile the cash/deposit total according to your cash register with your manual count of cash/deposit items. The calculation of cash register items starts with the **TOTAL SALES** figure; it then deducts sales items that are not included in a cash deposit and adds items that are not included in sales but are included in a cash deposit. This

formula assumes that all credit card vouchers are deposited directly in your bank account, as though they were cash. The formula also assumes that the **TOTAL BY TENDER** figure is total settlement received from customers and does not represent net cash. To calculate the net cash deposited, you must deduct the **PAID-OUTS** figure from the **TOTAL BY TENDER** figure.

If there is a difference between the figure based on what your cash register reports and the figure based on your manual count, the spreadsheet advises in Cell O20 that you check for errors in your manual counts and in your input of cash register journal/report tape data, before you record the amount shown in Cell K20 as an overage or shortage.

Step 19. Enter the following formula in Cell K28:

```
+G31+G39+G46
```

This formula calculates your daily cash deposit by adding your manual counts of cash, credit card vouchers, and miscellaneous income.

Step 20. Enter the following formula in Cell K30:

```
+G31+G39+G45-G47
```

This formula attempts to provide a figure for true sales. True sales are assumed by this spreadsheet to be sales not including the following:

1. Sales tax
2. Charged tips paid out as cash
3. Miscellaneous income
4. Promotional sales in the form of coupons, discounts, or free food and beverage

The figure for true sales does account for any overage or shortage in cash. True sales may be thought of as all receipts of payment for food and beverage sold, not including sales tax, promotional coupons, tips, and miscellaneous income.

The true sales figure from this spreadsheet is used in the Daily and Period-to-date Report spreadsheet described in Chapter 7 to help produce a more accurate representation of operational ratios than would appear if total sales were used.

Step 21. Enter each formula given in table 6-8 into the corresponding cell of Cell Range M13..M20. (For a complete list of Lotus's math-

TABLE 6-8. STEP 21 FORMULAS.

Cell	Formula
M13	@IF(K13<>0,''<--ERROR!'', ''O.K.'')
M14	@IF(K14<>0,''<--ERROR!'', ''O.K.'')
M15	@IF(K15<>0,''<--ERROR!'', ''O.K.'')
M16	@IF(K16<8.0,''<--ERROR!'', ''O.K.'')
M17	@IF(K17<>0,''<--ERROR!'', ''O.K.'')
M18	@IF(K18<>0,''<--ERROR!'', ''O.K.'')
M19	@IF(K19<>0,''<--ERROR!'', ''O.K.'')
M20	@IF(K20<>0,''<--ERROR!'', ''O.K.'')

ematical operators, including <> [not equal to] see table 2-6, page 23.)

Rendered in English, the formula in Cell M13 reads: "If Cell K13 is not equal to 0, then display the label <--ERROR! in Cell M13; otherwise, display the label O.K..

Similarly, the formula in Cell M16 reads: "If Cell K16 is less than 8.0 [the IRS's tip allocation factor], then display the label <--ERROR! in Cell M16; otherwise, display the label O.K..

For more information on the @IF command, see page 72.

Step 22. Enter each formula given in table 6-9 into the corresponding cell of Cell Range O13..O20.

Step 23. Recalculate your spreadsheet by pressing the CALC function key, <F9>. As soon as you press this key, Lotus will automatically begin evaluating and calculating all expressions or your spreadsheet. See page 37 for more information about forcing a manual recalculation of your spreadsheet.

Protecting Your Spreadsheet

Step 24. Use the /Worksheet Global Protection Enable command sequence, followed by Unprotect commands for the shaded areas of the spreadsheet, to protect the cells in the nonshaded areas of the spreadsheet from accidentally being filled (by you or by other spreadsheet users) with unwanted data. Begin by entering the following command string:

```
/WGPE
```

This string is an abbreviated expression for the /Worksheet Global Protection Enable command, which protects every cell in the spreadsheet from entry and alteration.

The next step is to unprotect the cells in the shaded areas of the spreadsheet by entering the /Range Unprotect commands indicated in table

TABLE 6-9. STEP 22 FORMULAS.

Cell	Formula
O13	@IF(M13=''<--ERROR!'',''RECOUNT CASH !!!!'',''NONE...GO HOME !!'')
O14	@IF(M14=''<--ERROR!'',''RECOUNT CR.CARD VCHRS!'',''NONE...GO HOME !!'')
O15	@IF(M15=''<--ERROR!'',''RECOUNT OVERRING VCHRS !'',''NONE...GO HOME !!'')
O16	@IF(M16=''<--ERROR!'',''REPORTED TIPS TOO LOW !'',''NONE...GO HOME !!'')
O17	@IF(M17=''<--ERROR!'',''RECOUNT CHG.TIP VCHRS !'',''NONE...GO HOME !!'')
O18	@IF(M17=''<--ERROR!'',''RECOUNT PROMO VCHRS !'',''NONE...GO HOME !!'')
O19	@IF(M19=''<--ERROR!'',''REPROGRAM TAX RATE !'',''NONE...GO HOME !!'')
O20	@IF(M20=''<--ERROR!'',''CHECK ALL ERRORS !!'',''NONE...GO HOME !!'')

TABLE 6-10. STEP 24 /RANGE UNPROTECT COMMANDS.

Cells to Unprotect	Command to Enter		
C5..C8	/RU	[point to C8]	<Return>
C14..C19	/RU	[point to C19]	<Return>
C24..C25	/RU	[point to C25]	<Return>
C30..C31	/RU	[point to C31]	<Return>
C37..C40	/RU	[point to C40]	<Return>
G14..G29	/RU	[point to G29]	<Return>
G34..G37	/RU	[point to G37]	<Return>
G42..G46	/RU	[point to G46]	<Return>

6-10. Before entering each command, place your cell pointer on the first named cell of each cell range that you want to unprotect.

Printing Your Spreadsheet

Step 25. Turn your printer on, align the paper in it, place your cell pointer on Cell A1 by pressing the <Home> key on your cursor/arrow keypad, and print your spreadsheet by issuing the following series of commands:

```
/PPR.    <End>      <Home>
<Return>     AGPQ
```

This abbreviated command language means: "Print to the printer the spreadsheet range A1 through O47. The paper is aligned in the printer, so the spreadsheet should begin printing at the top of the page. Go and print the spreadsheet. Then page-eject the paper in the printer to the top of a new page, and quit the print commands."

You may need to consult your Lotus manual for information on how to adjust Lotus's printer settings for footers, margins, borders, page length, and special set-up strings.

Saving LABOR.WK1

If you would like to stop and take a break at this point, save the spreadsheet you are working on by performing Step 26. Otherwise, skip Step 26 and go on to Step 27.

Step 26. You can save the Daily Sales/Cash Report spreadsheet you have created so far, by entering the following /File Save command:

```
/FSB:CASH     <Return>
```

CASH is the file name for the Daily Sales/Cash Report spreadsheet and will be written onto the disk in drive B. If you have a hard disk or a single floppy drive system, save the CASH spreadsheet onto the appropriate drive and directory. When you save this file under the name CASH, Lotus will automatically add a period and the file name extension WK1 to the name CASH. When you look at a directory of files on drive B, you will see this file displayed as CASH WK1. The WK1 extension identifies this file to you and to Lotus as a file in a spreadsheet format.

Using a Menu Macro to Enter Data in the Daily Sales/Cash Report

The shaded areas where you or your manager will enter the dollar amounts from your journal tape and your manual cash counts must be erased every day when you retrieve the Daily Sales/Cash Report spreadsheet from disk. Erasing this area leaves a clean slate on which to enter data from the day's sales/cash activity. At that point, you will begin moving from cell to cell entering your sales/cash data.

Instead of performing these preliminary steps manually every day, you can create a macro to perform the steps for you automatically.

This chapter explains how to create three different macros (see figure 6-2)—each consisting of several different commands, and each performing a different function. In addition, it explains how to tie all three macros together into a single menu macro. The menu macro is a curly-bracket macro that allows you to create a Lotus-like menu of up to eight macros from which you may select any one to execute. Instead of trying to remember three different backslash-letter names, you will only need to remember one—the one that executes the menu. Once you reach the menu, you may select any of the three macros identified there.

The first of these three macros will be named ENTER—SALES. It will automatically erase the

```
                  Q        R         S            T              U           V      W     X     Y     Z      AA
 2
 3
 4
 5
 6
 7
 8
 9
10  ==================================================================================   ======================================
11  MACRO NAME                        MACRO COMMAND                                          COMMAND EXPLANATION
12  =========          ================================================================   ======================================
13    \M              {MENUBRANCH ENTER_SALES}                                             * Display menu.
14
15  ENTER_SALES        Sales Input          Cash Input           Print                 Quit  * Menu choice.
16                     Enter SALES DATA     Enter PAYMENTS/VOUCHERS  Print Daily Sales/Cash Report Press ESC !!  * Menu help/information.
17                     /REDEPT_SALES~       {BRANCH ENTER_CASH}   {BRANCH PRINT_DSR}         * Erase DEPARTMENT SALES.
18                     /RESALES_BY_TAX~                                                      * Erase SALES BY TAX STATUS.
19                     /RESALES_BY_TENDER~                                                   * Erase SALES BY TENDER.
20                     /REMISC~                                                              * Erase MISCELLANEOUS.
21                     /RIA1..C47~                                                           * Enter header data and SALES DATA .
22                     {MENUBRANCH ENTER_SALES}                                              * Branch back to menu.
23
24
25  ENTER_CASH         /RECASH~                                                              * Erase CASH.
26                     /RECREDIT_CARDS~                                                      * Erase CREDIT CARDS.
27                     /REVOUCHERS_MISC~                                                     * Erase VOUCHERS & MISC.
28                     /RIE9..G47~ ~                                                         * Enter PAYMENTS/VOUCHERS.
29                     {CALC}                                                                * Recalculate spreadsheet.
30                     {GOTO}I10~                                                            * GOTO Cell I10: view ERRORS/CORRECTIVE ACTION.
31                     {MENUBRANCH ENTER_SALES}                                              * Branch back to menu.
32
33
34  PRINT_DSR          /PPRA1..O47~AGPQ                                                      * Print the Daily Sales/Cash Report.
35                     {MENUBRANCH ENTER_SALES}                                              * Branch back to menu.
```

6-2. \M menu macro.

previous day's sales data from the SALES DATA column of the spreadsheet, allowing you to enter the current day's sales data into empty cells.

The second macro will be named ENTER_CASH. It will automatically erase the previous day's cash count data from the PAYMENTS/VOUCHERS column of the spreadsheet, allowing you to enter the current day's manual cash counts into empty cells.

The third macro will be named PRINT_DSR. It will automatically perform the com-

mand in Step 25 to print the Daily Sales/Cash Report.

Before creating these macros, however, you have to name the areas of the spreadsheet that will be manipulated by the macros.

Step 27. Enter the /Range Name commands given in the far right-hand column of table 6-11 to create the range names listed in the middle column of the table. To proceed, first place your cell pointer on the first cell indicated in the far left-hand column of table 6-11 (this is the first cell

TABLE 6-11. STEP 27 /RANGE NAME COMMANDS.

Cell Range	Range Name	/Range Name Command to Enter
C14..C19	DEPT_SALES	/RNCDEPT_SALES \<Return\> C14..C19 \<Return\>
C24..C25	SALES_BY_TAX	/RNCSALES_BY_TAX \<Return\> C24..C25 \<Return\>
C30..C31	SALES_BY_TENDER	/RNCSALES_BY_TENDER \<Return\> C30..C31 \<Return\>
C37..C40	MISC	/RNCMISC \<Return\> C14..C19 \<Return\>
G14..G29	CASH	/RNCCASH \<Return\> G14..G29 \<Return\>
G34..G37	CREDIT_CARDS	/RNCCREDIT_CARDS \<Return\> G34..G37 \<Return\>
G42..G46	VOUCHERS_MISC	/RNCVOUCHERS_MISC \<Return\> G42..G46 \<Return\>
S13	\M	/RNC\M \<Return\> S13..S13 \<Return\>
S15	ENTER_SALES	/RNCENTER_SALES \<Return\> S15..S15 \<Return\>
S25	ENTER_CASH	/RNCENTER_CASH \<Return\> S25..S25 \<Return\>
S34	PRINT_DSR	/RNCPRINT_DSR \<Return\> S34..S34 \<Return\>

of the range we want to name); then enter the corresponding command.

Step 28. Begin creating the \M menu macro (see Figure 6-2) by entering the following menu macro command into Cell S13.

```
{MENUBRANCH ENTER_SALES}
```

Next, enter the following command explanation into Cell X13:

```
* Display menu.
```

The {MENUBRANCH *cell*} command is a special curly-bracket command used only in macros.* It tells Lotus to branch to a custom menu that begins at *cell*—the cell location of the upper left-hand corner of the menu. Cell S15 of the ENTER_SALES macro (see figure 6-2), forms the upper left-hand corner of the menu that is branched to.

Menu Macro Rule #1. The cell location that is branched to is assumed to contain a Lotus menu. After moving to this cell, Lotus pauses to let the user make a selection.

Menu Macro Rule #2. The user may select an option on the menu either by striking the key of the first character in the name of the option chosen or by positioning the cell pointer over the name of the desired option and pressing <Return>. This selection process emulates the process by which Lotus commands are chosen from Lotus command menus.

Menu Macro Rule #3. The branched-to menu must conform to certain formatting conditions. These may be expressed row-by-row in the following terms:

1. First row of the menu (see figure 6-2, row 15, cells S15 through V15): You may have up to eight horizontally adjacent cells containing

*This curly-bracket command does not exist in Lotus versions 1 and 1A. Instead, these versions use a more cryptic slash X (/X) command to perform the same function as the {MENUBRANCH *cell*} command. Specifically, these versions use the /XM*cell*˜ command where /XM is the command to display a custom menu beginning at *cell* to the user. The tilde (˜) initiates this special command. If you are using Lotus version 1 or 1A, use the slash X command in place of the curly-bracket command.

menu options. Limit the words used for menu options to one or two short words. A maximum of seventy-nine characters may be used for all words in this entire first row. In the present case, four menu options are entered in horizontally adjacent cells:
   - Sales Input
   - Cash Input
   - Print
   - Quit

2. Second row of the menu (see figure 6-2, row 16, cells S16 through V16): In each cell you must enter a brief description of what the menu option in the cell directly above does. These descriptions are to provide further help and information on the menu options in the first row. You may have up to 256 characters for each description, but only the first 79 characters will be displayed. If you do not want to provide a menu description, you may enter a label of blank spaces instead—but you must enter a label.

3. Third row of the menu (see figure 6-2, row 17, cells S17 through V17): For any menu option that involves a macro command, you must enter the first command corresponding to the menu option above it. If you do not enter anything, the macro will terminate and return control to you. In the present case, Cell S17 contains the first macro command, /REDEPT_SALES˜, of the Sales Input menu option. Cells T17 and U17, containing the Cash Input and Print menu options, use a special curly-bracket command. {BRANCH *cell*}. This special macro command instructs Lotus to branch to the indicated cell—which in the first instance is Cell S25 of the ENTER_CASH macro, and in the second is Cell S34 of the PRINT_DSR macro—and to continue executing the macro commands. The final menu option, Quit, has no associated macro command in the third row; consequently, if chosen, this option terminates macro execution and returns control to the user.

Menu Macro Rule #4. The cell to the right of the last menu option must be blank. You may not offer more than eight options in a single menu.

Menu Macro Rule #5. Each menu option should begin with a unique capital letter. If the

TABLE 6-12. STEP 29 MACRO COMMANDS (OR LABELS) AND EXPLANATIONS.

Cell	Command or Label	Command Explanation
S15	Sales Input	* Menu choice.
S16	Enter SALES DATA	* Menu help/information.
S17	'/REDEPT_SALES~	* Erase DEPARTMENT SALES.[1]
T15	Cash Input	
T16	Enter PAYMENTS/VOUCHERS	
T17	{BRANCH ENTER_CASH}	
U15	Print	
U16	Print Daily Sales/Cash Report	
U17	{BRANCH PRINT_DSR}	

1. All command explanations from here on in this column refer to commands in the corresponding row of column S of the spreadsheet and not to MENUBRANCH or BRANCH macro commands in columns T or U.

first character of each menu option is not unique and you make a menu selection by pressing the first letter of your choice, Lotus will execute the left-most option beginning with that letter, whether or not it is the one you wanted.

Step 29. Enter the row 15 menu choices, the row 16 descriptive messages, and the row 17 first macro commands (and associated column X command explanations) for the four menu options, as specified in table 6-12.

Step 30. Enter the remainder of the ENTER_SALES macro, together with the corresponding column X command explanations, as specified in table 6-13.

The /Range Input command in Cell S21 restricts user entry to the unprotected cells in the range indicated in the command (Cell Range A1..C47 in the present case). It allows you to use the cursor movement keys to move from one unprotected cell to another within the allowed range and to enter values in these cells. The /Range Input command can be terminated either by pressing the <Esc> key or by hitting the <Return> key without first entering a value in a cell. When the /Range Input command is termi-

nated in the ENTER_SALES macro, the macro automatically executes the next command, {MENUBRANCH ENTER_SALES}, which returns you to the menu of macro choices.

Step 31. Enter the ENTER_CASH macro, together with the corresponding column X command explanations, as specified in table 6-14.

Step 32. Enter the PRINT_DSR macro, together with the corresponding column X command explanations, as specified in table 6-15.

Step 33. Enter the macro names \M, ENTER_SALES, ENTER_CASH, and PRINT_DSR into cells Q13, Q15, Q25, and Q34, respectively.

Saving CASH.WK1

Step 34. Save the Daily Sales/Cash Report spreadsheet (including your newly created macros) by entering the following command:

    /FSB:CASH   <Return>

If you already saved the Daily Sales/Cash Report spreadsheet in Step 26, you will have to tell

TABLE 6-13. STEP 30 MACRO COMMANDS AND COMMAND EXPLANATIONS.

Cell	Command	Command Explanation
S18	'/RESALES_BY_TAX~	* Erase SALES BY TAX STATUS.
S19	'/RESALES_BY_TENDER~	* Erase SALES BY TENDER.
S20	'/REMISC~	* Erase MISCELLANEOUS.
S21	'/RIA1..C47~	* Enter header data and SALES DATA.
S22	{MENUBRANCH ENTER_SALES}	* Branch back to menu.

TABLE 6-14. STEP 31 MACRO COMMANDS AND COMMAND EXPLANATIONS.

Cell	Command	Command Explanation
S25	'/RECASH~	* Erase CASH.
S26	'/RECREDIT__CASH~	* Erase CREDIT CARDS.
S27	'/REVOUCHERS__MISC~	* Erase VOUCHER MISC.
S28	'/RIE9..G47~	* Enter PAYMENTS/VOUCHERS.
S29	{CALC}	* Recalculate spreadsheet.
S30	{GOTO}I10~	* GOTO Cell I10; view ERRORS/CORRECTIVE ACTION
S31	{MENUBRANCH ENTER__SALES}	* Branch back to menu.

Lotus to overwrite the existing file CASH.WK1 that is on disk, replacing it with your latest version, as follows:

```
/FS [point to CASH.WK1]  <Return>  R
```

Step 35. Execute the \M menu macro, by pressing the <Alt> key and the M key simultaneously. Notice that the menu macro displays a menu in the second line of the control panel in the left-hand corner of your screen. As you move the menu pointer from one option to another notice that the menu choice description changes in the third line of the control panel.

Play with the various options on the menu until you feel confident that you know how the menu macro works, how each macro is used to automate user entry, and how each command is used in each macro.

Step 36. If you have been playing with your newly created CASH.WK1 spreadsheet and menu macros, do not save the spreadsheet you have been playing with. If you do, Lotus will overwrite the doctored-up version of the CASH.WK1 spreadsheet onto the original version you saved in Step 34. If you do not save your spreadsheet with data that make sense, the spreadsheet in chapter 7 will not work properly. For more review of what it means to work with an existing spreadsheet that has been retrieved from disk and put into memory, see page 41.

Using the Information in This Spreadsheet

Cash Count Errors

Cash count errors (calculated by the spreadsheet) equal the amount of cash according to the manual cash count minus the combined cash according to the journal tape and cash amounts paid out according to the journal tape. Use the readouts for cash count errors (cells I13 through O13) to identify discrepancies between your manual count of cash and what the cash register says should be in the cash drawer. If discrepancies remain after you have re-counted the cash in the cash drawer and no documentation of cashier errors is present, consult your cashier(s) for explanation(s) of the difference.

Credit Card Count Errors

Credit card errors (calculated by the spreadsheet) equal the manual credit card voucher count minus the credit card settlements according to the journal tape. Use the readouts for credit card errors (cells I14 through O14) to identify discrepancies between your manual count of credit card vouchers and what the cash register reports should be in the cash drawer. If discrepancies remain after you have re-counted the vouchers in the cash drawer, consult your servers and cash-

TABLE 6-15. STEP 32 MACRO COMMANDS AND COMMAND EXPLANATIONS.

Cell	Command	Command Explanation
S34	'/PPRA1..C47~AGPQ	* Print the Daily Sales/Cash Report.
S35	{MENUBRANCH ENTER__SALES}	* Branch back to menu.

iers for missing vouchers and/or vouchers not rung up on the cash register.

Over-ring Count Errors

Over-ring count errors (calculated by the spreadsheet) equal the manual count of over-ring vouchers minus the over-rings according to the journal tape. Use the readouts for over-ring count errors (cells I15 through O15) to identify discrepancies between your manual count of over-rings and what the cash register reports as over-rings. This requires that your cashier not only document over-rings on paper, but also enter them in the cash register, using the over-ring key. If a difference between your count and the amount given in the journal tape report remains after you have re-counted the over-ring vouchers, question your cashier about possible failure to document or ring up over-rings.

Charged Tip Allocation Errors

Charged tip allocation errors (calculated by the spreadsheet) equal the manual count of credit card tips divided by total credit card sales. Use the readouts for charged tip allocation errors (cells I16 through O16) to establish whether or not charged tips received by employees meet the Internal Revenue Service's 8 percent factor—used for calculating tip allocation shortfalls (see chapter 8 for tip allocation calculations).

Charged Tips Count Errors

Charged tips count errors (calculated by the spreadsheet) equal the manual count of credit card tips minus the manual count of paid-out tip vouchers. Use the readouts for charged tips count errors (cells I17 through O17) to determine if more cash was paid out of the cash register for credit card tips than was owing to servers, or if a server was shortchanged for tips earned.

If errors appear in both credit card count and charged tips count (as is the case in the computations shown in figure 6-1), part or all of the problem with the out-of-balance credit card count may be due to an erroneous count of charged tips.

Promotional Sales Count Errors

Promotional sales count errors (calculated by the spreadsheet) equal the manual count of promotional vouchers/coupons minus the promotional sales according to the journal tape. Use the readouts for promotional sales count errors (cells I18 through O18) to identify discrepancies between your manual count of vouchers/coupons redeemed and what your cash register reports as promotional sales. If differences remain after re-counting, consult your cashier for an explanation.

Sales Tax Errors

Sales tax errors (calculated by the spreadsheet) equal the spreadsheet calculation of sales tax minus the sales tax according to the journal tape. Use the readouts for sales tax errors (cells I19 through O19) to make sure that your cash register is calculating sales tax properly. If any discrepancies show up, call your cash register dealer/vendor to rewrite your cash register's sales tax formula or check the sales tax rate in Cell C7 to make sure that it is correct.

Cash Over/Short Errors

Cash over/short errors (calculated by the spreadsheet) equal the manual count of all monies deposited in the bank minus all monies deposited in the bank according to the journal tape. Use the readouts for cash over/short errors (cells I20 through O20) to alert you to internal cash control problems in your operation. An error reading in this category may indicate one of the following:

1. Theft is occurring in one of several ways:
   a. A cashier's intentional failure to ring up sales on the cash register.
   b. An employee's pocketing of cash directly from the cash drawer.
   c. Collusion between a cashier and another cash-handling employee.
2. There are differences between credit card vouchers (on the one hand) and associated guest checks rung up on the cash register (on

TABLE 6-16. LEDGER ENTRIES OBTAINABLE FROM THE SPREADSHEET IN FIGURE 6-1c.

Item	Debits	Credits
Debit Cash	$1,209.31	
Debit Expenses (paid-outs)	$ 2.50	
Debit Promotional Expense/Sales	$ 36.75	
Debit Sales: Over-rings (Under-rings)	$ 3.50	
Credit Sales		$1,154.35
Credit Sales Tax Payable		$ 71.93
Credit Cash Over/ (Short)		$ 20.78
Credit Miscellaneous Income		$ 5.00
Total Debits/Credits:	$1,252.06	$1,252.06

the other)—such as errors in transferring amounts from the guest check to the credit card voucher.

3. Poor cash control and cash-handling procedures are being used.

4. Cashier errors are responsible:
   a. Mistakes in counting change.
   b. Errors in buying coin and paper money change from a manager.
   c. Errors in counting starting and ending cash register banks.
   d. Errors in ringing up guest checks.

Making Accounting Entries for the Day's Sales Activities

The Daily Sales/Cash Report spreadsheet may be used to make direct entries to your general ledger, sales journal, cash receipts journal, accounts receivable subsidiary ledger, and other subsidiary ledgers and journals. From the data illustrated in Figure 6-1, the entries shown in table 6-16 could be made in the general ledger.

Problems

1. What is the purpose of the Daily Sales/Cash Report?

2. What is a settlement?
3. List and describe types of settlement used by restaurant customers.
4. How may sales information from a cash register journal tape or ECR/POS report be organized?
5. How is the term *true sales* defined by the Daily Sales/Cash Report in this chapter? Why is this quantity called *true sales*?
6. Why might it be important to indicate the weather on a Daily Sales/Cash Report?
7. Explain what is meant by *overage* and *shortage*, and distinguish between the two.
8. Why does the dollar amount for TOTAL SALES BY DEPT differ from the dollar amount for TOTAL BY TENDER in figure 6-1?
9. Why does the total cash amount in Cell G31 of figure 6-1 differ from the cash deposit amount in Cell K28?
10. Explain how the following Lotus commands work and how they may be used in a spreadsheet:
    • /Range Input
    • {MENUBRANCH *cell*}
    • {BRANCH *cell*}

Cases

1. Enter the sales data (journal tape) information and manual cash/voucher data counts that follow into the Daily Sales/Cash Report spreadsheet you have created. Use the \M menu macro created in steps 27 through 33 to automate entry of the data.

   Analyze the Daily Sales/Cash Report that results when you have entered all of the preceding data. Explain what may be the cause of the errors. What would you look for and what action might you take—other than the action suggested in column P of the spreadsheet—to resolve some of the out-of-balance Daily Sales/Cash Report categories? What general ledger entries might you make from this Daily Sales/Cash Repo t?

SALES DATA FROM CASH REGISTER JOURNAL TAPE

Appetizers	$ 400.00
Entrées	$1,100.00
Desserts	$ 75.00
Wine	$ 400.00
Beer	$ 125.00
Promotional Sales	$ 0.00
Taxable Sales	$2,000.00
Nontaxable Sales	$ 100.00
Cash	$1,693.60
Credit Card	$ 536.40
Paid-outs	$ 25.00
Miscellaneous Income	$ 0.00
Over-rings	$ 15.00
Sales Tax	$ 130.00

MANUAL CASH/VOUCHER COUNTS

Pennies	$ .75
Nickels	$ 2.65
Dimes	$ 10.60
Quarters	$ 27.00
Half dollars	$ 0.00
Silver dollars	$ 0.00
$1 Bills	$ 215.00
$2 Bills	$ 0.00
$5 Bills	$ 255.00
$10 Bills	$ 340.00
$20 Bills	$ 420.00
$50 Bills	$ 50.00
$100 Bills	$ 100.00
$1,000 Bills	$ 0.00
Personal Checks	$ 36.00
Traveler's Checks	$ 40.00
Bankamericard	$ 15.97
Visa	$ 266.25
MasterCard	$ 213.00
Credit Card Tips	$ 35.00
Over-rings	$ 15.00
Cr. Card Tips Paid Out	$ 50.00
Promo Sales	$ 0.00
Paid-outs	$ 25.00
Misc. Income	$ 0.00

7. Daily and Period-to-date (DAP) Report

The Daily and Period-to-date (DAP) Report spreadsheet is the last in the series of daily report spreadsheets that includes the Daily Purchases Register spreadsheet, the Daily Labor Analysis spreadsheet, the Daily Sales/Cash Report spreadsheet, and the Daily Inventory and Valuation spreadsheet. Summary totals from these four spreadsheets are transferred to the DAP Report spreadsheet automatically by means of a macro, allowing direct comparisons of labor to sales and of food use to sales. Because food and labor cost as a percentage of sales is used throughout the foodservice industry as a basis for setting cost control standards, the DAP Report spreadsheet can become an important tool in analyzing your operation on a daily basis.

You should be aware of several factors before deciding to use the DAP Report spreadsheet for your own foodservice business. First, you may need to redesign the spreadsheet in order to make it suitable for your operation; it is certainly not perfect for every operation in the exact form it takes in this book. Second, the only way to calculate food costs precisely (for entry into the DAP report spreadsheet) is to start with an accurate daily ending inventory, and the only way to get an accurate ending inventory is to take a physical inventory.

A somewhat less accurate daily ending inventory value can be achieved by keeping a perpetual inventory. This involves deducting the recipe ingredients of a menu item from an inventory record on paper or computer every time you sell that item. A perpetual inventory, however, lacks the accuracy of a physical inventory.

Taking a complete physical inventory every day is not realistic for most foodservice operations. Keeping a perpetual inventory is also unrealistic unless you have a sophisticated, inte-

```
        A           B         C        D         E        F       G        H         I       J        K        L       M      N
1  DAILY AND PERIOD-TO-DATE REPORT:                            *******  TODAY'S TRUE SALES:        *******
2                                                              *******  TRUE SALES-TO-DATE:        *******
3          TODAY'S DATE:   03/01/86                            *******  TODAY'S TOTAL MAN-HOURS:   *******
4                  DAY: SATURDAY                               *******  TODAY'S SALES/MAN-HOUR:  ERR *******
5               PERIOD: MARCH 1986                             *******  TODAY'S CUSTOMER COUNT:    *******
6                 NAME: JOEL CHABAN                            *******  TODAY'S AVERAGE CHECK:   ERR *******
7  MONTH OF LAST PHYSICAL(1-12):      2
8                                       *******)   L A B O R   C O S T   R E C A P      (*******
```

	REGULAR	OVERTIME	GROSS	AM	PM	AM	PM	AM	PM	AM	PM	AM	PM
	PAY	PAY	PAY	OFFICE	OFFICE	BAR	BAR	D.R.	D.R.	KITCHEN	KITCHEN	JANITORIAL	JANIT
TODAY'S LABOR:													
AS A % OF TODAY'S GROSS PAY:	ERR	ERR	ERR	ERR	ERR	ERR	ERR	ERR	ERR	ERR	ERR	ERR	
AS A % OF TODAY'S SALES:	ERR	ERR	ERR	ERR	ERR	ERR	ERR	ERR	ERR	ERR	ERR	ERR	
PERIOD-TO-DATE LABOR:													
AS A % OF PTD GROSS PAY:	ERR	ERR	ERR	ERR	ERR	ERR	ERR	ERR	ERR	ERR	ERR	ERR	
AS A % OF PTD SALES:	ERR	ERR	ERR	ERR	ERR	ERR	ERR	ERR	ERR	ERR	ERR	ERR	

```
21  /////////////////////////////////     *******)   F O O D   C O S T   R E C A P   (*******   ///////////
```

FOOD CATEGORY	BEGINNING INVENTORY	TODAY'S PURCHASES	PTD PURCHASES	AVG. END INVENTORY	PTD COST OF GOODS	PERCENT OF PTD SALES
BEVERAGE:				$288.54	($288.54)	ERR
CHEESE:				$110.14	($110.14)	ERR
DAIRY:				$61.35	($61.35)	ERR
EGGS:				$49.00	($49.00)	ERR
FROZEN:				$456.46	($456.46)	ERR
GROCERY:				$327.27	($327.27)	ERR
GRAINS:				$45.33	($45.33)	ERR
MEAT/FISH/POULTRY:				$276.07	($276.07)	ERR
PRODUCE:				$227.64	($227.64)	ERR
PAPER/PLASTIC:				$542.19	($542.19)	ERR
TRANSFERS IN:					$0.00	ERR
TRANSFERS OUT:					$0.00	ERR
CREDITS/RETURNS:					$0.00	ERR
TOTAL:	$0.00	$0.00	$0.00	$2,383.97	($2,383.97)	ERR

```
42  COPY BEGINNING INVENTORY FROM B25..B34 TO THE CORRESPONDING MONTH BELOW:
44                            *******)  C A L C U L A T I O N   O F   E N D I N G   I N V E N T O R Y   A V E R A G E S     (*******
```

FOOD CATEGORY	JANUARY	FEBRUARY	MARCH	APRIL	MAY	JUNE	JULY	AUGUST	SEPTEMBER	OCTOBER	NOVEMBER	DECEMBER	AVER
BEVERAGE:	$323.58	$253.50											$28
CHEESE:	$125.87	$94.40											$1
DAIRY:	$84.90	$37.80											$6
EGGS:	$89.00	$9.00											$4
FROZEN:	$568.12	$344.80											$45
GROCERY:	$257.84	$396.70											$32
GRAINS:	$34.25	$56.40											$4
MEAT/FISH/POULTRY:	$458.64	$93.50											$27
PRODUCE:	$168.57	$286.70											$22
PAPER/PLASTIC:	$289.47	$794.90											$54
TOTAL:	$2,400.24	$2,367.70	$0.00	$0.00	$0.00	$0.00	$0.00	$0.00	$0.00	$0.00	$0.00	$0.00	$2,38

7-1. Daily and Period-to-date Report spreadsheet (DAP-FORM.WK1).

grated POS/back-office computer system capable of maintaining the recipe, inventory, and sales data necessary for accuracy.

The procedure used in this chapter for valuing ending inventory on a daily basis is to calculate an average year-to-date ending inventory from month-end physical inventories. Average ending inventory is calculated by taking each month's ending inventory and computing an average inventory-to-date. Although this method is not as accurate as taking a physical inventory every day, it is less time-consuming and it eliminates the awkward and burdensome job of trying to keep a perpetual inventory. Food cost calculations, which are expressed as a percentage of sales, are derived from ending inventory averages rather than from a daily physical inventory or from the current perpetual inventory data. This means that, on a daily basis, food cost calculations are at best only approximately accurate.

```
  P   G      R      S      T   U      V   W      X    Y        

            *******) D A I L Y   G R O S S   P R O F I T   A N D   L O S S  (*******
            ----------------------------------------------------------------------------
            TODAY        %              PTD          %
            ----------------------------------------------------------------------------
TRUE SALES:  $0.00       ERR            $0.00        ERR
            ----------------------------------------------------------------------------
BEGIN INVENTORY:  $0.00                 $0.00
PURCHASES:        $0.00    ERR          $0.00        ERR
AVG. END INVENTORY: $2,383.97           $2,383.97
            ----------------------------------------------------------------------------
COST OF GOODS SOLD: ($2,383.97)  ERR    ($2,383.97)  ERR
            ----------------------------------------------------------------------------
LABOR:        $0.00       ERR           $0.00        ERR
            ----------------------------------------------------------------------------
GROSS PROFIT: $2,383.97   ERR           $2,383.97    ERR
            ============================================================================
```

The first six rows of the DAP Report spreadsheet (see figure 7-1), in columns H through J, contain totals for sales for the day, sales to date, and other overall statistics; these statistics are discussed in detail on pages 110–13 of this chapter. The first two major sections on the left side of the spreadsheet, labeled LABOR COST RECAP and FOOD COST RECAP, use these overall sales figures in establishing control percentages.

The LABOR COST RECAP shows today's labor as a percentage of today's sales and shows period-to-date labor as a percentage of period-to-date sales. The FOOD COST RECAP determines the cost of goods for the period and calculates food costs as a percentage of period-to-date sales.

The major section on the right side of the DAP Report spreadsheet, labeled DAILY GROSS PROFIT AND LOSS, shows gross profit for the day and keeps track of period-to-date gross profit.

The major section on the bottom left-hand side of the report, labeled CALCULATION OF ENDING INVENTORY AVERAGES, calculates the average ending inventory to date, eliminating the need for you to take a daily physical inventory or keep a perpetual inventory.

Formatting, Headings, and Labels

Step 1. Reformat columns A through W from the normal, default Lotus column width of nine characters to the widths indicated in table 7-2.

The last command, /WGC12, globally sets the width of all remaining columns in the spreadsheet to a width of twelve characters.

Step 2. Begin re-creating the spreadsheet example shown in figure 7-1, by entering the appropriate headings and labels into columns A through Y, rows 1 through 60, exactly as specified in table 7-3.

You may need to pad some of your cell entries with blank spaces to get your headings to look like those pictured in figure 7-1. Any heading beginning with one of the three Lotus label alignment prefixes (', ", and ^) signifies a label to be padded with blank spaces or to be given a special cell alignment. Remember that the prefix ' aligns text to the left margin of the cell, the prefix " aligns text to the right margin of the cell, and the prefix ^ centers text within the cell. Unless a label alignment prefix is indicated in table 7-3, do not use one of these prefixes to begin a label or heading.

TABLE 7-2. STEP 1 FORMATTING COMMANDS.

Column	Width	Command to Enter	
A	30	/WCS30	<Return>
B	12	/WCS12	<Return>
C	18	/WCS18	<Return>
O	9	/WCS9	<Return>
P	9	/WCS9	<Return>
Q	9	/WCS9	<Return>
R	20	/WCS20	<Return>
All remaining	12	/WGC12	<Return>

TABLE 7-3. STEP 2 HEADINGS.

Cell	Heading
A1	DAILY AND PERIOD-TO-DATE REPORT:
A3	''TODAY'S DATE:
A4	''DAY:
A5	''PERIOD:
A6	''NAME:
A7	''MONTH OF LAST PHYSICAL (1-12):
G1	*******
G2	*******
G3	*******
G4	*******
G5	*******
G6	*******
H1	' TODAY'S TRUE SALES:
H2	' TRUE SALES TO DATE:
H3	TODAY'S TOTAL MAN HOURS:
H4	' TODAY'S SALES/MAN-HOUR:
H5	' TODAY'S CUSTOMER COUNT:
H6	' TODAY'S AVERAGE CHECK:
K1	' *******
K2	' *******
K3	' *******
K4	' *******
K5	' *******
K6	' *******
C8	' *******>
D8	' L A B O R C O S T R E C A P
H8	<*******
S5	''*******>
T5	D A I L Y G R O S S P R O F I T A N D L O S S
Y5	<*******
B10	^REGULAR
C10	^OVERTIME
D10	^GROSS
E10	^AM
F10	^PM
G10	^AM
H10	^PM
I10	^AM
J10	^PM
K10	^AM
L10	^PM
M10	^AM
N10	^PM
B11	^PAY
C11	^PAY

Cell	Heading
D11	^PAY
E11	^OFFICE
F11	^OFFICE
G11	^BAR
H11	^BAR
I11	^D.R.
J11	^D.R.
K11	^KITCHEN
L11	^KITCHEN
M11	^JANITORIAL
N11	^JANITORIAL
A13	''TODAY'S LABOR:
A14	''AS A % OF TODAY'S GROSS PAY:
A15	''AS A % OF TODAY'S SALES:
A17	''PERIOD-TO-DATE LABOR:
A18	''AS A % OF PTD GROSS PAY:
A19	''AS A % OF PTD SALES:
C21	' *******>
D21	' F O O D C O S T R E C A P
G21	<*******
A23	^FOOD CATEGORY
B22	''BEGINNING
B23	''INVENTORY
C22	^TODAY'S
C23	^PURCHASES
D22	^PTD
D23	^PURCHASES
E22	^AVG. END
E23	^INVENTORY
F22	^PTD COST
F23	^OF GOODS
G22	^PERCENT OF
G23	^PTD SALES
A25	''BEVERAGE:
A26	''CHEESE:
A27	''DAIRY:
A28	''EGGS:
A29	''FROZEN:
A30	''GROCERY:
A31	''GRAINS:
A32	''MEAT/FISH/POULTRY:
A33	''PRODUCE:
A34	''PAPER/PLASTIC:
A35	''TRANSFERS IN:
A36	''TRANSFERS OUT:
A37	''CREDITS/RETURNS:
A39	''TOTAL:

Continued.

TABLE 7-3. CONTINUED.

Cell	Heading
A42	COPY BEGINNING INVENTORY FROM B25..B34 TO THE CORRESPONDING MONTH BELOW:
C44	*******>
D44	' C A L C U L A T I O N O F E N D I N G I N V E N T O R Y A V E R A G E S
M44	<*******
A45	^FOOD CATEGORY
B45	''JANUARY
C45	''FEBRUARY
D45	''MARCH
E45	''APRIL
F45	''MAY
G45	''JUNE
H45	''JULY
I45	''AUGUST
J45	''SEPTEMBER
K45	''OCTOBER
L45	''NOVEMBER
M45	''DECEMBER
N45	''AVERAGES
A47	''BEVERAGE:
A48	''CHEESE:
A49	''DAIRY:
A50	''EGGS:
A51	''FROZEN:
A52	''GROCERY:
A53	''GRAINS:
A54	''MEAT/FISH/POULTRY:
A55	''PRODUCE:
A56	''PAPER/PLASTIC:
A58	''TOTAL:
R9	''TRUE SALES:
R11	''BEGIN INVENTORY:
R12	''PURCHASES:
R13	''AVG. END INVENTORY:
R15	''COST OF GOODS SOLD:
R17	''LABOR:
R19	''GROSS PROFIT:
S7	^TODAY
T7	^%
V7	^PTD
W7	^%

Step 3. Enter dashed lines and double-dashed lines into the spreadsheet, as indicated in table 7-4. Use the backslash (\) key at the beginning of each cell entry to signal to Lotus that the charac-

ter immediately following it is to be repeated across the cell from end to end.

To repeat a character across several individual cells, use Lotus's /Copy command, as indicated in table 7-4. Use the pointing method described on page 34 to define the last cell of a cell range when performing the /Copy operation. Remember to place the cell pointer on the originating cell (the cell being copied from) before you begin to enter each command listed in table 7-4.

Step 4. Format the cells and cell ranges identified in table 7-5, as indicated there. Enter each command given in the far right-hand column of the table exactly as it appears, by typing the characters shown and then hitting the <Return> key. When formatting a cell range, use the pointing method to define the last cell in each indicated cell range. Be sure to place the cell pointer on the first cell indicated in the far left-hand column of table 7-5 before entering the associated command.

Daily Operator Input

Step 5. The only daily operator input required by this spreadsheet is the operator's name, which must be entered into Cell B6. On the first day of the period, however, the three additional entries specified in table 7-6 are necessary.

The remainder of this spreadsheet is automatically generated when you execute the macro described later in this chapter.

Formulas

Some of the steps that follow contain instructions about making cells absolute when copying formulas and cell references. The meaning of absolute and relative cells is discussed on pages 34–35.

Do not be concerned when the label ERR appears in cells of your spreadsheet, as illustrated in figure 7-1. These are cells into which you will be entering formulas. The label ERR (for *error*) appears because the formulas in these cells reference one of the cells containing a $.00 (zero) or blank displayed value that may be used as a denominator for division in formulas; and because a number may not be divided by 0, Lotus

TABLE 7-4. STEP 3 REPEAT AND /COPY COMMANDS.

Cell	REPEAT Command to Enter	/Copy Command to Enter		
A9	\/	/CA9	\<Return\>	B9..N9	\<Return\>
A10	\\				
A11	\/				
A12	\\	/CA12	\<Return\>	B12..N12	\<Return\>
A16	\-	/CA16	\<Return\>	B16..N16	\<Return\>
A20	\=	/CA20	\<Return\>	B20..N20	\<Return\>
A21	\/	/CA21	\<Return\>	B21..B21	\<Return\>
H21	\/				
A24	\\	/CA24	\<Return\>	B24..H24	\<Return\>
A38	\-	/CA38	\<Return\>	B38..G38	\<Return\>
A40	\=	/CA40	\<Return\>	B40..N40	\<Return\>
A43	\/	/CA43	\<Return\>	B43..N43	\<Return\>
A46	\\	/CA46	\<Return\>	B46..N46	\<Return\>
A57	\-	/CA57	\<Return\>	B57..N57	\<Return\>
A59	\=	/CA59	\<Return\>	B59..N59	\<Return\>
S6	\-	/CS6	\<Return\>	T6..Y6	\<Return\>
S10	\-	/CS10	\<Return\>	T10..Y10	\<Return\>
S14	\-	/CS14	\<Return\>	T14..Y14	\<Return\>
S16	\-	/CS16	\<Return\>	T16..Y16	\<Return\>
S18	\-	/CS18	\<Return\>	T18..Y18	\<Return\>
S20	\=	/CS20	\<Return\>	T20..Y20	\<Return\>

returns the error message in that cell. When numbers greater than 0 are entered in these cells and the spreadsheet is recalculated, however, the ERR labels disappear.

Step 6. Enter the following Lotus calendar function into Cell B3:

@NOW

TABLE 7-5. STEP 4 /RANGE FORMAT COMMANDS.

Cell(s)	Format/Alignment	Command to Enter		
B3	date type 4	/RFD4	\<Return\>		
J1..J2	currency	/RFC2	\<Return\>	J1..J2	\<Return\>
J3	Fixed—two decimal places	/RFF2	\<Return\>	J3	\<Return\>
J4	currency	/RFC2	\<Return\>	J4	\<Return\>
J6	currency	/RFC2	\<Return\>	J6	\<Return\>
B13..N13	currency	/RFC2	\<Return\>	B13..N13	\<Return\>
B14..N15	percent	/RFP2	\<Return\>	B14..N15	\<Return\>
B17..N17	currency	/RFC2	\<Return\>	B17..N17	\<Return\>
B18..N19	percent	/RFP2	\<Return\>	B18..N19	\<Return\>
B25..F37	currency	/RFC2	\<Return\>	B25..F37	\<Return\>
B39..F39	currency	/RFC2	\<Return\>	B39..F39	\<Return\>
B47..N58	currency	/RFC2	\<Return\>	B47..N58	\<Return\>
G25..G39	percent	/RFP2	\<Return\>	G25..G39	\<Return\>
S9..S19	currency	/RFC2	\<Return\>	S9..S19	\<Return\>
T9..T19	percent	/RFP2	\<Return\>	T9..T19	\<Return\>
V9..V19	currency	/RFC2	\<Return\>	V9..V19	\<Return\>
W9..W19	percent	/RFP2	\<Return\>	W9..W19	\<Return\>

TABLE 7-6. DAILY INPUT INTO THE DAP REPORT SPREADSHEET.

Cell(s)	Input
B5	`PERIOD.` Enter the accounting period. If your accounting period is one month, enter the month and year. If your accounting period is based on thirteen periods per year, enter the number and year of the new period.
B7	`MONTH OF LAST PHYSICAL.` Enter the number of the month of the last ending physical inventory taken. If the new period were March, for example, the last ending physical inventory would have been taken in February, and you would enter 2 for February.
Rows 47 through 58	After updating the DAP Report with information from the first day of the new period (using the macro explained later in this chapter), you will need to copy the `BEGINNING INVENTORY` data from cells B25 through B34 into the corresponding cells in proper month of columns B through N, rows 47 through 58. Use the following command: `/CB25..B34` \<Return\> `_47` \<Return\> You must fill in the blank that precedes row 47 in the above command with the correct letter of the column containing the month of the last ending physical inventory.

If the target cell is formatted for date (as Cell B3 is), the @NOW function automatically gets today's date from the system date you entered when you first turned on your computer or from the date maintained by an automatic, battery-operated clock/calendar (if your computer has this feature). If the target cell is formatted for time, the time of day is returned when the @NOW function is entered.

Step 7. Enter the following formula into Cell B4 (this is a long formula, so take your time to prevent entry errors):

```
@CHOOSE(@MOD(@DATE(@YEAR(@NOW),
@MONTH(@NOW),@DAY(@NOW)),7),
''SATURDAY'',''SUNDAY'',''MONDAY'',
''TUESDAY'',''WEDNESDAY'',
''THURSDAY'',''FRIDAY'')
```

Although the formula is reproduced here on two lines, it should be typed into your computer without any break, as though it were a single long word. This formula automatically determines the day of the week (Sunday through Saturday). For a more detailed explanation of how this lengthy formula works, see pages 67–70.

Step 8. Enter the period into Cell B5, your name into cell B6, and the number of the month in which the last physical ending inventory was taken into Cell B7.

Step 9. Enter the following formula into Cell B14:

```
+B13/$D$13
```

This formula calculates regular pay as a percentage of gross pay.

The dollar signs in front of the column and row reference of Cell D13 designate the cell as absolute. This means that when this formula is copied, the reference to Cell D13 will not change; in contrast, the reference to Cell B13 will change as it is copied.

Now copy the formula from Cell B14 into cells C14 through N14, placing your cell pointer on Cell B14 and entering the following /Copy command:

```
/C   <Return>   [point to Cell C14].
[point to Cell N14]   <Return>
```

Step 10. Enter the following formula into Cell B15:

```
+B13/$J$1
```

This formula calculates regular pay as a percentage of today's sales.

Now copy the formula from Cell B15 into cells C15 through N15, placing your cell pointer on

Cell B15 and entering the following /Copy command:

```
/C    <Return>    [point to Cell C15].
[point to Cell N15]    <Return>
```

Step 11. Enter the following formula into Cell B18:

```
+B17/$D$17
```

This formula calculates period-to-date regular pay as a percentage of period-to-date gross pay.

Now copy the formula from Cell B18 into cells C18 through N18, placing your cell pointer on Cell B18 and entering the following /Copy command:

```
/C    <Return>    [point to Cell C18].
[point to Cell N18]    <Return>
```

Step 12. Enter the following formula into Cell B19:

```
+B17/$J$2
```

This formula calculates period-to-date regular pay as a percentage of sales to date.

Now copy the formula from Cell B19 into cells C19 through N19, placing your cell pointer on Cell B19 and entering the following /Copy command:

```
/C    <Return>    [point to Cell C19].
[point to Cell N19]    <Return>
```

Step 13. Enter the following cell reference into Cell E25:

```
+N47
```

Cell N47 references the average ending inventory for beverages and is used in the calculation of period-to-date cost of goods in Cell F25.

Now copy the formula from Cell E25 into cells E26 through E34, placing your cell pointer on Cell E25 and entering the following /Copy command:

```
/C    <Return>    [point to Cell E26].
[point to Cell E34]    <Return>
```

Average ending inventory values in the referenced cells are transferred to the corresponding cells in column E from the CALCULATIONS OF ENDING INVENTORY AVERAGES section of the spreadsheet (column N, rows 47 through 56).

Step 14. Enter the following formula into Cell F25:

```
+B25+D25-E25
```

This formula calculates period-to-date cost of goods for the BEVERAGES category. It is based on a traditional cost-of-goods formula according to which beginning inventory is added to period-to-date purchases and then average ending inventory is subtracted from this sum.

Now copy the formula from Cell F25 into cells F26 through F37, placing your cell pointer on Cell F25 and entering the following /Copy command:

```
/C    <Return>    [point to Cell F26].
[point to Cell F37]    <Return>
```

Step 15. Enter the following formula into Cell G25:

```
+F25/$J$2
```

This formula calculates period-to-date cost of goods as a percentage of sales to date.

Now copy the formula from Cell G25 into cells G26 through G37, placing your cell pointer on Cell G25 and entering the following /Copy command:

```
/C    <Return>    [point to Cell G26].
[point to Cell G37]    <Return>
```

Step 16. Enter each formula given in table 7-7 into the corresponding cell.

The cell reference and formulas in table 7-7 return the sum total of their respective column ranges.

Step 17. Enter the following formula into Cell N47:

```
@SUM(B47..M47)/$B$7
```

This formula calculates the average ending inventory for the BEVERAGES category.

TABLE 7-7. STEP 16 FORMULAS.

Cell	Formula
B39	@SUM(B24..B38)
C39	@SUM(C24..C38)
D39	@SUM(D24..D38)
E39	+N58
F39	@SUM(F24..F38)
G39	+F39/$J$2

Now copy the formula from Cell N47 into cells N48 through N56, placing your cell pointer on Cell N47 and entering the following /Copy command:

```
/C    <Return>    [point to Cell N48].
[point to Cell N56]    <Return>
```

Step 18. Enter the following formula into Cell B58:

```
@SUM(B46..B57)
```

This formula calculates the total inventory for January.

Now copy the formula from Cell B58 into cells C58 through N58, placing your cell pointer on Cell B58 and entering the following command:

```
/C    <Return>    [point to Cell C58].
[point to Cell N58]    <Return>
```

Step 19. Enter the following formula into Cell J4:

```
+J1/J3
```

This formula calculates sales per man-hour by dividing the day's sales by the total number of labor hours for the day.

Step 20. Enter the following formula into Cell J6:

```
+J1/J5
```

This formula calculates the average check per customer by dividing the day's sales by the total number of customers for the day.

Step 21. Enter each formula or cell reference given in table 7-8 for the DAILY GROSS PROFIT AND LOSS section of the spreadsheet into the cell indicated.

Protecting Your Spreadsheet

Step 22. Use the /Worksheet Global Protection Enable command sequence, followed by an Unprotect command for the shaded area near the top of the spreadsheet, to protect the cells in the nonshaded areas of the spreadsheet from accidentally being filled (by you or by other spreadsheet users) with unwanted data. Begin by entering the following command string:

```
/WGPE
```

This string is an abbreviated expression for the /Worksheet Global Protection Enable command, which protects every cell in the spreadsheet from entry and alteration.

The next step is to unprotect the cells in the shaded area near the top of the spreadsheet by means of the /Range Unprotect command. Before entering the command, place your cell pointer on Cell B5, the first cell of Cell Range B5..B7—the

TABLE 7-8. STEP 21 FORMULAS AND CELL REFERENCES.

Cell	Formula/Cell Reference
S9	+J1
T9	+S9/J1
V9	+J2
W9	+V9/J2
S11	+B39
V11	+B39
S12	+C39
T12	+S12/J1
V12	+D39
W12	+V12/J2
S13	+E39
V13	+E39
S15	+S11+S12−S13
T15	+S15/J1
V15	+V11+V12−V13
W15	+V15/J2
S17	+D13
T17	+S17/J1
V17	+D17
W17	+V17/J2
S19	+S9−S15−S17
T19	+S19/J1
V19	+V9−V15−V17
W19	+V19/J2

cell range that you want to unprotect. Then enter the following command:

```
/RU [point to B7]    <Return>
```

Saving DAP-FORM.WK1

If you would like to stop and take a break at this point, save the spreadsheet you are working on by performing Step 23. Otherwise, skip Step 23 and go on to Step 24.

Step 23. You can save the DAP-FORM spreadsheet you have created so far, by entering the following /File Save command:

```
/FSB:DAP-FORM    <Return>
```

DAP-FORM is the file name for the Daily and Period-to-date Report spreadsheet and will be written onto the disk in drive B. If you have a hard disk or a single floppy drive system, save the DAP-FORM spreadsheet onto the appropriate drive and directory. When you save this file under the name DAP-FORM, Lotus will automatically add a period and the file name extension WK1 to the name DAP-FORM. When you look at a directory of files on disk drive B, you will see this file displayed as `DAP-FORM WK 1`. The WK1 extension identifies this file to you and to Lotus as a file in a spreadsheet format.

DAP-FORM will be retrieved as a blank worksheet form at the beginning of each month's Daily and Period-to-date Report. Use this form on the first day of each period. When you have completed DAP-FORM on the first day, use the /File Save command to save it onto disk under the file name DAP-__, filling in the blank space with the number of the relevant monthly period. If you were using DAP-FORM on January 1, for example, you should save the file to disk by calling it DAP-1 because the number 1 represents January (the first month of the year).

You would then use DAP-1 throughout the month of January; and DAP-FORM.WK1 would not be needed until February 1. When you filled in the blank DAP-FORM form on February 1, you would save it onto disk under the file name DAP-2.

Using a Macro to Transfer Data to the Daily and Period-to-date Report

Your next task is to create a macro that will use the /File Combine command to consolidate the totals from previous spreadsheets in your Daily and Period-to-date Report spreadsheet. This macro will transfer data from the following spreadsheets:

- The Daily Purchases Register spreadsheet
- The Physical Inventory and Valuation spreadsheet
- The Daily Labor Report spreadsheet
- The Daily Sales/Cash Report spreadsheet

It will transfer selected data and summary totals from these spreadsheets to your current DAP-__ spreadsheet. The macro, named \U (for *update*), will specify where the data are to be retrieved from and where in your DAP Report the data are to be placed. For the period-to-date accumulated totals that your DAP Report maintains, macro commands will specify that the data being transferred from one of the other spreadsheets is automatically to be added to the previous day's period-to-date accumulated totals. This feature ensures that a running balance will be kept for all your period-to-date totals.

WARNING: Whenever the \U macro is executed, it adds the selected daily totals to the period-to-date totals. Therefore, if the macro is executed twice in the same day, it is likely to add the daily totals to the accumulated totals a second time, creating an error in the accumulated totals. For this reason, do not execute the \U macro more than once each day for updating the DAP Report.

Step 24. Begin creating the \U macro (see figure 7-2) by entering each macro command into the appropriate cell, as indicated in table 7-9. The command explanation in the far right-hand column of the table documents the action initiated by the macro command; each explanation should be entered into column V, opposite the command to which it refers.

The \U macro repeatedly uses Lotus's /File Combine Copy/Add command to transfer selected data from the previous four spreadsheets

```
        R         S        T        U        V        W        X        Y        Z
24
25     MACRO NAME              MACRO                      COMMAND EXPLANATION
26  =================  ==============================  ========================================================
27     \U          /WGRM                     * Turns automatic recalculation off.
28                 /WGPD                     * Unprotect the entire worksheet.
29                 {GOTO}J1~                 * Go to Cell J1.
30                 /FCCNK30~CASH~            * /File Combine cell K30 from CASH.WK1 to cell J1 in DAP-___.WK1.
31                 {GOTO}J2~                 * Go to Cell J2.
32                 /FCANK30~CASH~            * /File Combine cell K30 from CASH.WK1 by adding to the value in cell J2.
33                 {GOTO}J3~                 * Go to Cell J3.
34                 /FCCNK21~LABOR~           * /File Combine cell K21 from LABOR.WK1 to cell J3 in DAP-___.WK1.
35                 {GOTO}J5~                 * Go to Cell J5.
36                 /FCCNC8~CASH~             * /File Combine cell C8 from CASH.WK1 to cell J5 in DAP-___.WK1.
37                 /RPJ5~                    * Protect Cell J5.
38                 {GOTO}B13~                * Go to Cell B13.
39                 /FCCNN21..Z21~LABOR~      * /File Combine cell range N21..Z21 from LABOR.WK1 to cells B13..N13 in DAP-___.WK1.
40                 {GOTO}B17~                * Go to Cell B17.
41                 /FCANN21..Z21~LABOR~      * /File Combine cell range N21..Z21 from LABOR.WK1 by adding to the values in cells B17..N17.
42                 {GOTO}B25~                * Go to Cell B25.
43                 /FCCNF68..F77~INVENTRY~   * /File Combine cell range F68..F77 from INVENTRY.WK1 to cells B25..B34 in DAP-___.WK1.
44                 {GOTO}C25~                * Go to Cell C25.
45                 /FCCNJ27..J39~PURCHASE~   * /File Combine cell range J27..J39 from PURCHASE.WK1 to cells C25..C37 in DAP-___.WK1.
46                 {GOTO}D25~                * Go to Cell D25.
47                 /FCANJ27..J39~PURCHASE~   * /File Combine cell range J27..J39 from PURCHASE.WK1 by adding to the values in cells D25..D37.
48                 {CALC}                    * Recalculate spreadsheet.
49                 /WGPE                     * Protect entire worksheet.
50                 {HOME}                    * Go to Cell A1.
51                                           * END OF MACRO
52
```

7-2. \U *macro.*

automatically. For this command to work, however, you must already have used the /File Retrieve command, to retrieve the spreadsheet that you want to transfer the data to, so that it is the current spreadsheet you are using. In addition, the cell pointer must be positioned on the receiving cell or on the cell that forms the upper left-hand corner of the receiving range (the cell or range to which the data are being transferred). The /File Combine command has the following form and sequence:

```
/FileCombine [C (for Copy),
A (for Add), or S (for Subtract)]
[originating cell/cell range]
<Return>   [originating file
name]   <Return>
```

Notice how the /File Combine command works (according to the command explanations in table 7-9) and how each of these commands is preceded by a {GOTO} command to ensure that the cell pointer is properly positioned to receive the data in the appropriate cell.

When you execute the \U macro, it performs three general actions on the DAP-__.WK1 spreadsheet (see figure 7-3). First, it turns off automatic recalculation and unprotects the entire worksheet. Second, it file–combines selected data from external spreadsheet files in one of two

ways depending on whether the values being transferred are to be accumulated (added to the previous day's transfers) or not. If the values being transferred are not to be accumulated, the /File Combine Copy command is used to replace the values in the DAP-__.WK1 spreadsheet with the values being transferred. If the values being transferred are to be accumulated (added to the previous day's accumulated totals), the /File Combine Add command is used to add the values in the DAP-__.WK1 spreadsheet to the values being transferred. Third, it forces an automatic recalculation of the spreadsheet, recalculates all spreadsheet cells on the basis of the newly transferred data, protects the entire worksheet, and ends after moving the cell pointer to Cell A1.

The \U macro described in table 7-9 will only work properly if all the spreadsheets used for data transfer reside on disk drive B. Alternatively, you may specify a different drive letter before the file name in each /File Combine command. If you specify a different drive letter, Lotus will find the file on the drive you specify; however, all files in use should reside on the same floppy or hard disk. If you store the files on different floppy disks, you will have to change disks during execution of the macro.

Step 25. Name the \U macro you have just created, by placing the cell pointer on cell S27 (the

TABLE 7-9. STEP 24 MACRO COMMANDS AND COMMAND EXPLANATIONS.

Cell	Command	Command Explanation
S27	'/WGRM	* Turn automatic recalc off.
S28	'/WGPD	* Unprotect entire worksheet.
S29	{GOTO}J1~	* Go to Cell J1.
S30	'/FCCNK30~B:CASH~	* Transfer value in Cell K30 from the CASH.WK1 spreadsheet to Cell J1 in the DAP-_.WK1 spreadsheet.
S31	{GOTO}J2~	* Go to Cell J2.
S32	'/FCANK30~B:CASH~	* Transfer value in Cell K30 from the CASH.WK1 spreadsheet to Cell J2 in the DAP-_.WK1 spreadsheet, and add value in Cell K30 to value in Cell J2.
S33	{GOTO}J3~	* Go to Cell J3.
S34	'/FCCNK21~B:LABOR~	* Transfer value in Cell K21 from the LABOR.WK1 spreadsheet to Cell J3 in the DAP-_.WK1 spreadsheet.
S35	{GOTO}J5~	* Go to Cell J5.
S36	'/FCCNC8~B:CASH~	* Transfer value in Cell C8 from the CASH.WK1 spreadsheet to Cell J5 in the DAP-_.WK1 spreadsheet.
S37	'/RPJ5~	* Protect Cell J5.
S38	{GOTO}B13~	* Go to Cell B13.
S39	'/FCCNN21..Z21~B:LABOR~	* Transfer values in Cell Range N21..Z21 from the LABOR.WK1 spreadsheet to Cell B13 in the DAP-_.WK1 spreadsheet.
S40	{GOTO}B17~	* Go to Cell B17.
S41	'/FCANN21..Z21~B:LABOR~	* Transfer value in Cell Range N21..Z21 from the LABOR.WK1 spreadsheet to Cell B17 in the DAP-_.WK1 spreadsheet, and add values in Cell Range N21..Z21 to corresponding values in Cell Range B17..N17.
S42	{GOTO}B25~	* Go to Cell B25.
S43	'/FCCNF68..F77~B:INVENTRY~	* Transfer values in Cell Range F68..F77 from the INVENTRY.WK1 spreadsheet to Cell Range B25..B34 in the DAP-_.WK1 spreadsheet.
S44	{GOTO}C25~	* Go to Cell C25.
S45	'/FCCNJ27..J39~B:PURCHASE~	* Transfer values in Cell Range J27..J39 from the PURCHASE.WK1 spreadsheet to Cell Range C25..C37 in the DAP-_.WK1 spreadsheet.
S46	{GOTO}D25~	* Go to Cell D25.
S47	'/FCANJ27..J39~B:PURCHASE~	* Transfer values in Cell Range J27..J39 from the PURCHASE.WK1 spreadsheet to Cell Range D25..D37 in the DAP-_.WK1 spreadsheet, and add values from PURCHASE.WK1 to values in Cell Range D25..D37 of DAP-_.WK1.
S48	{CALC}	* Recalculate spreadsheet.
S49	'/WGPE	* Protect entire worksheet.
S50	{HOME}	* Go to Cell A1.

first cell of the macro) and entering the following /Range Name command:

```
/RNC\U    <Return>    <Return>
```

Enter the following label into Cell R27:

```
\U
```

Saving DAP-FORM.WK1

Step 26. Save the Daily and Period-to-date Report spreadsheet (including your newly created macro) by entering the following command:

```
/FSB:DAP-FORM    <Return>
```

If you already saved the Daily and Period-to-date Report spreadsheet in Step 23, you will have to tell Lotus to overwrite the existing DAP-FORM.-WK1 file that is on disk, replacing it with your latest version, as follows:

```
/FS [point to DAP-FORM.WK1]
<Return>    R
```

Step 27. Execute the \U macro by pressing the <Alt> key and the U key simultaneously.

Play with the \U macro until you feel comfortable about your knowledge of how it works and how each macro command is used.

Step 28. If you have been playing with your newly created DAP-FORM.WK1 spreadsheet, do not save the spreadsheet you have been playing with. If you do, Lotus will overwrite the doctored-up version of the DAP-FORM.WK1 spreadsheet onto the original version that you saved in Step 26. You need to save your DAP-FORM spreadsheet without data so that it can be used as a fresh template on which to begin each month's accumulation of activity.

When using this spreadsheet on a daily basis, after you have started a new period (using DAP-FORM.WK1 as your fresh, blank template) and have executed the \U macro, you will save your updated Daily and Period-to-date Report spreadsheet to a file called DAP-__.WK1. You fill in the blank in the file name with the number of the period. If this month were June, for example, you would fill in the blank with 6 because June is the

sixth month of the year. But, to reiterate, do not save the altered and data-laden DAP-FORM form back to the DAP-FORM.WK1 file. For more review of what it means to work with an existing spreadsheet that has been retrieved from disk and put into memory, see page 41.

Printing Your Spreadsheet

Step 29. Turn your printer on, align the paper in it, place your cell pointer on Cell A1 by pressing the <Home> key on your cursor/arrow keypad, and print your spreadsheet by issuing the following series of commands:

```
/PPR.    <End>    <Home>
<Return>    AGPQ
```

This abbreviated command language means: "Print to the printer the spreadsheet range A1 through Z59. The paper is aligned in the printer, so the spreadsheet should begin printing at the top of the page. Go and print the spreadsheet. Then page-eject the paper in the printer to the top of a new page, and quit the print commands."

You may need to consult your Lotus manual for information on how to adjust Lotus's printer settings for footers, margins, borders, page length and special set-up strings.

Using the Information in This Spreadsheet

Accuracy of This Spreadsheet

As was mentioned on page 98 the DAP Report presents some inherent inaccuracies because it uses an average ending inventory—instead of using an accurate physical inventory valuation or maintaining a somewhat accurate perpetual inventory—to calculate cost of goods. These inaccuracies are obvious if you look at the following entries in figure 7-3:

1. PTD COST OF GOODS, in column F of the FOOD COST RECAP section and in row 15 of the DAILY GROSS PROFIT AND LOSS

	A	B	C	D	E	F	G	H	I	J	K	L	M	N
1	DAILY AND PERIOD-TO-DATE REPORT:						*******	TODAY'S TRUE SALES:	$1,134.88 *******					
2							*******	TRUE SALES-TO-DATE:	$1,134.88 *******					
3	TODAY'S DATE: 03/01/86						*******	TODAY'S TOTAL MAN-HOURS:	86.6 *******					
4	DAY: SATURDAY						*******	TODAY'S SALES/MAN-HOUR:	$13.10 *******					
5	PERIOD: MARCH 1986						*******	TODAY'S CUSTOMER COUNT:	200 *******					
6	NAME: JOEL CHABAN						*******	TODAY'S AVERAGE CHECK:	$5.67 *******					
7	MONTH OF LAST PHYSICAL(1-12): 2													
8			*******>	L A B O R C O S T R E C A P			<*******							
9	///													
10	\\\\\\\\\\\\\\\\\\\\\\\	REGULAR	OVERTIME	GROSS	AM	PM	AM	PM	AM	PM	AM	PM	AM	PM
11	//////////////////////	PAY	PAY	PAY	OFFICE	OFFICE	BAR	BAR	D.R.	D.R.	KITCHEN	KITCHEN	JANITORIAL	JANITORIAL
12	\\\\\\\\\\\\\\\\\\\\\\\													
13	TODAY'S LABOR:	$478.77	$19.36	$498.13	$61.60	$47.31	$38.67	$89.62	$35.59	$31.80	$55.63	$74.80	$32.55	$30.57
14	AS A % OF TODAY'S GROSS PAY:	96.11%	3.89%	100.00%	12.37%	9.50%	7.76%	17.99%	7.15%	6.38%	11.17%	15.02%	6.53%	6.14
15	AS A % OF TODAY'S SALES:	42.19%	1.71%	43.89%	5.43%	4.17%	3.41%	7.90%	3.14%	2.80%	4.90%	6.59%	2.87%	2.69
16														
17	PERIOD-TO-DATE LABOR:	$478.77	$19.36	$498.13	$61.60	$47.31	$38.67	$89.62	$35.59	$31.80	$55.63	$74.80	$32.55	$30.57
18	AS % OF PTD GROSS PAY:	96.11%	3.89%	100.00%	12.37%	9.50%	7.76%	17.99%	7.15%	6.38%	11.17%	15.02%	6.53%	6.14
19	AS A % OF PTD SALES:	42.19%	1.71%	43.89%	5.43%	4.17%	3.41%	7.90%	3.14%	2.80%	4.90%	6.59%	2.87%	2.69
20	===													
21	///////////////////////////////////		*******>	F O O D C O S T R E C A P		<*******	///////////						
22		BEGINNING	TODAY'S	PTD	AVG. END	PTD COST	PERCENT OF							
23	FOOD CATEGORY	INVENTORY	PURCHASES	PURCHASES	INVENTORY	OF GOODS	PTD SALES							
24	\\													
25	BEVERAGE:	$147.40	$85.00	$85.00	$288.54	($56.14)	-4.95%							
26	CHEESE:	$286.05	$156.60	$156.60	$110.14	$332.52	29.30%							
27	DAIRY:	$87.13	$60.59	$60.59	$61.35	$86.37	7.61%							
28	EGGS:	$60.30	$125.00	$125.00	$49.00	$136.30	12.01%							
29	FROZEN:	$250.96	$276.35	$276.35	$456.46	$70.85	6.24%							
30	GROCERY:	$118.05	$249.53	$249.53	$327.27	$40.31	3.55%							
31	GRAINS:	$218.25	$16.88	$16.88	$45.33	$189.81	16.72%							
32	MEAT/FISH/POULTRY:	$141.63	$765.77	$765.77	$276.07	$631.33	55.63%							
33	PRODUCE:	$210.95	$83.24	$83.24	$227.64	$66.56	5.86%							
34	PAPER/PLASTIC:	$89.54	$56.00	$56.00	$542.19	($396.64)	-34.95%							
35	TRANSFERS IN:		$18.63	$18.63		$18.63	1.64%							
36	TRANSFERS OUT:		($36.99)	($36.99)		($36.99)	-3.26%							
37	CREDITS/RETURNS:		($15.25)	($15.25)		($15.25)	-1.34%							
38														
39	TOTAL:	$1,610.27	$1,841.35	$1,841.35	$2,383.97	$1,067.65	94.08%							
40	===													
41														
42	COPY BEGINNING INVENTORY FROM B25..B34 TO THE CORRESPONDING MONTH BELOW:													
43	///													
44			*******>	C A L C U L A T I O N O F E N D I N G I N V E N T O R Y A V E R A G E S							<*******			
45	FOOD CATEGORY	JANUARY	FEBRUARY	MARCH	APRIL	MAY	JUNE	JULY	AUGUST	SEPTEMBER	OCTOBER	NOVEMBER	DECEMBER	AVERAGES
46	\\													
47	BEVERAGE:	$323.58	$253.50											$288.54
48	CHEESE:	$125.87	$94.40											$110.14
49	DAIRY:	$84.90	$37.80											$61.35
50	EGGS:	$89.00	$9.00											$49.00
51	FROZEN:	$568.12	$344.80											$456.46
52	GROCERY:	$257.84	$396.70											$327.27
53	GRAINS:	$34.25	$56.40											$45.33
54	MEAT/FISH/POULTRY:	$458.64	$93.50											$276.07
55	PRODUCE:	$168.57	$286.70											$227.64
56	PAPER/PLASTIC:	$289.47	$794.90											$542.19
57														
58	TOTAL:	$2,400.24	$2,367.70	$0.00	$0.00	$0.00	$0.00	$0.00	$0.00	$0.00	$0.00	$0.00	$0.00	$2,383.97
59	===													
60														

7-3. *Daily and Period-to-date Report spreadsheet after execution of the \U macro.*

section of the spreadsheet: the totals for several food categories show preposterous negative dollar values.

2. PERCENT OF SALES, in column G of the FOOD COST RECAP section and in "Cost of Goods Sold" in the DAILY GROSS PROFIT AND LOSS section of the spreadsheet: percentages for several food categories show preposterous negative percentages.

3. GROSS PROFIT, in row 19 of the DAILY GROSS PROFIT AND LOSS section of the spreadsheet: the calculation of gross profit reflects the inaccuracies in the PTD COST OF GOODS.

These calculations will usually be inaccurate in the beginning of a period, when you first begin accumulating period-to-date purchases (column D in the FOOD COST RECAP section), because period-to-date purchases will be less than the average ending inventories calculated for the various inventory food categories. This can create an im-

```
: P :: G ::     R    :: S :: T :: U :: V :: W :: X :: Y :: Z

                    *******> D A I L Y   G R O S S   P R O F I T   A N D   L O S S  <*******
                    -------------------------------------------------------------------------
                    TODAY        %              PTD         %
                    -------------------------------------------------------------------------
      TRUE SALES:   $1,134.88    100.00%        $1,134.88   100.00%
                    -------------------------------------------------------------------------
 BEGIN INVENTORY:   $1,610.27                   $1,610.27
       PURCHASES:   $1,841.35    162.25%        $1,841.35   162.25%
AVG. END INVENTORY: $2,383.97                   $2,383.97
                    -------------------------------------------------------------------------
COST OF GOODS SOLD: $1,067.65    94.08%         $1,067.65   94.08%
                    -------------------------------------------------------------------------
          LABOR:    $498.13      43.89%         $498.13     43.89%
                    -------------------------------------------------------------------------
   GROSS PROFIT:    ($430.90)    -37.97%        ($430.90)   -37.97%
                    =========================================================================
```

possible situation of negative inventory dollar values and also makes accurate calculation of the cost of goods sold in the TODAY columm (column S) of the DAILY GROSS PROFIT AND LOSS section of the spreadsheet extremely difficult.

The period-to-date calculations become more and more accurate, however, as the period progresses, as you begin accumulating more and more days of activity in the DAP Report, and as period-to-date purchases begin to exceed average ending inventory calculations.

Reviewing the DAP Report Daily

Reviewing the DAP Report daily is a good way to keep in touch with business activity in your foodservice operation. The DAP Report has been designed to present various comparisons of food costs and labor costs to sales. These comparisons provide ratios from which you can develop standards of performance and allowable deviations for your operation. Because the DAP Report is updated daily, it allows you to pinpoint problems in your operation accurately and in a timely fashion.

Today's True Sales

Today's true sales are a net sales figure representing sales that include any overage or shortage in cash but do not include sales tax, charged tips, or miscellaneous income. Use this figure as an effective measure of the day's actual sales of food and beverage and to measure how well your restaurant is meeting its budget projections (see chapter 10). The figure for today's true sales is used throughout the DAP Report spreadsheet to calculate ratios of food cost to sales and labor cost to sales—ratios you can use to improve the management and control of your operation.

True Sales to Date

True sales to date, also referred to as period-to-date sales, represent a cumulative total of sales for the period. Use this figure to measure how well your foodservice operation is meeting its budget projections. This cumulative total is used throughout the DAP Report spreadsheet to calculate ratios of food cost to sales and labor cost to sales.

Today's Total Man-hours

Today's total man-hours are the day's total labor (in hours) required to produce the day's sales in your operation. The labor goal of management is to optimize the labor schedule, minimizing total labor hours without jeopardizing the quality of service to customers. The figure for total man-hours may be used to measure management's progress toward this goal and as a historical reference when setting up weekly and monthly labor schedules and when projecting labor budgets.

Today's Sales per Man-hour

The figure for today's sales per man-hour measures employee productivity in your operation by comparing total labor hours to sales. The more dollar sales per labor-hour your staff can produce, the more productive your staff is. A low figure for sales per labor-hour may indicate one or more of the following problems:

1. Management is scheduling too many employees.
2. Employees are not being trained properly in how to be productive.
3. Employees are being scheduled for too many hours.
4. Employees are incurring too much overtime.
5. Sales are too low. Attention to marketing and sales may be lacking.
6. Hiring procedures are improper or lax.

Too high a figure for sales per labor-hour may indicate that your staff is jeopardizing the quality of service to customers. An understaffed operation cannot properly service a high-volume operation. Loss of business through being understaffed may be more dangerous to the health of your operation than loss of operating expenses through being overstaffed. Be wary of both potential problems by setting allowable deviations from the figure you set for standard or average sales per man-hour.

Today's Customer Count

Today's customer count is an indicator of how well your operation is meeting its budget projections (see chapter 10) in attracting new business. Many operators use customer counts, rather than sales, as a guage of their operation's performance in attracting new business, since increases in sales may be the result of factors other than new customers—such as increases in menu prices or greater volume in sales of higher-priced menu items than in sales of lower-priced menu items.

Today's Average Check

Today's average check equals today's true sales divided by today's customer count. Today's aver-age check measures how well your service staff has been selling the products on your menu. The better your staff is at selling extras on your menu—such as appetizers, desserts, and wine—the higher the average check will be. One goal of foodservice operators is to increase the average check by training their service staff in selling and service techniques that increase the average check amount. Set minimum and maximum deviations from the average check. When your servers increase the amount of the average check above the maximum deviation, reward them. If the amount of the average check falls below the minimum deviation, have your managers put more emphasis on server training and motivation.

Today's Labor as a Percentage of Gross Pay

Use the figures for today's labor as a percentage of gross pay (in row 14) to develop daily labor standards and allowable deviations from the standard for percentage of gross pay. Using past Daily Labor Reports, your budget, and the DAP Report spreadsheet as planning tools, set minimum and maximum allowable percentages for each department's total pay. Set similar standards for each department, and treat deviations below the minimum allowable percentage and above the maximum allowable percentage as indicators of problems in the labor department involved.

You can also use these derived standards and deviations in conjunction with similar standards and deviations established for today's labor as a percentage of today's sales.

Today's Labor as a Percentage of Today's Sales

Set standards and allowable deviations from the standard for today's labor as a percentage of today's sales, as described previously. Treat excessive deviations from these daily percentages as indicators of labor problems such as poor scheduling, inappropriate hiring techniques, and improper or lax training and management practices.

Period-to-date Labor as a Percentage of PTD Gross Pay

Set standards and allowable deviations from the standard for period-to-date labor as a percentage of period-to-date gross pay, as described previously. Treat excessive deviations from these daily percentages as indicators of labor problems in scheduling, hiring, training, and management.

Period-to-date Labor as a Percentage of PTD Sales

Set standards and allowable deviations from the standard for period-to-date labor as a percentage of period-to-date sales, as described previously. Treat excessive deviations from these daily percentages as indicators of labor problems in scheduling, hiring, training, and management.

Cost of Goods as a Percentage of PTD Sales

Calculations of cost of goods as a percentage of period-to-date sales (in column G of the FOOD COST RECAP section of the DAP Report spreadsheet) represent each inventory food category as a percentage of sales. Over time, these percentages will fall into a pattern from which you can develop standards and averages for each inventory category. Deviations from these standards may indicate one or more of the following:

- Menu trends of your customers toward or away from a particular food category
- Overpurchasing or underpurchasing in a particular food category
- Pilferage or theft in a specific food category
- Food wastage in a particular food category
- Overportioning or underportioning by your kitchen crew in a particular food category
- Menu prices that are out of alignment with food costs in a particular food category

Cost of Goods Sold

The cost of goods sold, in the DAILY GROSS PROFIT AND LOSS section of the spreadsheet, is a general indicator of how well food and beverage costs are being managed in your oper-ation. Use the cost of goods sold and its associated percentage of true sales as your day-to-day indicator of food and beverage costs.

Use both today's and the period-to-date cost of goods sold figures to measure your performance in keeping to your budget (see chapter 9). Take immediate action if the cost of goods becomes too low or too high. If the cost of goods figure is too high, this may indicate one of the following problems:

1. Menu prices are too low.
2. Food and beverage are being wasted.
3. Servings are being overportioned.
4. Employees are pilfering inventory or stealing money.
5. Purchasing activities and procedures are not being performed properly.

If cost of goods is too low, this may indicate one of the following problems:

1. Menu prices are too high.
2. Food and beverage are being underportioned.

Labor

Like cost of goods sold, labor is a general indicator of how well labor is being managed in your operation. Use labor and its associated percentage of true sales as your day-to-day indicator of labor costs.

Use both today's and period-to-date labor figures to measure your performance in keeping to your labor budget (see chapter 9). Take immediate action if the labor costs become too low or too high. For a review of labor problems in situations where labor costs are too high or too low, see pages 76–78.

Gross Profit

Gross profit measures how much money you have left to cover fixed expenses after paying for the day's and the period-to-date's primary variable expenses, food, beverage, and labor. As with the cost of goods sold, use both today's and period-to-date gross profit figures to measure your performance in keeping to your budget. Compare this figure with your budget's fixed cost and break-even calculations to assess whether your operation is maintaining itself at better than break-even.

Author's Note

During the revision of this book, a problem was discovered with version 2 of Lotus 1-2-3 regarding the /File Combine Copy command. Specifically, the problem affects the macro used in chapter 7 to transfer daily activity from the spreadsheets developed in chapters 3 through 6 to the spreadsheet developed in chapter 7. As of December 1986, the /File Combine Copy command of the present version of Lotus 1-2-3 Release 2 not only transfers values to the spreadsheet in chapter 7, it also transfers formulas con-taining erratic cell references from these other spreadsheets. The /File Combine Copy command, as explained to me by the technical support staff at Lotus, is not supposed to transfer formulas.

By the time you purchase this book, Lotus Development Corporation may already have solved the problems posed by this command. If so, the macro in the main text of chapter 7 should work properly, as presented.

The macro presented below is an alternative to the one presented in the main text of chapter 7. It is not as efficient as the macro presented there, but it will work. Therefore, if you have problems with your Lotus software as described above when you try to use the macro in the main text of chapter 7, use the alternative macro that follows.

Cell	Command	Command Explanation
S27	'/WGRM	* Turn automatic recalc off.
S28	'/WGPD	* Unprotect entire worksheet.
S29	{GOTO}J1~	* Go to Cell J1.
S30	'/REJ1~	* Erase old value in Cell J1.
S31	'/FCANK30~B:CASH~	* Transfer value in Cell K30 from the CASH.WK1 spreadsheet to Cell J1 in the DAP-_.WK1 spreadsheet.
S32	{GOTO}J2~	* Go to Cell J2.
S33	'/FCANK30~B:CASH~	* Transfer value in Cell K30 from the CASH.WK1 spreadsheet to Cell J2 in the DAP-_.WK1 spreadsheet, and add value in Cell K30 to value in Cell J2.
S34	{GOTO}J3~	* Go to Cell J3.
S35	'/REJ3~	* Erase old value in Cell J3.
S36	'/FCANK21~B:LABOR~	* Transfer value in Cell K21 from the LABOR.WK1 spreadsheet to Cell J3 in the DAP-_.WK1 spreadsheet.
S37	{GOTO}J5~	* Go to Cell J5.
S38	'/REJ5~	* Erase old value in Cell J5.
S39	'/FCANC8~B:CASH~	* Transfer value in Cell C8 from the CASH.WK1 spreadsheet to Cell J5 in the DAP-_.WK1 spreadsheet.
S40	'/RPJ5~	* Protect Cell J5.
S41	{GOTO}B13~	* Go to Cell B13.
S42	'/REB13..N13~	* Erase old values in Cell Range B13..N13.
S43	'/FCANN21..Z21~B:LABOR~	* Transfer values in Cell Range N21..Z21 from the LABOR.WK1 spreadsheet to Cell B13 in the DAP-_.WK1 spreadsheet.

Continued

Cell	Command	Command Explanation
S44	{GOTO}B17~	* Go to Cell B17.
S45	'/FCANN21..Z21~B:LABOR~	* Transfer the value in Cell Range N21..Z21 from the LABOR.WK1 spreadsheet to Cell B17 in the DAP-_.WK1 spreadsheet, and add values in Cell Range N21..Z21 to corresponding values in Cell Range B17..N17.
S46	{GOTO}B25~	* Go to Cell B25.
S47	'/REB25..B34~	* Erase old values in Cell Range B25..B34.
S48	'/FCANF68..F77~B:INVENTRY~	* Transfer values in Cell Range F68..F77 from the INVENTRY.WK1 spreadsheet to Cell Range B25..B34 in the DAP-_.WK1 spreadsheet.
S49	{GOTO}C25~	* Go to Cell C25.
S50	'/REC25..C37~	* Erase old values in Cell Range C25..C37.
S51	'/FCANJ27..J39~B:PURCHASE~	* Transfer values in Cell Range J27..J39 from the PURCHASE.WK1 spreadsheet to Cell Range C25..C37 in the DAP-_.WK1 spreadsheet.
S52	{GOTO}D25~	* Go to Cell D25.
S53	'/FCANJ27..J39~B:PURCHASE~	* Transfer values in Cell Range J27..J39 from the PURCHASE.WK1 spreadsheet to Cell Range D25..D37 in the DAP-_.WK1 spreadsheet, and add values from PURCHASE.WK1 to corresponding values in Cell Range D25..D37 of DAP-_.WK1.
S54	{CALC}	* Recalculate spreadsheet.
S55	'/WGPE	* Protect entire worksheet.
S56	{HOME}	* Go to Cell A1.

Problems

1. Briefly describe each of the four major sections of the Daily and Period-to-date Report spreadsheet.
2. Explain why ending inventory averages are used in the DAP Report. How are they calculated?
3. Explain how, why, and when the PTD COST OF GOODS column (column F, rows 22 through 40) can have negative dollar totals in several food categories. How and when will these negative dollar totals become positive dollar totals?
4. Describe the inherent inaccuracies in the DAP Report. Why do these inaccuracies exist, and why do these inaccuracies grow less significant as the period progresses?
5. Explain how you might use the following ratios reported by the DAP Report spreadsheet to manage/control a foodservice operation:

- Today's sales per man-hour
- Today's average check
6. Explain how the following ratios may be used to manage/control a foodservice operation:
   - Today's labor as a percentage of today's gross pay
   - Today's labor as a percentage of today's sales
7. Explain how the following ratios may be used to manage/control a foodservice operation:
   - Period-to-date labor as a percentage of PTD gross pay
   - Period-to-date labor as a percentage of PTD sales
8. Explain on a chronological basis how the DAP Report spreadsheet might be maintained as a tool for developing standard ratios and deviations from standards that you could then apply in the management and control of your foodservice operation.
9. What disastrous event will happen to your DAP Report spreadsheet if, after executing the upgrade (\U) macro, you add suppliers to the Daily Purchases Register spreadsheet in chapter 3? How can you prevent this disaster from occurring?
10. How will adding inventory items to the Daily Inventory and Valuation spreadsheet in chapter 4 affect the DAP Report spreadsheet when you run the upgrade (\U) macro? What remedy do you suggest?
11. How will adding new employees to the Daily Labor Report spreadsheet in chapter 5 affect the DAP Report spreadsheet when you run the

upgrade (\U) macro? What solution do you suggest?

Cases

1. Discuss the advantages of using spreadsheets in a foodservice operation, with regard to the following:
   - Timeliness of information
   - Information produced by using spreadsheets versus manual reporting methods
   - Management and control of a foodservice operation
2. Discuss the disadvantages of using spreadsheets, with regard to the following:
   - Computer file handling, housekeeping, and management
   - Data integrity and corruption
   - Data security and insecurity
   - Delegating responsibility for spreadsheet data entry to other employees
   - Developing complex file interrelationships
3. How might you alter the spreadsheets in chapters 3 through 7 to enhance their use?
4. What management and/or accounting applications might you want to develop using spreadsheets (other than the applications described in the chapters of this book)?
5. What management and/or accounting applications and uses would you not consider appropriate for spreadsheet development because of the disadvantages of spreadsheets?

8. Tip Allocation

TABLE 8-1. SUMMARY OF LOTUS COMMANDS USED IN THIS CHAPTER.

Commands Used

Command String Abbreviation	Command Name	Functions Used
/C	/Copy	@IF
/FS	/File Save	@SUM
/PP	/Print Printer	
/RF	/Range Format	
/RU	/Range Unprotect	
/WCS	/Worksheet Column Set-width	
/WGC	/Worksheet Global Column	
/WGP	/Worksheet Global Protect	

Federal tip reporting and allocation rules are complex and have puzzled many restaurateurs since their promulgation in the Tax Equity and Fiscal Responsibility Act (TEFRA) of December 1982. This chapter is intended to help you understand what some of these rules require and how tip allocations are calculated. You can gain a lot of insight simply by going through the process of constructing the spreadsheet.

The Tip Allocation spreadsheet is used to calculate end-of-year or end-of-payroll-period tip allocations for your employees. Calculations are based on the Internal Revenue Service's standard tip allocation formulas in effect on April 15, 1984.

How to Use the Tip Allocation Spreadsheet

Based either on gross receipts for each employee or on hours worked by each employee, the Tip Allocation spreadsheet calculates each employee's shortfall (unless an employee does not have a reporting shortfall) and consequent tip allocation. The IRS recommends these two methods of calculating tip allocations for foodservice operations that qualify under TEFRA rules and do not adopt a good-faith agreement. The two methods are called, respectively, the Hours Worked method and the Gross Receipts method. Both methods are described in this chapter.

The Internal Revenue Service explains its allocation rules in Publication 539 (Revision Nov. 1983), *Employment Taxes*, as follows:

> **Allocation rules.** You may allocate tips under a formula agreed to by both you and your employees. If you cannot agree on a formula, you must allocate them according to Internal Revenue Service regulations. If you allocate tips according to a good-faith agreement between you and your employees or according to the regulations, you will not be liable to any employee if any amount is allocated improperly.
>
> According to the formula in the regulations, you make tip allocations only to your directly tipped employees. A directly tipped employee is any employee who receives tips directly from customers, even if the tips are turned over to a tip pool. For example, waiters, waitresses, and bar-

---

IMPORTANT

TEFRA (the Tax Equity and Fiscal Responsibility Act) was promulgated in December 1982 and took effect at the beginning of 1983. If any of TEFRA's provisions relating to the calculation of tip allocations are amended or changed in any way after November 12, 1986, the calculations described in this spreadsheet for determining your employees' tip allocations may be incorrect. If you are unsure about changes in TEFRA rules or about the applicability of this spreadsheet to your employees and your tip allocation reporting circumstances, seek the advice of a licensed Certified Public Accountant before using the Tip Allocation spreadsheet to calculate tip allocations for your employees.

In all cases, you should consult a qualified, licensed Certified Public Accountant to determine whether your foodservice operation qualifies for mandatory reporting of tip allocations under TEFRA rules. This spreadsheet does not perform the following TEFRA qualification tests:

1. It does not test whether or not your restaurant or foodservice operation(s) qualifies for mandatory reporting of tip allocations under TEFRA rules.
2. It does not test whether an employee qualifies as a directly tipped employee or as an indirectly tipped employee under TEFRA rules.
3. It does not test whether or not a person qualifies under TEFRA rules as an employee of the legal entity for which you are reporting.
4. It does not test to determine whether revenue categories should or should not be included in *gross receipts* (entered in Cell E6 of the spreadsheet), as the term is defined in TEFRA rules. If you are not familiar with TEFRA rules on the definition of *gross receipts,* consult a Certified Public Accountant.
5. It does not test whether a particular item should or should not be considered a charged receipt for purposes of calculating gross receipts.
6. It does not test whether a particular add-on charge should or should not be considered a charged tip.
7. Of special importance to operations that have adopted active good-faith agreements, this spreadsheet does not consider special tip allocation formulas created by a good-faith agreement.

---

tenders are usually considered directly tipped employees. An employee who does not normally receive tips directly from customers is an indirectly tipped employee. Busboys, service bartenders, and cooks are examples of indirectly tipped employees. If an employee receives tips both directly and indirectly, such as through a tip-splitting or tip-pooling arrangement, the employee is treated as a directly tipped employee.

You may allocate tips under the regulations on the basis of each directly tipped employee's share of gross receipts or on the basis of each directly tipped employee's share of the total hours worked.

Using the Gross Receipts formula or the Hours Worked formula necessitates that you keep accurate records. If you use the Hours Worked method, you must keep accurate records of the number of hours that each directly tipped employee has worked (this is required by payroll laws, anyway). If you use the Gross Receipts method, you must keep accurate records of each directly tipped employee's gross receipts—from waiting on tables or from any other source.

The Gross Receipts method may inspire you to purchase a point-of-sale system so that you can track sales for each employee, to hire extra bookkeepers to handle the additional bookkeeping that this method necessitates, or to switch to the Hours Worked method. Whichever method and formula you decide to use, you must always keep accurate records of tips re-

```
:   A    ::   B   ::   C   ::   D   ::   E   ::   F   ::   G   ::   H   :: I :: J  :
```

	A	B	C	D	E	F	G	H	I	J
1	TIP ALLOCATIONS BASED ON									
2	"HOURS WORKED" AND									
3	"GROSS RECEIPTS" METHODS			DATE:	03/01/86					
4	-------------------------------									
5										
6	1.			GROSS RECEIPTS FOR PERIOD:	$750,000.00 x .08 factor =	$60,000.00 = TOTAL ALLOCABLE TIPS				
7	2. TOTAL TIPS REPORTED BY INDIRECTLY TIPPED EMPLOYEES:				$5,000.00					
8	3. TOTAL TIPS ALLOCABLE TO DIRECTLY TIPPED EMPLOYEES:				$55,000.00					

HOURS WORKED METHOD

DIRECTLY TIPPED EMPLOYEES	HOURS WORKED IN PAYROLL PERIOD	REPORTED TIPS	DIRECTLY TIPPED EMPLOYEES SHARE OF 8% GROSS	HOURS WORKED RATIO TO TOTAL HOURS	EACH EMPLOYEES SHARE OF 8% GROSS	EACH EMPLOYEE'S SHORTFALL	ALLOCABLE SHORTFALL AMOUNT	SHORTFALL RATIO	TIP ALLOCATION
JOHN	1000	$3,200.00	$55,000.00	6.81%	$3,747.87	$547.87	$6,600.00	6.08%	$401.35
ELLEN	2000	$7,500.00	$55,000.00	13.63%	$7,495.74	$0.00	$6,600.00	0.00%	$0.00
BETH	2150	$9,800.00	$55,000.00	14.65%	$8,057.92	$0.00	$6,600.00	0.00%	$0.00
PAT	2000	$6,800.00	$55,000.00	13.63%	$7,495.74	$695.74	$6,600.00	7.72%	$509.68
STEVE	950	$2,200.00	$55,000.00	6.47%	$3,560.48	$1,360.48	$6,600.00	15.10%	$996.65
GLEN	1475	$4,100.00	$55,000.00	10.05%	$5,528.11	$1,428.11	$6,600.00	15.85%	$1,046.19
ANN	1800	$5,000.00	$55,000.00	12.27%	$6,746.17	$1,746.17	$6,600.00	19.38%	$1,279.19
MARY	1800	$5,200.00	$55,000.00	12.27%	$6,746.17	$1,546.17	$6,600.00	17.16%	$1,132.68
PRIMO	250	$1,600.00	$55,000.00	1.70%	$936.97	$0.00	$6,600.00	0.00%	$0.00
SUE	1250	$3,900.00	$55,000.00	8.52%	$4,684.84	$1,684.84	$6,600.00	18.70%	$1,234.26
	14675	$48,400.00		100.00%	$55,000.00	$9,009.37		100.00%	$6,600.00

GROSS RECEIPTS METHOD

DIRECTLY TIPPED EMPLOYEES	GROSS RECEIPTS IN PAYROLL PERIOD	REPORTED TIPS	DIRECTLY TIPPED EMPLOYEES SHARE OF 8% GROSS	GROSS RECEIPTS RATIO TO TOTAL RECEIPTS	EACH EMPLOYEES SHARE OF 8% GROSS	EACH EMPLOYEE'S SHORTFALL	ALLOCABLE SHORTFALL AMOUNT	SHORTFALL RATIO	TIP ALLOCATION
JOHN	$75,000.00	$3,200.00	$55,000.00	10.00%	$5,500.00	$2,300.00	$6,600.00	20.72%	$1,367.57
ELLEN	$125,000.00	$7,500.00	$55,000.00	16.67%	$9,166.67	$1,666.67	$6,600.00	15.02%	$990.99
BETH	$100,000.00	$9,800.00	$55,000.00	13.33%	$7,333.33	$0.00	$6,600.00	0.00%	$0.00
PAT	$110,000.00	$6,800.00	$55,000.00	14.67%	$8,066.67	$1,266.67	$6,600.00	11.41%	$753.15
STEVE	$50,000.00	$2,200.00	$55,000.00	6.67%	$3,666.67	$1,466.67	$6,600.00	13.21%	$872.07
GLEN	$90,000.00	$4,100.00	$55,000.00	12.00%	$6,600.00	$2,500.00	$6,600.00	22.52%	$1,486.49
ANN	$90,000.00	$5,000.00	$55,000.00	12.00%	$6,600.00	$1,600.00	$6,600.00	14.41%	$951.35
MARY	$75,000.00	$5,200.00	$55,000.00	10.00%	$5,500.00	$300.00	$6,600.00	2.70%	$178.38
PRIMO	$10,000.00	$1,600.00	$55,000.00	1.33%	$733.33	$0.00	$6,600.00	0.00%	$0.00
SUE	$25,000.00	$3,000.00	$55,000.00	3.33%	$1,833.33	$0.00	$6,600.00	0.00%	$0.00
	$750,000.00	$48,400.00		100.00%	$55,000.00	$11,100.00		100.00%	$6,600.00

8-1. Tip Allocation spreadsheet.

ported by both directly tipped and indirectly tipped employees.

Figure 8-1 shows calculations by the Hours Worked method in rows 10 through 27 and shows calculations by the Gross Receipts method in rows 29 through 46. Both methods access and apply the user-supplied and user-calculated data shown in rows 6 through 8 of the spreadsheet.

Although this chapter works through a single spreadsheet example using first the Hours Worked method and then the Gross Receipts method, you will use only one of these methods in your final spreadsheet. Your choice of which method to use should be based on how you qualify for tip allocations, on advice from your CPA, on the factors already mentioned in this introduction, and on factors unique to your own circumstances.

Where a time period is expressed in the Tip Allocation spreadsheet—by a label such as PAY-ROLL PERIOD or PERIOD—you can treat the period as your typical payroll period. Make sure that the amounts you use apply to the period you are using. On the subject of what periods you should report to the IRS, Publication 539, *Employment Taxes*, states the following:

> An allocation period can be your regular payroll period, the calendar year, or some reasonable division of a year, such as a calendar month or calendar quarter.

Your foodservice operation may require modifications in the Tip Allocation spreadsheet presented here. For example, you may need to expand the number of rows used, if you have more directly tipped employees than are represented in figure 8-1. You are free to make changes of this sort in adapting the spreadsheet to fit your own tip allocation requirements.

TABLE 8-2. STEP 1 FORMATTING COMMANDS.

Column(s)	Width	Command to Enter	
A	20	/WCS20	<Return>
I	9	/WCS9	<Return>
all remaining	15	/WGC15	<Return>

Gathering the Information You Need

Before you attempt to put together your own tip allocation spreadsheet—using your operation's data rather than the data shown in figure 8-1—you will need to gather the following data:

- The gross receipts for the allocation or payroll period
- The amount of total tips reported by indirectly tipped employees
- The name of each directly tipped employee who is or was employed during the allocation or payroll period
- The total hours worked in the payroll period by each directly tipped employee (if you use the Hours Worked method) or the gross receipts for each directly tipped employee in the payroll period (if you use the Gross Receipts method)
- The reported tips of each directly tipped employee

Common Spreadsheet Characteristics

The first seven steps identified in this chapter are common to both the Hours Worked method and the Gross Receipts method. After that, parallel procedures are described, first for the Hours Worked method and then for the Gross Receipts method. In each case, the parallel steps are numbered 8 through 19.

Formatting, Headings, and Labels

Step 1. Reformat columns A through J from the normal, default Lotus column width of nine characters to the widths indicated in table 8-2.

Step 2. Begin re-creating the spreadsheet example shown in figure 8-1, by entering the appropriate headings and labels into columns A through J, rows 1 through 46, exactly as specified in table 8-3.

You may need to pad some of your cell entries with blank spaces to get your headings to look like those pictured in figure 8-1. Any heading beginning with one of the three Lotus label alignment prefixes (', ", and ^) signifies a label to be padded with blank spaces or to be given a special cell alignment. Remember that the prefix ' aligns text to the left margin of the cell, the prefix " aligns text to the right margin of the cell, and the prefix ^ centers text within the cell. Unless a label alignment prefix is indicated in table 8-3, do not use one of these prefixes to begin a label or heading.

Step 3. Enter dashed lines and double-dashed lines into the spreadsheet, as indicated in table 8-4. Use the backslash (\) key at the beginning of each cell entry to signal to Lotus that the character immediately following it is to be repeated across the cell from end to end.

To repeat a character across several individual cells, use Lotus's /Copy command, as indicated in table 8-4. Use the pointing method described on page 34 to define the last cell of a cell range when performing the /Copy operation. Remember to place the cell pointer on the originating cell (the cell being copied from) before you begin to enter each command listed in table 8-4.

Step 4. Format the cells and cell ranges identified in table 8-5, as indicated there. Enter each command given in the far right-hand column of the table exactly as it appears, by typing the characters shown and then hitting the <Return> key. When formatting a cell range, use the pointing method to define the last cell in each indicated cell range. Be sure to place the cell pointer on the first cell indicated in the far left-hand column of table 8-5 before entering the associated command.

Step 5. Enter the following Lotus calendar function into Cell E3:

@NOW

If the target cell is formatted for date (as Cell E3 is), the @NOW function automatically gets today's date from the system date you entered when you first turned on your computer or from

TABLE 8-3. STEP 2 HEADINGS.

Cell	Heading
A1	TIP ALLOCATING BASED ON
A2	''''HOURS WORKED'' AND
A3	''''GROSS RECEIPTS'' METHODS
D3	''DATE:
A6	' 1. GROSS RECEIPTS FOR PERIOD:
H6	'= TOTAL ALLOCABLE TIPS
F6	× .08 factor =
A7	' 2. TOTAL TIPS REPORTED BY INDIRECTLY TIPPED EMPLOYEES:
A8	' 3. TOTAL TIPS ALLOCABLE TO DIRECTLY TIPPED EMPLOYEES:
E10	' *** HOURS WORKED METHOD *** =
B11	^HOURS WORKED
D11	^DIRECTLY TIPPED
E11	^HOURS WORKED
F11	^EACH
G11	^EACH
H11	^ALLOCABLE
A12	^DIRECTLY TIPPED
B12	^IN
C12	^REPORTED
D12	^EMPLOYEES SHARE
E12	^RATIO TO
F12	^EMPLOYEES SHARE
G12	^EMPLOYEE'S
H12	^SHORTFALL
I12	^SHORTFALL
J12	^TIP
A13	^EMPLOYEES
B13	^PAYROLL PERIOD
C13	^TIPS
D13	^OF 8% GROSS
E13	^TOTAL HOURS
F13	^OF 8% GROSS
G13	^SHORTFALL
H13	^AMOUNT
I13	^RATIO
J13	^ALLOCATION
E29	'*** GROSS RECEIPTS METHOD ***=
B30	^GROSS RECEIPTS
D30	^DIRECTLY TIPPED
E30	'' GROSS RECEIPTS
F30	^EACH
G30	^EACH
H30	^ALLOCABLE
A31	^DIRECTLY TIPPED
B31	^IN
C31	^REPORTED
D31	^EMPLOYEES SHARE
E31	^RATIO TO
F31	^EMPLOYEES SHARE

Continued.

TABLE 8-3. CONTINUED.

Cell	Heading
G31	^EMPLOYEE'S
H31	^SHORTFALL
I31	^SHORTFALL
J31	^TIP
A32	^EMPLOYEES
B32	^PAYROLL PERIOD
C32	^TIPS
D32	^OF 8% GROSS
E32	^TOTAL RECEIPTS
F32	^OF 8% GROSS
G32	^SHORTFALL
H32	^AMOUNT
I32	^RATIO
J32	^ALLOCATION

the date maintained by an automatic, battery-operated clock/calendar (if your computer has this feature). If the target cell is formatted for time, the time of day is returned when the @NOW function is entered.

Step 6. Enter the following formula into Cell G6:

```
+E6*.08
```

Rendered in English, this formula reads: "Multiply the value in Cell E6 by 0.08." The result of multiplying $750,000 by 0.08 is $60,000, which represents 8 percent of your establishment's gross receipts during the allocation period. If your employees report tips totaling less than 8 percent of your total sales, you must allocate an amount that—together with reported tips—equals 8 percent of total sales among all employees who receive tips directly from your customers (or among all tipped employees, if your good-faith agreement with your employees specifies allocating them this way).

Step 7. Enter the following formula into Cell E8:

```
+G6-E7
```

Rendered in English, this formula reads: "Subtract the value in Cell E7 from the value in Cell G6." The difference when total tips reported by indirectly tipped employes ($5,000.00) is subtracted from total allocable tips ($60,000.00) is $55,000, which represents total tips allocable to directly tipped employees.

TABLE 8-4. STEP 3 REPEAT AND /COPY COMMANDS.

Cell	REPEAT Command to Enter	/Copy Command to Enter		
A4	\-	/CA4	<Return>	B9 <Return>
A10	\=	/CA10	<Return>	B10..D10 <Return>
G10	\=	/CG10	<Return>	H10..J10 <Return>
A14	\-	/CA14	<Return>	B14..J14 <Return>
A25	\-	/CA25	<Return>	B25..J25 <Return>
A27	\=	/CA27	<Return>	B27..J27 <Return>
A29	\=	/CA29	<Return>	B29..D29 <Return>
G29	\=	/CG29	<Return>	H29..J29 <Return>
A33	\-	/CA33	<Return>	B33..J33 <Return>
A44	\-	/CA44	<Return>	B44..J44 <Return>
A46	\=	/CA46	<Return>	B46..J46 <Return>

TABLE 8-5. STEP 4 /RANGE FORMAT COMMANDS.

Cell(s)	Format/Alignment	Command to Enter			
E3	date type 4	`/RFD4`	`<Return>`		
E6..E8	currency	`/RFC2`	`<Return>`	`E6..E8`	`<Return>`
G6	currency	`/RFC2`	`<Return>`	`G6`	`<Return>`
C15..D45	currency	`/RFC2`	`<Return>`	`C15..D45`	`<Return>`
E15..E45	percent	`/RFP2`	`<Return>`	`E15..E45`	`<Return>`
F15..H45	currency	`/RFC2`	`<Return>`	`F15..H45`	`<Return>`
I15..I45	percent	`/RFP2`	`<Return>`	`I15..I45`	`<Return>`
J15..J45	currency	`/RFC3`	`<Return>`	`J15..J45`	`<Return>`

The Hours Worked Method

Steps 8 through 19 immediately following describe the procedures involved in the Hours Worked method. If you are interested only in the Gross Receipts method, skip to Step 8, page 126.

Operator Input

Step 8. Before entering the formulas for the Hours Worked method, enter the input given in table 8-6, representing the data in the upper two shaded areas of figure 8-1. The data in Columns A, B, C, and E constitute the only information that you normally must enter. The remainder of the spreadsheet is calculated automatically.

TABLE 8-6. STEP 8 INPUT DATA (HOURS WORKED METHOD).

Cell(s)	Input
E6	GROSS RECEIPTS FOR PERIOD. Enter the gross receipts for the period under consideration.
E7	TOTAL TIPS REPORTED BY INDIRECTLY TIPPED EMPLOYEES. Enter the total tips reported by indirectly tipped employees.
A15..A24	DIRECTLY TIPPED EMPLOYEES. Enter the names of directly tipped employees.
B15..B24	HOURS WORKED IN PAYROLL PERIOD. Enter the hours worked during the payroll period.
C15..C24	REPORTED TIPS. Enter the reported tips for each directly tipped employee.

Formulas

Some of the steps that follow contain instructions about making cells absolute when copying formulas and cell references. The meaning of absolute and relative cells is discussed on pages 34–35.

Step 9. Enter the following cell reference into Cell D15:

    +$E$8

Rendered in English, this cell reference reads: "Get the value in Cell E8 and put it in Cell D15." The value in Cell E8 represents the total tips allocable to directly tipped employees—$55,000.00.

Placing dollar signs in front of the column and row references of Cell E8 designates the cell as absolute. This means that, when this reference to Cell E8 is copied, it will not change.

Now copy the cell reference from Cell D15 into cells D16 through D24, placing your cell pointer on Cell D15 and entering the following / Copy command:

    /C   <Return>   [point to Cell D16].
    [point to Cell D24]   <Return>

Step 10. Enter the following formula into Cell E15:

    +B15/$B$26

Rendered in English, this formula reads: "Divide the value in Cell B15 (1,000 hours) by the value in Cell B26 (14,675 hours)." The result in Cell E15 (6.81 percent) is the hours worked ratio, which is the percentage of total hours that the first directly tipped employee on your list (John) has worked during the payroll or allocation period.

Placing dollar signs in front of the column and row references of Cell B26 designates the cell as absolute. This means that, when this formula is copied, the reference to Cell B26 will not change; in contrast, the reference to Cell B15 will change in each cell into which the formula is copied.

Now copy the formula from Cell E15 into cells E16 through E24, placing your cell pointer on Cell E15 and entering the following /Copy command:

```
/C    <Return>    [point to Cell E16].
[point to Cell E24]    <Return>
```

Step 11. Enter the following formula into Cell F15:

```
+E15*D15
```

Rendered in English, this formula reads: "Multiply the value in Cell E15 (6.81 percent) by the value in Cell D15 ($55,000.00)." The result in Cell F15 ($3,747.87) is the employee's share of the 8 percent gross tips allocable to directly tipped employees.

Now copy the formula from Cell F15 into cells F16 through F24, placing your cell pointer on Cell F15 and entering the following /Copy command:

```
/C    <Return>    [point to Cell F16].
[point to Cell F24]    <Return>
```

Step 12. Enter the following formula into Cell G15:

```
@IF(C15>F15,0,F15-C15)
```

Rendered in English, this formula reads: "If Cell C15 is greater than Cell F15, display $0.00 in Cell G15; otherwise, display the result of Cell C15 subtracted from Cell F15." The first part of this formula, IF(C15>F15, tests to see if the first employee has a shortfall. If the employee's reported tips in Cell C15 ($3,200.00, in the case of John) are greater than the employee's share of

the 8 percent gross tips in Cell F15 ($3,747.87, in the same case), the employee does not have a shortfall, and $0.00 is displayed in Cell G15. If the employee's reported tips are less than his or her share of the 8 percent gross tips, the employee has a shortfall—as is the case with John in figure 8-1. The amount displayed in Cell G15, the employee's shortfall ($547.87, in John's case), is calculated by subtracting the employee's reported tips in Cell C15 ($3,200.00) from the employee's share of the 8 percent gross in Cell F15 ($3,747.87).

Now copy the formula from Cell G15 into cells G16 through G24, placing your cell pointer on Cell G15 and entering the following /Copy command:

```
/C    <Return>    [point to Cell G16].
[point to Cell G24]    <Return>
```

Step 13. Enter the following formula into Cell H15:

```
+$G$6-($E$7+$C$26)
```

Rendered in English, this formula reads: "Subtract the sum of cells E7 and C26 from Cell G6." The result of this formula is the allocable shortfall amount ($6,600.00) that is applicable to all directly tipped employees who qualify for tip allocations. The total allocable shortfall amount in Cell H15 ($6,600.00) is determined by adding the reported tips of all directly tipped employees in Cell C26 ($48,400.00) and of all indirectly tipped employees in Cell E7 ($5,000.00), and then subtracting this sum from the amount of total allocable tips in Cell G6 ($60,000.00).

Placing dollar signs in front of the column and row references of the formula's cell references designates these cell references as absolute. This means that, when the formula is copied, these cell references will not change.

Now copy the formula from Cell H15 into cells H16 through H24, placing your cell pointer on Cell H15 and entering the following /Copy command:

```
/C    <Return>    [point to Cell H16].
[point to Cell H24]    <Return>
```

Step 14. Enter the following formula into Cell I15:

```
@IF(C15>F15,0,G15/$G$26)
```

Rendered in English, this formula reads: "If Cell C15 is greater than Cell F15, display 0.00% in Cell I15; otherwise, display the result of Cell G15 divided by Cell G26." The first part of this formula, IF(C15>F15, tests to see if the first employee has a shortfall. If the employee's reported tips in Cell C15 are greater than the employee's share of the 8 percent gross tips, the employee does not have a shortfall, and 0.00% is displayed in Cell I15. If the employee's reported tips are less than his or her share of the 8 percent gross tips, the employee has a shortfall. In figure 8-1, the shortfall ratio displayed in Cell I15 (6.08 percent), representing John's proportionate share of the total allocable shortfall amount, is calculated by dividing his individual shortfall in Cell G15 ($547.87) by the total of each employee's shortfall in Cell G26 ($9,009.37).

Placing dollar signs in front of the column and row references of Cell G26 designates the cell as absolute. This means that, when the formula is copied, the reference to Cell G26 will not change; in contrast, the remaining cell references in the formula will change as the formula is copied.

Now copy the formula from Cell I15 into cells I16 through I24, placing your cell pointer on Cell I15 and entering the following /Copy command:

```
/C    <Return>    [point to Cell I16].
[point to Cell I24]    <Return>
```

Step 15. Enter the following formula into Cell J15:

```
@IF(C15>F15,0,I15*H15)
```

Rendered in English, this formula reads; "If Cell C15 is greater than Cell F15, display $0.00 in Cell J15; otherwise, display the result of Cell I15 multiplied by Cell H15." The first part of this formula, IF(C15>F15, tests to see if the first employee has a shortfall. If the employee's reported tips in Cell C15 are greater than the employee's share of the 8 percent gross tips, the employee does not have a shortfall, $0.00 is displayed in Cell J15, and there is no allocation to that employee. If the employee's reported tips

are less than his or her share of the 8 percent gross tips, the employee has a shortfall. In figure 8-1, the amount displayed in Cell J15 ($401.35), representing John's tip allocation, is calculated by multiplying John's shortfall ratio in Cell I15 (6.08 percent) by the total allocable shortfall amount in Cell H15 ($6,600.00).

Now copy the formula from Cell J15 into cells J16 through J24, placing your cell pointer on Cell J15 and entering the following /Copy command:

```
/C    <Return>    [point to Cell J16].
[point to Cell J24]    <Return>
```

Step 16. Enter each formula indicated in table 8-7 into the corresponding cell. These formulas sum columns B, C, E, F, G, I, and J, for the HOURS WORKED METHOD portion of the spreadsheet shown in figure 8-1.

Protecting Your Spreadsheet

Step 17. Use the /Worksheet Global Protection Enable command sequence, followed by Unprotect commands for the shaded areas of the spreadsheet, to protect the cells in the nonshaded areas of the spreadsheet from accidentally being filled (by you or by other spreadsheet users) with unwanted data. Begin by entering the following command string:

```
/WGPE
```

This string is an abbreviated expression for the /Worksheet Global Protection Enable command, which protects every cell in the spreadsheet from entry and alteration.

TABLE 8-7. STEP 16 FORMULAS (HOURS WORKED METHOD).

Cell	Formula
B26	@SUM(B14..B25)
C26	@SUM(C14..C25)
E26	@SUM(E14..E25)
F26	@SUM(F14..F25)
G26	@SUM(G14..G25)
I26	@SUM(I14..I25)
J26	@SUM(J14..J25)

The next step is to unprotect the cells in the shaded portion of the spreadsheet by means of the /Range Unprotect command. Before entering the command, place your cell pointer on Cell A15 (the cell that forms the upper left-hand corner of Cell Range A15..C24). Then enter the following command:

```
/RU [point to C24]     <Return>
```

Saving Your Spreadsheet

Step 18. You can save the TIPS spreadsheet you have created, by entering the following /File Save command:

```
/FSB:TIPS     <Return>
```

TIPS is the file name for the Tip Allocation spreadsheet and will be written onto the disk in drive B. If you have a hard disk or a single floppy drive system, save the TIPS spreadsheet onto the appropriate drive and directory. When you save this file under the name TIPS, Lotus will automatically add a period and the file name extension WK1 to the name TIPS. When you look at a directory of files on disk drive B, you will see this file displayed as TIPS WK1. The WK1 extension identifies this file to you and to Lotus as a file in a spreadsheet format.

Printing Your Spreadsheet

Step 19. Turn your printer on, align the paper in it, place your cell pointer on Cell A1 by pressing the <Home> key on your cursor/arrow keypad, and print your spreadsheet by issuing the following series of commands:

```
/PPR.    <End>    <Home>
<Return>    AGPQ
```

This abbreviated command language means: "Print to the printer the spreadsheet range A1 to J27. The page is aligned in the printer, so the spreadsheet should begin printing at the top of the page. Go and print the spreadsheet. Then page-eject the paper in the printer to the top of a new page, and quit the print commands."

You may need to consult your Lotus manual for information on how to adjust Lotus's printer settings for footers, margins, borders, page length, and special set-up strings.

The Gross Receipts Method

Steps 8 through 19 immediately following describe the procedures involved in the Gross Receipts method. For the corresponding steps of the Hours Worked method, see page 123.

Operator Input

Step 8. Before entering the formulas for the Gross Receipts method, enter the input given in table 8-8, representing the data in the uppermost and lowermost shaded areas of figure 8-1. The data in Columns A, B, C, and E constitute the only information that you normally must enter. The remainder of the spreadsheet is calculated automatically once the formulas have been entered.

Formulas

Some of the steps that follow contain instructions about making cells absolute when copying for-

TABLE 8-8. STEP 8 INPUT DATA (GROSS RECEIPTS METHOD).

Cell(s)	Input
E6	GROSS RECEIPTS FOR PERIOD. Enter the gross receipts for the relevant period.
E7	TOTAL TIPS REPORTED BY INDIRECTLY TIPPED EMPLOYEES. Enter the total tips reported by indirectly tipped employees.
A34..A43	DIRECTLY TIPPED EMPLOYEES. Enter the names of directly tipped employees.
B34..B43	GROSS RECEIPTS IN PAYROLL PERIOD. Enter the gross receipts in payroll period.
C34..C43	REPORTED TIPS. Enter the reported tips for each directly tipped employee.

mulas and cell references. The meaning of absolute and relative cells is discussed on pages 34–35.

Step 9. Enter the following cell reference into Cell D34:

```
+$E$8
```

Rendered in English, this cell reference reads "Get the value in Cell E8 and put it in Cell D34." The value in Cell E8 represents the tips allocable to directly tipped employees—$55,000.00.

Placing dollar signs in front of the column and row references of Cell E8 designates the cell as absolute. This means that, when this reference to Cell E8 is copied, it will not change.

Now copy the cell reference from Cell D34 into cells D35 through D43, placing your cell pointer on Cell D34 and entering the following /Copy command:

```
/C     <Return>     [point to Cell D35].
[point to Cell D43]     <Return>
```

Step 10. Enter the following formula into Cell E34:

```
+B34/$B$45
```

Rendered in English, this formula reads: "Divide the value in Cell B34 ($75,000.00) by the value in Cell B45 ($750,000.00). The result in Cell E34 (10 percent) is the gross receipts ratio, which is the percentage of total gross receipts that the first directly tipped employee on your list (John) has earned for your restaurant during the payroll or allocation period.

Placing dollar signs in front of the column and row references of Cell B45 designates the cell as absolute. This means that, when this formula is copied, the reference to Cell B45 will not change; in contrast, the reference to Cell B34 will change in each cell to which the formula is copied.

Now copy the formula from Cell E34 into cells E35 through E43, placing your cell pointer on Cell E34 and entering the following /Copy command:

```
/C     <Return>     [point to Cell E35].
[point to Cell E43]     <Return>
```

Step 11. Enter the following formula into Cell F34:

```
+E34*D34
```

Rendered in English, this formula reads: "Multiply the value in Cell E34 (10 percent) by the value in Cell D34 ($55,000.00)." The result in Cell F34 ($5,500.00) is the employee's share of the 8 percent gross tips allocable to directly tipped employees.

Now copy the formula from Cell F34 into cells F35 through F43, placing your cell pointer on Cell F34 and entering the following command:

```
/C     <Return>     [point to Cell F35].
[point to Cell F43]     <Return>
```

Step 12. Enter the following formula into Cell G34:

```
@IF(C34>F34,0,F34-C34)
```

Rendered in English, this formula reads: "If Cell C34 is greater than Cell F34, display $0.00 in Cell G34; otherwise, display the result of Cell C34 subtracted from Cell F34." The first part of this formula, IF(C34>F34, tests to see if the first employee has a shortfall. If the employee's reported tips in Cell C34 ($3,200.00, in the case of John) is greater than the employee's share of the 8 percent gross tips in Cell F34 ($5,500.00, in the same case) the employee does not have a shortfall, and $0.00 is displayed in Cell G34. If the employee's reported tips are less than his or her share of the 8 percent gross tips, the employee has a shortfall—as is the case with John in figure 8-1. The amount displayed in Cell G34, the employee's shortfall ($2,300.00, in John's case), is calculated by subtracting the employee's reported tips in Cell C34 ($3,200.00) from the employee's share of the 8 percent gross in Cell F34 ($5,500.00).

Now copy the formula from Cell G4 into cells G35 through G43, placing your cell pointer on Cell G34 and entering the following /Copy command:

```
/C     <Return>     [point to Cell G35].
[point to Cell G43]     <Return>
```

Step 13. Enter the following formula into Cell H34:

```
+$G$6-($E$7+$C$45)
```

Rendered in English, this formula reads: "Subtract the sum of cells E7 and C45 from Cell G6." The result of this formula is the allocable shortfall amount ($6,600.00) that is applicable to all directly tipped employees who qualify for tip allocations. The total allocable shortfall amount in Cell H34 ($6,600.00) is determined by adding the reported tips of all directly tipped employees in Cell C45 ($48,400.00) and of all indirectly tipped employees in Cell E7 ($5,000.00), and then subtracting this sum from the amount of total allocable tips in Cell G6 ($60,000.00).

Placing dollar signs in front of the column and row references of the formula's cell references designates these cell references as absolute. This means that, when the formula is copied, these cell references will not change.

Now copy the formula from Cell H34 into cells H35 through H43, placing your cell pointer on Cell H34 and entering the following /Copy command:

```
/C    <Return>    [point to Cell H35].
[point to Cell H43]    <Return>
```

Step 14. Enter the following formula into Cell I34:

```
@IF(C34>F34,0,G34/$G$45)
```

Rendered in English, this formula reads: "If Cell C34 is greater than Cell F34, display 0.00% in Cell I34; otherwise, display the result of Cell G34 divided by Cell G45." The first part of this formula, IF(C34>F34, tests to see if the first employee has a shortfall. If the employee's reported tips in Cell C34 are greater than the employee's share of the 8 percent gross tips, the employee does not have a shortfall, and 0.00% is displayed in Cell I34. If the employee's reported tips are less than his or her share of the 8 percent gross tips, the employee has a shortfall. In figure 8-1, the shortfall ratio displayed in Cell I34 (20.72 percent), representing John's proportionate share of the total allocable shortfall amount, is calcu-

lated by dividing his individual shortfall in Cell G34 ($2,300.00) by the total of each employee's shortfall in Cell G45 ($11,100.00).

Placing dollar signs in front of the column and row references of Cell G45 designates the cell as absolute. This means that, when the formula is copied, the reference to Cell G45 will not change; in contrast, the remaining cell references in the formula will change as the formula is copied.

Now copy the formula from Cell I34 into cells I35 through I43, placing your cell pointer on Cell I34 and entering the following /Copy command:

```
/C    <Return>    [point to Cell I35].
[point to Cell I43]    <Return>
```

Step 15. Enter the following formula into Cell J34:

```
@IF(C34>F34,0,I34*H34)
```

Rendered in English, this formula reads: "If Cell C34 is greater than Cell F34, display $0.00 in Cell J34; otherwise, display the result of Cell I34 multiplied by Cell H34." The first part of this formula, IF(C34>F34, tests to see if the first employee has a shortfall. If the employee's reported tips in Cell C34 are greater than the emloyee's share of the 8 percent gross tips, the employee does not have a shortfall, $0.00 is displayed in Cell J34, and there is no allocation to that employee. If the employee's reported tips are less than his or her share of the 8 percent gross tips, the employee has a shortfall. In figure 8-1, the amount displayed in Cell J34 ($1,367.57), representing John's tip allocation, is calculated by multiplying John's shortfall ratio in Cell I34 (20.72 percent) by the total allocable shortfall amount in Cell H34 ($6,600.00).

Now copy the formula from Cell J34 into cells J35 through J43, placing your cell pointer on Cell J34 and entering the following /Copy command:

```
/C    <Return>    [point to Cell J35].
[point to Cell J43]    <Return>
```

Step 16. Enter each formula indicated in table 8-9 into the corresponding cell. These formulas sum columns B, C, E, F, G, I, and J for the GROSS

TABLE 8-9. STEP 16 FORMULAS (GROSS RECEIPTS METHOD).

Cell	Formula
B45	@SUM(B33..B44)
C45	@SUM(C33..C44)
E45	@SUM(E33..E44)
F45	@SUM(F33..F44)
G45	@SUM(G33..G44)
I45	@SUM(I33..I44)
J45	@SUM(J33..J44)

RECEIPTS METHOD portion of the spreadsheet shown in figure 8-1.

Protecting Your Spreadsheet

Step 17. Use the /Worksheet Global Protection Enable command sequence, followed by Unprotect commands for the shaded areas of the spreadsheet, to protect the cells in the nonshaded areas of the spreadsheet from accidentally being filled (by you or by other spreadsheet users) with unwanted data. Begin by entering the following command string:

    /WGPE

This string is an abbreviated expression for the /Worksheet Global Protection Enable command, which protects every cell in the spreadsheet from entry and alteration.

The next step is to unprotect the cells in the shaded portion of the spreadsheet by means of the /Range Unprotect command. Before entering the command, place your cell pointer on Cell A34 (the cell that forms the upper left-hand corner of the cell range that you want to unprotect). Then enter the following command:

    /RU [point to C43]   <Return>

Saving Your Spreadsheet

Step 18. You can save the TIPS spreadsheet you have created, by entering the following /File Save command:

    /FSB:TIPS   <Return>

TIPS is the file name for the Tip Allocation spreadsheet and will be written onto the disk in drive B. If you have a hard disk or a single floppy drive system, save the TIPS spreadsheet onto the appropriate drive and directory. When you save this file under the name TIPS, Lotus will automatically add a period and the file name extension WK1 to the name TIPS. When you look at a directory of files on disk drive B1, you will see this file displayed as TIPS WK1. The WK1 extension identifies this file to you and to Lotus as a file in a spreadsheet format.

Printing Your Spreadsheet

Step 19. Turn your printer on, align the paper in it, place your cell pointer on Cell A1 by pressing the <Home> key on your cursor/arrow keypad, and print your spreadsheet by issuing the following series of commands:

    /PPR.   <End>   <Home>
    <Return>   AGPQ

This abbreviated command language means: "Print to the printer the spreadsheet range A1 to J46. The page is aligned in the printer, so the spreadsheet should begin printing at the top of the page. Go and print the spreadsheet. Then page-eject the paper in the printer to the top of a new page, and quit the print commands."

You may need to consult your Lotus manual for information on how to adjust Lotus's printer settings for footers, margins, borders, page length, and special set-up strings.

Using the Information in This Spreadsheet

Reporting Tip Allocations to Federal and State Taxing Agencies

Use GROSS RECEIPTS FOR PERIOD (Cell E6), REPORTED TIPS (column C), and TIP ALLOCATIONS (column J) from the spreadsheet for reporting to the relevant state taxing agency—if your state requires tip reporting) and to the federal taxing agency—the Internal Revenue Service. The IRS requires restaurants that have tipped employees or that typically employ more than ten full-time employees, whether or not they are tipped, to file IRS Form 8027— "Annual Information Return of Tip Income and Allocated Tips." As of this writing, the Form 8027 for the previous year must be filed by February 28 of the new year.

For more information about tip reporting rules and policies, contact the Internal Revenue Service.

Problems

1. What are three alternative methods of calculating tip allocations?
2. What two methods of calculating tip allocations are recommended by the IRS for foodservice operations that do not adopt a good-faith agreement?
3. What is the difference between the two IRS-recommended methods?
4. What is a good-faith agreement?
5. What is the difference between a directly tipped employee and an indirectly tipped employee?
6. Identify the records an employer must keep for each of the following:
   - Tip reporting in general

- The Hours Worked method specifically
- The Gross Receipts method specifically
7. Explain the difference between **TOTAL TIPS ALLOCABLE TO DIRECTLY TIPPED EMPLOYEES** in Cell E8 of figure 8-1 and total **REPORTED TIPS** in Cell C26.
8. Explain what is meant by the term *shortfall*.
9. How is the hours worked ratio used in calculating tip allocations?
10. How is the shortfall ratio used in calculating tip allocations?

Cases

1. Explain in your own words how tip allocations are determined, using either the Hours Worked method or the Gross Receipts method.
2. Assume that you have a part-time employee who works 3 hours per day during the busiest part of the day as a directly tipped bartender, and assume that this part-time employee does not report any tips. How could this affect tip allocations to directly tipped full-time (8 hours per day) employees who work during slow times of the day? (Assume, too, that total reported tips by all directly tipped employees are less than 8 percent of total tips allocable to directly tipped employees—thereby creating an allocable shortfall amount.) Assume that the Hours Worked method is used to determine tip allocations.

9. Budgeting

TABLE 9-1. SUMMARY OF LOTUS COMMANDS USED IN THIS CHAPTER.

Commands Used

Command String Abbreviation	Command Name	Functions Used
/C	/Copy	@SUM
/FR	/File Retrieve	
/FS	/File Save	
/PP	/Print Printer	
/RF	/Range Format	
/RNC	/Range Name Create	
/RU	/Range Unprotect	
/WCS	/Worksheet Column Set-width	
/WGC	/Worksheet Global Column	
/WGP	/Worksheet Global Protect	

A budget is a financial plan that establishes business performance and financial goals for a specified period of time. Budgeting and setting goals go hand-in-hand in business planning, and they form the basis for the following actions:

- Making business decisions
- Measuring actual business performance
- Allocating financial resources
- Planning financial requirements
- Planning labor and other direct operating requirements

- Encouraging team effort among employees
- Providing direction to management and employees
- Taking action to avoid problems rather than merely reacting to them after they occur

Of the several types of budgets widely used in business, the most common (and the one that this chapter is concerned with) is the operating budget. Other types of budgets include the cash-flow budget, the labor budget, and specialized budgets focusing on a department, a special activity, or a special project of the business.

The operating budget discussed in this chapter analyzes the projected monthly profit, loss, and expenses of operations for a year. Creating the operating budget or any other type of budget is a three-phase process that consists of the following:

- Forecasting future business events
- Projecting and preparing your operating budget based on your forecasts
- Analyzing the budget

Assume that your foodservice operation has been in business for one year, and that—like many people who are new to the foodservice business—you did not plan your first year in business as well as you would have liked. Your great talent, innate business acumen, and luck enabled you to have a successful first year, but the limits of your success and a sense that things were not as well organized as you would have liked impel you to set down on paper your operation's financial and performance goals. Once these have been set, you will share them in part with your managers and employees, who will participate in achieving them.

Because you have read this book, you know that you ought to begin planning by formulating an operating budget for the next year.

As mentioned earlier, forecasting is the first phase of formulating a budget. An operating budget is based on forecasted sales, and forecast sales for restaurants generally are calculated on a forecast average check per customer multiplied by anticipated customer counts for each month of the year.

Forecasting is the most difficult part of budgeting because it relies partly on your ability to make intuitive judgments about the future. Because it is an intangible quality, intuition is virtually impossible to teach. It develops over time from your experience and always involves an element of transcendental guessing.

If you were opening your first restaurant and wanted to forecast an operating budget, you might have to rely entirely on your market research (if you had done any) and your best guesses in forecasting sales. But because the assumption in this chapter's example is that you have been in business for a year, you can use the year's experience as a basis for your sales forecasts. This makes budgeting much easier.

Look at the FORECASTS section at the top of the operating budget in figure 9-1 or the breakout of this section in figure 9-2. It shows separate forecasts of sales for lunch and dinner for each month of the year. Column D presents a summary for the entire year. Sales for each meal period (lunch and dinner) are based on forecast customer counts and average checks for each month.

This chapter is necessarily limited to a generalized description of the steps involved in formulating an operating budget. Your actual budget, however, may be much more detailed than the one described here. For instance, you may want to achieve greater accuracy by having your spreadsheet break sales forecasts down to daily or weekly projections, as well as monthly projections. In fact,

greater detail is the rule rather than the exception, because accuracy in budgeting is the goal.

The customer count forecasts shown in figure 9-2 assume that your business fluctuates seasonally and that your business's two peak seasons are the fall months and the spring months. This assumption reflects the common experience that business is slow during the summer (when customers are away on vacation) and during the winter (when dining out is inhibited by adverse weather conditions). Customer counts follow these seasonal patterns.

In planning your actual budget, you might try using your prior year's history of customer counts, increased by a percentage by which you feel your customer count will improve in the following year, as the basis for your forecasting. For instance, if your customer count was 5,000 customers last January and you expect a 5 percent increase in business this year, you would forecast 5,250 customers for the coming January, as follows:

Last January's customer count:	5,000 customers
times Forecast percentage increase in business:	× 5%
equals	
Net increase in customers:	250 customers
plus Last January's customer count:	+ 5,000 customers
equals	
This year's forecast customer count for January:	5,250 customers

You can easily adjust the percentage increase on a computer spreadsheet until you feel comfortable with your customer count forecasts. The example in this chapter does not handle this forecasting calculation; it starts with forecast customer counts already in place.

Notice that the average check in figure 9-2, rows 9 and 15, increases every few months for both lunch and dinner. This increase is based on the assumption that your food costs will increase as a result of rising prices in the commodities market, and that you will have to increase your menu prices in April and again in October.

Once you feel somewhat comfortable about your sales forecasts, you may begin formulating your operating budget. The operating budget shown in figure 9-3 is in a typical summarized profit-and-loss statement format, as prescribed by most professional foodservice industry accountants. The division of expenses into controllable and noncontrollable categories is also typical. Controllable expenses are those that management has control or strong influence over; noncontrollable expenses are those that management has little or no control over.

The dollar amounts for sales and expenses in the operating budget are determined by any of several factors.

Sales are determined by your forecasts. The ratio breakdown between food and beverage sales is usually determined by previous sales experience and/or by market analyses.

Expenses are generally determined in one of three ways:

1. An expense such as hourly wages fluctuates with sales, although it consumes a constant percentage of the gross sales from day to day. The higher the sales are, the more hourly labor is needed, and vice versa. The dollar amount budgeted for such expenses is calculated by multiplying sales by a fixed percentage. This type of expense is identified in column A of the spreadsheet with a *V*, indicating that it is a *variable* expense.
2. An expense such as a manager's salary is fixed at a constant dollar amount and does not change whether sales increase or decrease. The budgeted dollar amount for such expenses is not calculated; it is simply plugged into the budget. This type of expense is identified in column A of the spreadsheet with an *F*, indicating that it is a *fixed* expense.
3. An expense may be partly fixed and partly variable. Because of its inherent ambiguity and computational complexity, this type of expense is not illustrated in the example in this chapter. As an example, however, assume that your landlord charges a fixed base rent per month plus 1 percent of your monthly sales. In this case, you would calculate rent in your budget as both a fixed and a variable expense: you would add the fixed dollar amount to an amount calculated by multiplying your forecast monthly sales by 1 percent.

The third and final phase of formulating your operating budget is the budget analysis, shown at the bottom of figure 9-1 and in the breakout of this section in figure 9-4. Each ratio and statistic calculated in this analysis is explained in detail on pages 154–55. For now, you only need to know that the purpose of the budget analysis is to condense your forecast budget into numerical ratios and statistics that can be used in the following ways:

1. They can be compared to industry standards to help you plan.
2. They can be compared with your foodservice operation's actual activity, to measure actual performance against the forecast budget.
3. They can be employed as performance and financial goals in your operation.

Formatting, Headings, and Labels

Step 1. Reformat columns A through Q from the normal, default Lotus column width of nine characters to the widths indicated in table 9-2.

Step 2. Begin re-creating the spreadsheet example in figure 9-1, by entering the appropriate headings and labels into columns A through Q, rows 1 through 115, exactly as specified in table 9-3.

You may need to pad some of your cell entries with blank spaces to get your headings to look like those pictured in figure 9-1. Any heading beginning with one of the three Lotus label alignment prefixes (', ", and ^) signifies a label to be padded with blank spaces or to be given a special cell alignment. Remember that the prefix ' aligns text to the left margin of the cell, the prefix " aligns text to the right margin of the cell, and the prefix ^ centers text within the cell. Unless a label alignment prefix is indicated in table 9-3, do not use one of these prefixes to begin a label or heading.

Step 3. Copy the calendar month headings in row 6, columns D through Q, into row 26 by entering the following /Copy command:

```
/CD6..Q6    <Return>    D26    <Return>
```

Again copy the calendar month headings in row 6, columns D through Q—this time into row 102, by entering the following /Copy command:

```
:  A  ::        B        ::  C ::   D   ::::    F    ::    G    ::    H    ::    I    ::
```

```
********** >>>>>>> FORECASTS <<<<<<< ********************************************************
```

	ANNUAL	JANUARY	FEBRUARY	MARCH	APRIL
LUNCH FORECASTS:					
CUSTOMER COUNT	51250	4500	4500	4500	4600
AVERAGE LUNCH CHECK	$6.68	$6.25	$6.25	$6.25	$6.75
TOTAL ESTIMATED LUNCH SALES	$342,600.00	$28,125.00	$28,125.00	$28,125.00	$31,050.00
DINNER FORECASTS:					
CUSTOMER COUNT	70500	5500	6000	6000	6500
AVERAGE DINNER CHECK	$10.81	$9.50	$9.50	$9.50	$11.00
TOTAL ESTIMATED DINNER SALES	$762,375.00	$52,250.00	$57,000.00	$57,000.00	$71,500.00
TOTAL FORECASTED SALES	$1,104,975.00	$80,375.00	$85,125.00	$85,125.00	$102,550.00

```
*****************************************************************************************
********** >>>>> OPERATING BUDGET <<<<< ***********************************************
```

TYPE OF EXPENSE:		% OF SALES					
F=FIXED			ANNUAL	JANUARY	FEBRUARY	MARCH	APRIL
V=VARIABLE	SEASONAL INDEX -->	100.00%		7.27%	7.70%	7.70%	9.28%

		%	ANNUAL	JANUARY	FEBRUARY	MARCH	APRIL
REVENUE **							
	FOOD SALES	75.00%	$828,731.25	$60,281.25	$63,843.75	$63,843.75	$76,912.50
	BEVERAGE SALES	25.00%	$276,243.75	$20,093.75	$21,281.25	$21,281.25	$25,637.50
	TOTAL REVENUE	100.00%	$1,104,975.00	$80,375.00	$85,125.00	$85,125.00	$102,550.00
COST OF GOODS SOLD **							
V	FOOD	38.00%	$314,917.88	$22,906.88	$24,260.63	$24,260.63	$29,226.75
V	BEVERAGE	25.00%	$69,060.94	$5,023.44	$5,320.31	$5,320.31	$6,409.38
	TOTAL CST OF GDS SLD	34.75%	$383,978.81	$27,930.31	$29,580.94	$29,580.94	$35,636.13
GROSS PROFIT		65.25%	$720,996.19	$52,444.69	$55,544.06	$55,544.06	$66,913.88
CONTROLLABLE EXPENSES **							
F	SALARIES	5.12%	$56,600.00	$4,716.67	$4,716.67	$4,716.67	$4,716.67
V	HOURLY WAGES	21.00%	$232,044.75	$16,878.75	$17,876.25	$17,876.25	$21,535.50
V	EMPLOYEE BENEFITS	5.00%	$55,248.75	$4,018.75	$4,256.25	$4,256.25	$5,127.50
V	DIRECT OPERATING	5.50%	$60,773.63	$4,420.63	$4,681.88	$4,681.88	$5,640.25
F	UTILITIES	2.20%	$24,300.00	$2,025.00	$2,025.00	$2,025.00	$2,025.00
F	ADMINISTRATIVE AND GENERAL	5.43%	$60,000.00	$5,000.00	$5,000.00	$5,000.00	$5,000.00
F	MARKETING	1.49%	$16,500.00	$1,200.20	$1,271.13	$1,271.13	$1,531.32
F	MAINTENANCE AND REPAIR	1.70%	$18,800.00	$1,566.67	$1,566.67	$1,566.67	$1,566.67
	TOTAL CONTROLLABLE EXPENSES	47.45%	$524,267.13	$39,826.66	$41,393.83	$41,393.83	$47,142.91
TOTAL OPERATING PROFIT BEFORE OCCUPATION AND NON-CONTROLLABLE EXPENSES		17.80%	$196,729.06	$12,618.03	$14,150.23	$14,150.23	$19,770.97
NON-CONTROLLABLE EXPENSES **							
F	RENT	6.30%	$69,600.00	$5,800.00	$5,800.00	$5,800.00	$5,800.00
F	INSURANCE	1.36%	$15,000.00	$1,250.00	$1,250.00	$1,250.00	$1,250.00
F	PROPERTY TAXES	.18%	$2,000.00	$166.67	$166.67	$166.67	$166.67
F	OTHER TAXES	.40%	$4,400.00	$366.67	$366.67	$366.67	$366.67
F	INTEREST	1.00%	$11,000.00	$916.67	$916.67	$916.67	$916.67
	TOTAL NON-CONTROLLABLE EXP.	9.23%	$102,000.00	$8,500.00	$8,133.33	$8,163.89	$8,133.33
PROFIT BEFORE DEPRECIATION		8.57%	$94,729.06	$4,118.03	$6,016.89	$5,986.34	$11,637.63
DEPRECIATION & AMORTIZATION							
F	DEPRECIATION	1.10%	$12,200.00	$1,016.67	$1,016.67	$1,016.67	$1,016.67
F	AMORTIZATION	.80%	$8,832.00	$736.00	$736.00	$736.00	$736.00
	TOTAL DEPREC. & AMORT.	1.90%	$21,032.00	$1,752.67	$1,752.67	$1,752.67	$1,752.67
NET PROFIT BEFORE TAXES		6.67%	$73,697.06	$2,365.37	$4,264.23	$4,233.67	$9,884.97

```
********************************************************************************************
********** >>>>> BUDGET ANALYSIS <<<<< ***********************************************
```

	ANNUAL	JANUARY	FEBRUARY	MARCH	APRIL
TURNOVER:					
INVENTORY TURNOVER	54.85	3.99	4.23	4.23	5.09
SEAT TURNOVERS PER DAY (95 SEATS)	4.11	4.05	4.25	4.25	4.49
BREAKEVEN:					
BREAK-EVEN SALES	$886,613.33	$73,366.51	$72,490.25	$72,580.78	$73,261.21
BREAK-EVEN PER HOUR (OPEN 12 HRS/DAY)	$236.81	$235.15	$232.34	$232.63	$234.81
BREAK-EVEN PER SEAT (95 SEATS)	$9,332.77	$772.28	$763.06	$764.01	$771.17
SALES PER SEAT (95 SEATS)	$11,631.32	$846.05	$896.05	$896.05	$1,079.47
GROSS PROFIT PER CUSTOMER:					
LUNCH FOOD: GROSS PROFIT PER CUSTOMER	$3.11	$2.91	$2.91	$2.91	$3.14
DINNER FOOD: GROSS PROFIT PER CUSTOMER	$5.03	$4.42	$4.42	$4.42	$5.12

9-1. Budget spreadsheet, showing forecasts, operating budget, and budget analysis.

MAY	JUNE	JULY	AUGUST	SEPTEMBER	OCTOBER	NOVEMBER	DECEMBER
4250	4000	3500	3500	4250	4500	4500	4650
$6.75	$6.75	$6.75	$6.75	$6.75	$7.00	$7.00	$7.00
$28,687.50	$27,000.00	$23,625.00	$23,625.00	$28,687.50	$31,500.00	$31,500.00	$32,550.00
6500	6000	5500	5000	6000	6000	6000	5500
$11.00	$11.00	$11.00	$11.00	$11.00	$11.75	$11.75	$11.75
$71,500.00	$66,000.00	$60,500.00	$55,000.00	$66,000.00	$70,500.00	$70,500.00	$64,625.00
$100,187.50	$93,000.00	$84,125.00	$78,625.00	$94,687.50	$102,000.00	$102,000.00	$97,175.00

MAY	JUNE	JULY	AUGUST	SEPTEMBER	OCTOBER	NOVEMBER	DECEMBER
9.07%	8.42%	7.61%	7.12%	8.57%	9.23%	9.23%	8.79%
$75,140.63	$69,750.00	$63,093.75	$58,968.75	$71,015.63	$76,500.00	$76,500.00	$72,881.25
$25,046.88	$23,250.00	$21,031.25	$19,656.25	$23,671.88	$25,500.00	$25,500.00	$24,293.75
$100,187.50	$93,000.00	$84,125.00	$78,625.00	$94,687.50	$102,000.00	$102,000.00	$97,175.00
$28,553.44	$26,505.00	$23,975.63	$22,408.13	$26,985.94	$29,070.00	$29,070.00	$27,694.88
$6,261.72	$5,812.50	$5,257.81	$4,914.06	$5,917.97	$6,375.00	$6,375.00	$6,073.44
$34,815.16	$32,317.50	$29,233.44	$27,322.19	$32,903.91	$35,445.00	$35,445.00	$33,768.31
$65,372.34	$60,682.50	$54,891.56	$51,302.81	$61,783.59	$66,555.00	$66,555.00	$63,406.69
$4,716.67	$4,716.67	$4,716.67	$4,716.67	$4,716.67	$4,716.67	$4,716.67	$4,716.67
$21,039.38	$19,530.00	$17,666.25	$16,511.25	$19,884.38	$21,420.00	$21,420.00	$20,406.75
$5,009.38	$4,650.00	$4,206.25	$3,931.25	$4,734.38	$5,100.00	$5,100.00	$4,858.75
$5,510.31	$5,115.00	$4,626.88	$4,324.38	$5,207.81	$5,610.00	$5,610.00	$5,344.63
$2,025.00	$2,025.00	$2,025.00	$2,025.00	$2,025.00	$2,025.00	$2,025.00	$2,025.00
$5,000.00	$5,000.00	$5,000.00	$5,000.00	$5,000.00	$5,000.00	$5,000.00	$5,000.00
$1,496.05	$1,388.72	$1,256.19	$1,174.07	$1,413.92	$1,523.11	$1,523.11	$1,451.06
$1,566.67	$1,566.67	$1,566.67	$1,566.67	$1,566.67	$1,566.67	$1,566.67	$1,566.67
$46,363.44	$43,992.05	$41,063.90	$39,249.27	$44,548.81	$46,961.44	$46,961.44	$45,369.52
$19,008.90	$16,690.45	$13,827.66	$12,053.54	$17,234.78	$19,593.56	$19,593.56	$18,037.17
$5,800.00	$5,800.00	$5,800.00	$5,800.00	$5,800.00	$5,800.00	$5,800.00	$5,800.00
$1,250.00	$1,250.00	$1,250.00	$1,250.00	$1,250.00	$1,250.00	$1,250.00	$1,250.00
$166.67	$166.67	$166.67	$166.67	$166.67	$166.67	$166.67	$166.67
$366.67	$366.67	$366.67	$366.67	$366.67	$366.67	$366.67	$366.67
$916.67	$916.67	$916.67	$916.67	$916.67	$916.67	$916.67	$916.67
$8,135.88	$8,133.33	$8,133.55	$8,133.33	$8,133.35	$8,133.33	$8,133.33	$8,133.33
$10,873.02	$8,557.11	$5,694.12	$3,920.21	$9,101.43	$11,460.22	$11,460.22	$9,903.83
$1,016.67	$1,016.67	$1,016.67	$1,016.67	$1,016.67	$1,016.67	$1,016.67	$1,016.67
$736.00	$736.00	$736.00	$736.00	$736.00	$736.00	$736.00	$736.00
$1,752.67	$1,752.67	$1,752.67	$1,752.67	$1,752.67	$1,752.67	$1,752.67	$1,752.67
$9,120.36	$6,804.45	$3,941.45	$2,167.54	$7,348.76	$9,707.56	$9,707.55	$8,151.17

MAY	JUNE	JULY	AUGUST	SEPTEMBER	OCTOBER	NOVEMBER	DECEMBER
4.97	4.62	4.18	3.90	4.70	5.06	5.06	4.82
4.35	4.05	3.64	3.44	4.15	4.25	4.25	4.11
$73,164.22	$72,838.67	$72,446.63	$72,202.66	$72,913.39	$73,236.87	$73,236.88	$73,023.39
$234.50	$233.46	$232.20	$231.42	$233.70	$234.73	$234.73	$234.05
$770.15	$766.72	$762.60	$760.03	$767.51	$770.91	$770.91	$768.67
$1,054.61	$978.95	$885.53	$827.63	$996.71	$1,073.68	$1,073.68	$1,022.89
$3.14	$3.14	$3.14	$3.14	$3.14	$3.26	$3.26	$3.26
$5.12	$5.12	$5.12	$5.12	$5.12	$5.46	$5.46	$5.46

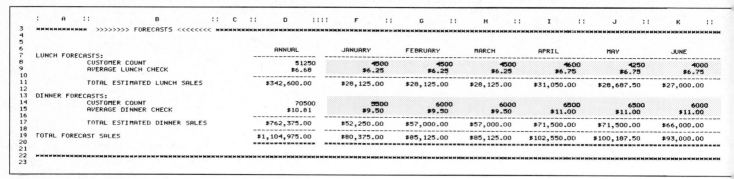

	ANNUAL	JANUARY	FEBRUARY	MARCH	APRIL	MAY	JUNE
FORECASTS							
LUNCH FORECASTS:							
CUSTOMER COUNT	51250	4500	4500	4500	4600	4250	4000
AVERAGE LUNCH CHECK	$6.68	$6.25	$6.25	$6.25	$6.75	$6.75	$6.75
TOTAL ESTIMATED LUNCH SALES	$342,600.00	$28,125.00	$28,125.00	$28,125.00	$31,050.00	$28,687.50	$27,000.00
DINNER FORECASTS:							
CUSTOMER COUNT	70500	5500	6000	6000	6500	6500	6000
AVERAGE DINNER CHECK	$10.81	$9.50	$9.50	$9.50	$11.00	$11.00	$11.00
TOTAL ESTIMATED DINNER SALES	$762,375.00	$52,250.00	$57,000.00	$57,000.00	$71,500.00	$71,500.00	$66,000.00
TOTAL FORECAST SALES	$1,104,975.00	$80,375.00	$85,125.00	$85,125.00	$102,550.00	$100,187.50	$93,000.00

9-2. Forecasts section of the Budget spreadsheet.

OPERATING BUDGET

TYPE OF EXPENSE:
F=FIXED
V=VARIABLE

		% OF SALES ANNUAL	JANUARY	FEBRUARY	MARCH	APRIL	MAY	JUNE
SEASONAL INDEX -->		100.00%	7.27%	7.70%	7.70%	9.28%	9.07%	8.42%
	REVENUE ▪▪							
	FOOD SALES	75.00% $828,731.25	$60,281.25	$63,843.75	$63,843.75	$76,912.50	$75,140.63	$69,750.00
	BEVERAGE SALES	25.00% $276,243.75	$20,093.75	$21,281.25	$21,281.25	$25,637.50	$25,046.88	$23,250.00
	TOTAL REVENUE	100.00% $1,104,975.00	$80,375.00	$85,125.00	$85,125.00	$102,550.00	$100,187.50	$93,000.00
	COST OF GOODS SOLD ▪▪							
V	FOOD	38.00% $314,917.88	$22,906.88	$24,260.63	$24,260.63	$29,226.75	$28,553.44	$26,505.00
V	BEVERAGE	25.00% $69,060.94	$5,023.44	$5,320.31	$5,320.31	$6,409.38	$6,261.72	$5,812.50
	TOTAL COST OF GOODS SOLD	34.75% $383,978.81	$27,930.31	$29,580.94	$29,580.94	$35,636.13	$34,815.16	$32,317.50
	GROSS PROFIT	65.25% $720,996.19	$52,444.69	$55,544.06	$55,544.06	$66,913.88	$65,372.34	$60,682.50
	CONTROLLABLE EXPENSES ▪▪							
F	SALARIES	5.12% $56,600.00	$4,716.67	$4,716.67	$4,716.67	$4,716.67	$4,716.67	$4,716.67
V	HOURLY WAGES	21.00% $232,044.75	$16,878.75	$17,876.25	$17,876.25	$21,535.50	$21,039.38	$19,530.00
V	EMPLOYEE BENEFITS	5.00% $55,248.75	$4,018.75	$4,256.25	$4,256.25	$5,127.50	$5,009.38	$4,650.00
V	DIRECT OPERATING	5.50% $60,773.63	$4,420.63	$4,681.88	$4,681.88	$5,640.25	$5,510.31	$5,115.00
F	UTILITIES	2.20% $24,300.00	$2,025.00	$2,025.00	$2,025.00	$2,025.00	$2,025.00	$2,025.00
F	ADMINISTRATIVE AND GENERAL	5.43% $60,000.00	$5,000.00	$5,000.00	$5,000.00	$5,000.00	$5,000.00	$5,000.00
F	MARKETING	1.49% $16,500.00	$1,200.20	$1,271.13	$1,271.13	$1,531.32	$1,496.05	$1,388.72
F	MAINTENANCE AND REPAIR	1.70% $18,800.00	$1,566.67	$1,566.67	$1,566.67	$1,566.67	$1,566.67	$1,566.67
	TOTAL CONTROLLABLE EXPENSES	47.45% $524,267.13	$39,826.66	$41,393.83	$41,393.83	$47,142.91	$46,363.44	$43,992.05
	TOTAL OPERATING PROFIT BEFORE OCCUPATION AND NONCONTROLLABLE EXPENSES	17.80% $196,729.06	$12,618.03	$14,150.23	$14,150.23	$19,770.97	$19,008.90	$16,690.45
	NONCONTROLLABLE EXPENSES ▪▪							
F	RENT	6.30% $69,600.00	$5,800.00	$5,800.00	$5,800.00	$5,800.00	$5,800.00	$5,800.00
F	INSURANCE	1.36% $15,000.00	$1,250.00	$1,250.00	$1,250.00	$1,250.00	$1,250.00	$1,250.00
F	PROPERTY TAXES	.18% $2,000.00	$166.67	$166.67	$166.67	$166.67	$166.67	$166.67
F	OTHER TAXES	.40% $4,400.00	$366.67	$366.67	$366.67	$366.67	$366.67	$366.67
F	INTEREST	1.00% $11,000.00	$916.67	$916.67	$916.67	$916.67	$916.67	$916.67
	TOTAL NONCONTROLLABLE EXP.	9.23% $102,000.00	$8,500.00	$8,133.33	$8,163.89	$8,133.33	$8,135.88	$8,133.33
	PROFIT BEFORE DEPRECIATION	8.57% $94,729.06	$4,118.03	$6,016.89	$5,986.34	$11,637.63	$10,873.02	$8,557.11
	DEPRECIATION & AMORTIZATION							
F	DEPRECIATION	1.10% $12,200.00	$1,016.67	$1,016.67	$1,016.67	$1,016.67	$1,016.67	$1,016.67
F	AMORTIZATION	.80% $8,832.00	$736.00	$736.00	$736.00	$736.00	$736.00	$736.00
	TOTAL DEPREC. & AMORT.	1.90% $21,032.00	$1,752.67	$1,752.67	$1,752.67	$1,752.67	$1,752.67	$1,752.67
	NET PROFIT BEFORE TAXES	6.67% $73,697.06	$2,365.37	$4,264.23	$4,233.67	$9,884.97	$9,120.36	$6,804.45

9-3. Operate budget section (projected from the forecasts section) of the Budget spreadsheet.

```
/CD6..Q6   <Return>   D102   <Return>
```

Step 4. Enter dashed lines and double-dashed lines into the spreadsheet, as indicated in table

9-4. Use the backslash (\) key at the beginning of each cell entry to signal to Lotus that the character immediately following it is to be repeated across the cell from end to end.

L	M	N	O	P	Q
JULY	AUGUST	SEPTEMBER	OCTOBER	NOVEMBER	DECEMBER
3500	3500	4250	4500	4500	4650
$6.75	$6.75	$6.75	$7.00	$7.00	$7.00
$23,625.00	$23,625.00	$28,687.50	$31,500.00	$31,500.00	$32,550.00
5500	5000	6000	6000	6000	5500
$11.00	$11.00	$11.00	$11.75	$11.75	$11.75
$60,500.00	$55,000.00	$66,000.00	$70,500.00	$70,500.00	$64,625.00
$84,125.00	$78,625.00	$94,687.50	$102,000.00	$102,000.00	$97,175.00

L	M	N	O	P	Q
JULY 7.61%	AUGUST 7.12%	SEPTEMBER 8.57%	OCTOBER 9.23%	NOVEMBER 9.23%	DECEMBER 8.79%
$63,093.75	$58,968.75	$71,015.63	$76,500.00	$76,500.00	$72,881.25
$21,031.25	$19,656.25	$23,671.88	$25,500.00	$25,500.00	$24,293.75
$84,125.00	$78,625.00	$94,687.50	$102,000.00	$102,000.00	$97,175.00
$23,975.63	$22,408.13	$26,985.94	$29,070.00	$29,070.00	$27,694.88
$5,257.81	$4,914.06	$5,917.97	$6,375.00	$6,375.00	$6,073.44
$29,233.44	$27,322.19	$32,903.91	$35,445.00	$35,445.00	$33,768.31
$54,891.56	$51,302.81	$61,783.59	$66,555.00	$66,555.00	$63,406.69
$4,716.67	$4,716.67	$4,716.67	$4,716.67	$4,716.67	$4,716.67
$17,666.25	$16,511.25	$19,884.38	$21,420.00	$21,420.00	$20,406.75
$4,206.25	$3,931.25	$4,734.38	$5,100.00	$5,100.00	$4,858.75
$4,626.88	$4,324.38	$5,207.81	$5,610.00	$5,610.00	$5,344.63
$2,025.00	$2,025.00	$2,025.00	$2,025.00	$2,025.00	$2,025.00
$5,000.00	$5,000.00	$5,000.00	$5,000.00	$5,000.00	$5,000.00
$1,256.19	$1,174.07	$1,413.92	$1,523.11	$1,523.11	$1,451.06
$1,566.67	$1,566.67	$1,566.67	$1,566.67	$1,566.67	$1,566.67
$41,063.90	$39,249.27	$44,548.81	$46,961.44	$46,961.44	$45,369.52
$13,827.66	$12,053.54	$17,234.78	$19,593.56	$19,593.56	$18,037.17
$5,800.00	$5,800.00	$5,800.00	$5,800.00	$5,800.00	$5,800.00
$1,250.00	$1,250.00	$1,250.00	$1,250.00	$1,250.00	$1,250.00
$166.67	$166.67	$166.67	$166.67	$166.67	$166.67
$366.67	$366.67	$366.67	$366.67	$366.67	$366.67
$916.67	$916.67	$916.67	$916.67	$916.67	$916.67
$8,133.55	$8,133.33	$8,133.35	$8,133.33	$8,133.33	$8,133.33
$5,694.12	$3,920.21	$9,101.43	$11,460.22	$11,460.22	$9,903.83
$1,016.67	$1,016.67	$1,016.67	$1,016.67	$1,016.67	$1,016.67
$736.00	$736.00	$736.00	$736.00	$736.00	$736.00
$1,752.67	$1,752.67	$1,752.67	$1,752.67	$1,752.67	$1,752.67
$3,941.45	$2,167.54	$7,348.76	$9,707.56	$9,707.55	$8,151.17

To repeat a character across several individual cells, use Lotus's /Copy command, as indicated in table 9-4. Use the pointing method described on page 34 to define the last cell of a cell range

when performing the /Copy operation. Remember to place the cell pointer on the originating cell (the cell being copied from) before you begin to enter each command listed in table 9-4.

Step 5. Format the cell ranges identified in table 9-5, as indicated there. Enter the command in the far right-hand column of the table exactly as it appears, by typing the characters shown and then hitting the <Return> key. When formatting a cell range, use the pointing method to define the last cell in each indicated cell range. Be sure to place the cell pointer on the first cell indicated in the far left-hand column of table 9-5 before entering the associated command.

Saving BUDGET.WK1

If you would like to stop and take a break at this point, save the spreadsheet you are working on by means of Step 6. Otherwise, skip Step 6 and go on to Step 7.

Step 6. You can save the BUDGET spreadsheet you have created so far, by entering the following /File Save command:

    /FSB:BUDGET   <Return>

BUDGET is the file name for the Budget spreadsheet and will be written onto the disk in drive B. If you have a hard disk or a single floppy drive system, save the BUDGET spreadsheet onto the appropriate drive and directory. When you save this file under the name BUDGET, Lotus will automatically add a period and the file name extension WK1 to the name BUDGET. When you look at a directory of files on disk drive B, you will see this file displayed as BUDGET WK1. The WK1 extension identifies this file to you and to Lotus as a file in a spreadsheet format.

If you issue a /Quit command to Lotus or turn your computer off, you will need to retrieve the BUDGET spreadsheet from disk before you can resume work on it. To retrieve the BUDGET spreadsheet, enter the following /File Retrieve command:

    /FRB:BUDGET   <Return>

```
     :   A   ::          B          :: C ::    D    ::::    F    ::      G       ::    H      ::     I     ::    J      ::    K      ::
100 ************  >>>>> BUDGET ANALYSIS <<<<< *****************************************************************************************
101
102                                          ANNUAL         JANUARY      FEBRUARY       MARCH       APRIL         MAY         JUNE
103                                        ------------    ----------    ----------    ----------    ----------    ----------    ----------
104   TURNOVER:
105         INVENTORY TURNOVER               54.85          3.99          4.23          4.23          5.09          4.97          4.62
106         SEAT TURNOVERS PER DAY (95 SEATS) 4.11          4.05          4.25          4.25          4.49          4.35          4.05
107 BREAK-EVEN:
108         BREAK-EVEN SALES                $886,613.33   $73,366.51    $72,490.25    $72,580.78    $73,261.21    $73,164.22    $72,838.67
109         BREAK-EVEN PER HOUR (OPEN 12 HRS/DAY) $236.81    $235.15       $232.34       $232.63       $234.81       $234.50       $233.46
110         BREAK-EVEN PER SEAT (95 SEATS)  $9,332.77      $772.28       $763.06       $764.01       $771.17       $770.15       $766.72
111         SALES PER SEAT (95 SEATS)       $11,631.32     $846.05       $896.05       $896.05     $1,079.47     $1,054.61       $978.95
112 GROSS PROFIT PER CUSTOMER:
113         LUNCH FOOD: GROSS PROFIT PER CUSTOMER $3.11      $2.91         $2.91         $2.91         $3.14         $3.14         $3.14
114         DINNER FOOD: GROSS PROFIT PER CUSTOMER $5.03      $4.42         $4.42         $4.42         $5.12         $5.12         $5.12
115 ******************************************************************************************************************************
116
```

9-4. Budget analysis section of the Budget spreadsheet.

Operator Input

The operator input (in the shaded areas of the budget illustrated in figure 9-1) represents goals that you set for your operation. *Forecast* input comprises all goals involving customer counts and average check. *Revenue* input—how sales are divided between food and beverage sales—is primarily based on prior sales experience, although it may also be influenced by your own goals in this area.

When doing "what if" analysis of your budget, adjust the input (goals) illustrated in the shaded areas of figure 9-1 to fine-tune your budget so that it reflects the goals and projections of your operation for the next year.

Most foodservice operation control is based on maintaining the expense goals you set. Variable expense goals are expressed as a percentage of sales. If an actual percentage goal, such as food cost as a percentage of sales, varies from the budgeted percentage, there is good reason to suspect food control problems in your operation.

Fixed expense goals are expressed as a fixed dollar amount and may be used as a guide to limit spending during the year. If actual dollar amounts vary from those budgeted, problems exist that call for action to correct the variance or to amend the budget.

TABLE 9-2. STEP 1 FORMATTING COMMANDS.

Column	Width	Command to Enter	
A	12	/WCS12	<Return>
B	30	/WCS30	<Return>
C	9	/WCS9	<Return>
E	2	/WCS2	<Return>
all remaining	15	/WGC15	<Return>

Amending the budget once it has been set should not be a common practice nor a matter of whim. Once in a while, however, business opportunities or setbacks occur that force you to amend the budget. Having the budget set down on a spreadsheet makes it readily adjustable to reflect opportunities and setbacks.

Step 7. Enter the input specified in table 9-6, representing the data in the shaded areas of figure 9-1. This input is the only information you will normally be required to enter. The remainder of the spreadsheet (once created) is calculated automatically.

Formulas

Some of the steps that follow contain instructions about making cells absolute when copying formulas and cell references. The meaning of absolute and relative cells is discussed on pages 34–35.

Forecasting Formulas

Step 8. Enter the following formula into Cell D8:

    @SUM(F8..Q8)

This formula sums the forecast lunch customer counts for January through December.

Step 9. Enter the following formula into Cell D9:

    +D11/D8

This formula divides the total estimated lunch sales for the year by the total annual customer count, returning the annual average check in Cell D9.

L	::	M	::	N	::	O	::	P	::	Q	:

JULY	AUGUST	SEPTEMBER	OCTOBER	NOVEMBER	DECEMBER
4.18	3.90	4.70	5.06	5.06	4.82
3.64	3.44	4.15	4.25	4.25	4.11
$72,446.63	$72,202.66	$72,913.39	$73,236.87	$73,236.88	$73,023.39
$232.20	$231.42	$233.70	$234.73	$234.73	$234.05
$762.60	$760.03	$767.51	$770.91	$770.91	$768.67
$885.53	$827.63	$996.71	$1,073.68	$1,073.68	$1,022.89
$3.14	$3.14	$3.14	$3.26	$3.26	$3.26
$5.12	$5.12	$5.12	$5.46	$5.46	$5.46

TABLE 9-3. STEP 2 HEADINGS.

Cell	Heading
A1	''>>>>>>>>
A7	LUNCH FORECASTS:
A13	DINNER FORECASTS:
A19	TOTAL FORECAST SALES
A25	TYPE OF EXPENSE:
A26	F=FIXED
A27	V=VARIABLE
A104	''TURNOVER:
A107	''BREAK-EVEN:
A112	GROSS PROFIT PER CUSTOMER:
B1	OPERATING BUDGET <<<<<<<<
B3	^>>>>>>>> FORECASTS <<<<<<<<
B8	CUSTOMER COUNT
B9	AVERAGE LUNCH CHECK
B11	TOTAL ESTIMATED LUNCH SALES
B14	CUSTOMER COUNT
B15	AVERAGE DINNER CHECK
B17	TOTAL ESTIMATED DINNER SALES
B24	^>>>>> OPERATING BUDGET <<<<<
B27	''SEASONAL INDEX -->
B30	REVENUE **
B32	''FOOD SALES
B33	''BEVERAGE SALES
B35	TOTAL REVENUE
B38	COST OF GOODS SOLD **
B43	TOTAL COST OF GOODS SOLD
B47	GROSS PROFIT
B51	CONTROLLABLE EXPENSES **
B53	''SALARIES
B54	''HOURLY WAGES
B55	''EMPLOYEE BENEFITS
B56	''DIRECT OPERATING
B57	''UTILITIES
B58	''ADMINISTRATIVE AND GENERAL
B59	''MARKETING
B60	''MAINTENANCE AND REPAIR
B62	TOTAL CONTROLLABLE EXPENSES
B66	TOTAL OPERATING PROFIT BEFORE

TABLE 9-3. CONTINUED.

Cell	Heading
B67	OCCUPATION AND NONCONTROLLABLE
B68	EXPENSES
B72	NONCONTROLLABLE EXPENSES **
B74	''RENT
B75	''INSURANCE
B76	''PROPERTY TAXES
B77	''OTHER TAXES
B78	''INTEREST
B80	TOTAL NONCONTROLLABLE EXP.
B84	PROFIT BEFORE DEPRECIATION
B88	DEPRECIATION & AMORTIZATION
B90	''DEPRECIATION
B91	''AMORTIZATION
B93	TOTAL DEPREC. & AMORT.
B96	NET PROFIT BEFORE TAXES
B100	^>>>>> BUDGET ANALYSIS <<<<<
B105	INVENTORY TURNOVER
B106	SEAT TURNOVERS PER DAY (95 SEATS)
B108	BREAK-EVEN SALES
B109	BREAK-EVEN PER HOUR (OPEN 12 HRS/DAY)
B110	BREAK-EVEN PER SEAT (95 SEATS)
B111	SALES PER SEAT (95 SEATS)
B113	LUNCH FOOD: GROSS PROFIT PER CUSTOMER
B114	DINNER FOOD: GROSS PROFIT PER CUSTOMER
C25	% OF SALES
D6	^ANNUAL
F6	^JANUARY
G6	^FEBRUARY
H6	^MARCH
I6	^APRIL
J6	^MAY
K6	^JUNE
L6	^JULY
M6	^AUGUST
N6	^SEPTEMBER
O6	^OCTOBER
P6	^NOVEMBER
Q6	^DECEMBER

Step 10. Enter the following formula into Cell D11:

```
@SUM(F11..Q11)
```

TABLE 9-4. STEP 4 REPEAT AND /COPY COMMANDS.

Cell	REPEAT Command to Enter	/Copy Command to Enter			
A3	*	/CA3	<Return>	C3..Q3	<Return>
D7	\—	/CD7	<Return>	F7..Q7	<Return>
D10	\—	/CD10	<Return>	F10..Q10	<Return>
D16	\—	/CD16	<Return>	F16..Q16	<Return>
D18	\—	/CD18	<Return>	F18..Q18	<Return>
D20	\=	/CD20	<Return>	F20..Q20	<Return>
A22	*	/CA22	<Return>	B22..Q22	<Return>
A24	*	/CA24	<Return>	C24..Q24	<Return>
A28	\=	/CA28	<Return>	B28..D28	<Return>
F28	\=	/CF28	<Return>	.G28..Q28	<Return>
B29	\=				
B31	\=				
C34	\—	/CC34	<Return>	D34..D34	<Return>
F34	\—	/CF34	<Return>	G34..Q34	<Return>
C36	\—	/CC36	<Return>	D36..D36	<Return>
F36	\—	/CF36	<Return>	G36..Q36	<Return>
B37	\=				
B39	\=				
C42	\—	/CC42	<Return>	D42..D42	<Return>
F42	\—	/CF42	<Return>	G42..Q42	<Return>
C44	\—	/CC44	<Return>	D44..D44	<Return>
F44	\—	/CF44	<Return>	G44..Q44	<Return>
B46	*				
B48	*				
B50	\=				
B52	\=				
C61	\—	/CC61	<Return>	D61..D61	<Return>
F61	\—	/CF61	<Return>	G61..Q61	<Return>
C63	\—	/CC63	<Return>	D63..D63	<Return>
F63	\—	/CF63	<Return>	G63..Q63	<Return>
B65	*				
B69	*				
B71	\=				
B73	\=				
C79	\—	/CC79	<Return>	D79..D79	<Return>
F79	\—	/CF79	<Return>	G79..Q79	<Return>
C81	\—	/CC81	<Return>	D81..D81	<Return>
F81	\—	/CF81	<Return>	G81..Q81	<Return>
B83	*				
B85	*				
B87	\=				
B89	\=				
C92	\—	/CC92	<Return>	D92..D92	<Return>
F92	\—	/CF92	<Return>	G92..Q92	<Return>
C94	\—	/CC94	<Return>	D94..D94	<Return>
F94	\—	/CF94	<Return>	G94..Q94	<Return>
B95	*				
B97	*				
C97	\=	/CC97	<Return>	D97..D97	<Return>

Continued

TABLE 9-4. CONTINUED.

Cell	REPEAT Command to Enter	/Copy Command to Enter		
F97	\=	/CF97	\<Return\>	G97..Q97 \<Return\>
A98	*	/CA98	\<Return\>	B98..Q98 \<Return\>
A100	*	/CA100	\<Return\>	C100..Q100 \<Return\>
D103	\-	/CD103	\<Return\>	F103..Q103 \<Return\>
A115	*	/CA115	\<Return\>	B115..Q115 \<Return\>

This formula sums the total estimated lunch sales for January through December.

Step 11. Enter the following formula into Cell F11:

```
+F8*F9
```

This formula multiplies January's average lunch check by January's customer count, returning the total estimated lunch sales for January in Cell F11.

Now copy the formula from Cell F11 into cells G11 through Q11, placing your cell pointer on Cell F11 and entering the following /Copy command:

```
/C    <Return>    [point to Cell
G11] . [point to Cell Q11]    <Return>
```

Step 12. Repeat steps 8 through 11 for dinner forecasts, by entering each formula given in table 9-7 into the corresponding cell.

Now copy the formula from Cell F17 into cells G17 through Q17, placing your cell pointer on Cell F17 and entering the following /Copy command:

```
/C    <Return>    [point to Cell
G17] . [point to Cell Q17]    <Return>
```

Step 13. Enter the following formula into Cell D19:

```
+D11+D17
```

This formula adds the total estimated lunch sales to the total estimated dinner sales, returning the total forecast sales in Cell D19.

Now copy the formula from Cell D19 into cells F19 through Q19, placing your cell cursor on Cell D19 and entering the following Copy command:

```
/C    <Return>    [point to Cell
F19] . [point to Cell Q19]    <Return>
```

Saving BUDGET.WK1

If you would like to stop and take a break at this point, save the spreadsheet you are working now by means of the instructions given in Step 14. Otherwise, go on to Step 15.

Step 14. You can save the BUDGET spreadsheet you have created so far, by entering the following /File Save command:

```
/FSB:BUDGET    <Return>
```

If you saved BUDGET in Step 6, you must tell Lotus to overwrite the existing BUDGET.WK1 file on disk, replacing it with your latest version, as follows:

TABLE 9-5. STEP 5 /RANGE FORMAT COMMANDS.

Cell(s)	Format/Alignment	Command to Enter		
D9..Q11	currency	/RFC2	\<Return\>	D9..Q11 \<Return\>
D15..Q19	currency	/RFC2	\<Return\>	D15..Q19 \<Return\>
D27..Q27	percent	/RFP2	\<Return\>	D27..Q27 \<Return\>
C32..C97	percent	/RFP2	\<Return\>	C32..C97 \<Return\>
D32..Q97	currency	/RFC2	\<Return\>	D32..Q97 \<Return\>
D105..Q106	fixed—two decimal places	/RFF2	\<Return\>	D105..Q106 \<Return\>
D108..Q114	currency	/RFC2	\<Return\>	D108..Q114 \<Return\>

TABLE 9-6. STEP 7 DATA INPUT INTO THE BUDGET SPREADSHEET.

Cell(s)	Input
F8..Q8	CUSTOMER COUNT. Enter your forecast lunch customer counts.
F9..Q9	AVERAGE LUNCH CHECK. Enter your forecast average lunch check.
F14..Q14	CUSTOMER COUNT. Enter your forecast dinner customer counts.
F15..Q15	AVERAGE DINNER CHECK. Enter your forecast average dinner check.
COLUMN A	TYPE OF EXPENSE. Enter a *V* or *F* to indicate whether each expense is variable or fixed.
C32	FOOD SALES. Enter the percentage of sales that are food sales.
C33	BEVERAGE SALES. Enter the percentage of sales that are beverage sales.
C40	FOOD. Enter your percentage food cost goal.
C41	BEVERAGE. Enter your percentage beverage cost goal.
D53	SALARIES. Enter the fixed annual dollar amount for salaries.
C54..C56	HOURLY WAGES, EMPLOYEE BENEFITS, DIRECT OPERATING. Enter the percentage of sales that will be absorbed by hourly wages, employee benefits and direct operating expenses, respectively.
D57..D60	UTILITIES, ADMINISTRATIVE AND GENERAL MARKETING, MAINTENANCE AND REPAIR. Enter the fixed annual dollar amounts for utilities, administrative and general expenses, marketing, and maintenance and repair, respectively.
D74..D78	RENT, INSURANCE, PROPERTY TAXES, OTHER TAXES, INTEREST. Enter the fixed annual dollar amounts for rent, insurance, property taxes, other taxes, and interest, respectively.
D90..D91	DEPRECIATION AMORTIZATION. Enter the fixed annual dollar amounts for depreciation expenses and amortization expenses, respectively.

```
/FS [point to BUDGET.WK1]
<Return>    R
```

If you issue the /Quit and Exit commands to leave Lotus after saving your spreadsheet, you will have to retrieve the BUDGET file from disk before you can go on to Step 15. To retrieve your Daily Purchases Register spreadsheet, enter the following /File Retrieve command:

```
/FR [point to BUDGET.WK1]    <Return>
```

If only one file is listed on the third line of the control panel, you need not point to a file name; you may simply hit <Return> after entering /FR.

TABLE 9-7. STEP 12 FORMULAS.

Cell	Formula
D14	@SUM(F14..Q14)
D15	+D17/D14
D17	@SUM(F17..Q17)
F17	+F14*F15

Operating Budget Formulas

The Seasonal Index

The SEASONAL INDEX shown in figure 9-3, row 27, indicates each month's share of total sales for the year. This index is calculated by dividing each month's forecast sales by the annual total forecast sales. The index and the corresponding monthly share of sales is higher during busy, on-season months than during slow, off-season months. The seasonal index may be used in two ways:

1. It can be compared with the prior year's seasonal index to verify that your customer count forecasts are in line with real seasonal market fluctuations.

2. It can be used to allocate the proportion of annual fixed expense to each month, as the annual fixed expense, which is affected by seasonal volume, needs to be prorated among the months of the year. Even though a fixed expense allocated using the seasonal index may appear to fluctuate from month to month, which seems to contradict the definition of fixed expenses, it still adheres to the defini-

tion of a fixed expense when the expense is "fixed" on an annual basis.

Step 15. Enter the following formula into Cell D27:

```
@SUM(F27..Q27)
```

This formula sums the monthly seasonal index figures for January through December. The annual seasonal index should always add up to 100 percent.

Step 16. Enter the following formula into Cell F27:

```
+F19/$D$19
```

This formula divides the total estimated sales for January by the annual total estimated sales, returning the seasonal index for January in Cell F27.

Placing dollar signs in front of the column and row reference of Cell D19 designates the cell as absolute. This means that, when this formula is copied, the reference to Cell D19 will not change; in contrast, the reference to Cell F19 will be changed in each cell to which the formula is copied.

Now copy the formula from Cell F27 into cells G27 through Q27, placing your cell pointer on Cell F27 and entering the following /Copy command:

```
/C    <Return>    [point to Cell
G27] . [point to Cell Q27]    <Return>
```

Step 17. Enter the following formula into Cell D32:

```
+$C$32*D19
```

This formula multiplies the share of sales for food by the total forecast sales, returning annual food sales in Cell D32.

Now copy the formula from Cell D32 into cells F32 through Q32, placing your cell pointer on Cell D32 and entering the following /Copy command:

```
/C    <Return>    [point to Cell
F32] . [point to Cell Q32]    <Return>
```

Step 18. Enter the following formula into Cell D33:

```
+$C$33*D19
```

This formula multiplies the share of sales for beverages by the total forecast sales, returning annual beverage sales in Cell D33.

Now copy the formula from Cell D33 into cells F33 through Q33, placing your cell pointer on Cell D33 and entering the following /Copy command:

```
/C    <Return>    [point to Cell
F33] . [point to Cell Q33]    <Return>
```

Step 19. Enter the following formula into Cell C35:

```
@SUM(C32..C34)
```

This formula sums the percentage of sales for total revenue. The total revenue should always add up to 100 percent.

Now copy the formula from Cell C35 into cells D35 through Q35, placing your cell pointer on Cell C35 and entering the following /Copy command:

```
/C    <Return>    [point to Cell
D35] . [point to Cell Q35]    <Return>
```

Step 20. Enter the following formula into D40:

```
+$C$40*D32
```

This formula multiplies the percentage food cost by the food sales figure, returning the cost of food in Cell D40.

Now copy the formula from Cell D40 into cells F40 through Q40, placing your cell pointer on Cell D40 and entering the following /Copy command:

```
/C    <Return>    [point to Cell
F40] . [point to Cell Q40]    <Return>
```

Step 21. Enter the following formula into Cell D41:

```
+$C$41*D33
```

This formula multiplies the percentage beverage cost by the beverage sales figure returning the cost of beverages sold in Cell D41.

Now copy the formula from Cell D41 into cells F41 through Q41, placing your cell pointer on Cell D41 and entering the following command:

```
/C    <Return>    [point to Cell
F41] . [point to Cell Q41]    <Return>
```

Step 22. Enter the following formula into Cell C43:

```
+D43/D35
```

This formula divides the total annual cost of goods by the total revenue figure, returning the overall average percentage cost of goods in Cell C43.

Step 23. Enter the following formula into Cell D43:

```
@SUM(D40..D42)
```

This formula sums the food and beverage cost of goods.

Now copy the formula from Cell D43 into cells F43 through Q43, placing your cell pointer on Cell D43 and entering the following command:

```
/C    <Return>    [point to Cell
F43] . [point to Cell Q43]    <Return>
```

Step 24. Enter the following formula into Cell C47:

```
+D47/D35
```

This formula divides annual gross profit by total revenue, returning gross profit as a percentage of total revenue in Cell C47.

Step 25. Enter the following formula into Cell D47:

```
+D35-D43
```

This formula subtracts the total cost of goods sold from the total revenue figure, returning the gross profit in Cell D47.

Now copy the formula from Cell D47 into cells F47 through Q47, placing your cell pointer on

Cell D47 and entering the following /Copy command:

```
/C    <Return>    [point to Cell
F47] . [point to Cell Q47]    <Return>
```

Step 26. Enter the following formula into Cell C53:

```
+D53/$D$35
```

This formula divides total annual fixed salaries by annual total revenue, returning fixed salaries as a percentage of total revenue in Cell C53.

Now copy the formula from Cell C53 into cells C57 through C60, placing your cell pointer on Cell C53 and entering the following /Copy command:

```
/C    <Return>    [point to Cell
C57] . [point to Cell C60]    <Return>
```

Allocating Fixed Expenses Evenly Throughout the Year

In several of the remaining steps involving formula entry, the annual fixed expenses figure in column D is divided by 12 so that each month of the year is allotted an equal share of the expense. This equal allotment may not reflect the actual case, since it is not at all unusual for a fixed expense to be divided unevenly throughout the year. Later in this chapter, the seasonal index is used to allocate the monthly marketing expenses figure; even though this figure is fixed, it changes with the seasons of the year.

Step 27. Enter the following formula into Cell F53:

```
+$D$53/12
```

This formula divides the annual salaries figure evenly among the twelve months of the year.

Now copy the formula from Cell F53 into cells G53 through Q53, placing your cell pointer on Cell F53 and entering the following /Copy command:

```
/C    <Return>    [point to Cell
G53] . [point to Cell Q53]    <Return>
```

Step 28. Enter the following formula into Cell D54:

```
+D35*$C$54
```

This formula multiplies hourly wages as a percentage of sales by total revenue, returning annual hourly wages in Cell D54.

Now copy the formula from Cell D54 into cells F54 through Q54, placing your cell pointer on Cell D54 and entering the following /Copy command:

```
/C    <Return>    [point to Cell
F54] . [point to Cell Q54]    <Return>
```

Step 29. Enter the following formula into Cell D55:

```
+D35*$C$55
```

This formula multiplies employee benefits as a percentage of sales by total revenue, returning annual employee benefits in Cell D55.

Now copy the formula from Cell D55 into cells F55 through Q55, placing your cell pointer on Cell D55 and entering the following /Copy command:

```
/C    <Return>    [point to Cell
F55] . [point to Cell Q55]    <Return>
```

Step 30. Enter the following formula into Cell D56:

```
+D35*$C$56
```

This formula multiplies direct operating expenses as a percentage of sales by total revenue, returning the annual direct operating expenses in Cell D56.

Now copy the formula from Cell D56 into cells F56 through Q56, placing your cell pointer on Cell D56 and entering the following /Copy command:

```
/C    <Return>    [point to Cell
F56] . [point to Cell Q56]    <Return>
```

Step 31. Enter the following formula into Cell F57:

```
+$D$57/12
```

This formula divides the annual utilities figure evenly among the twelve months of the year.

Now copy the formula from Cell F57 into cells G57 through Q57, placing your cell pointer on Cell F57 and entering the following /Copy command:

```
/C    <Return>    [point to Cell
G57] . [point to Cell Q57]    <Return>
```

Step 32. Enter the following formula into Cell F58:

```
+$D$58/12
```

This formula divides the annual administrative and general expenses figure evenly among the twelve months of the year.

Now copy the formula from Cell F58 into cells G58 through Q58, placing your cell pointer on Cell F58 and entering the following /Copy command:

```
/C    <Return>    [point to Cell
G58] . [point to Cell Q58]    <Return>
```

Using the Seasonal Index to Allocate Fixed Expenses

A marketing rule of thumb is that it is best to advertise and promote your business during on-season months, when the potential customer population is at its peak and you can reach more people per marketing dollar. This translates into budgeting more dollars for marketing during on-season months and fewer for marketing during off-season months. A good indicator of how much to budget for seasonal fluctuations is the seasonal index, which is used in Step 33 for allocating marketing expense.

Step 33. Enter the following formula into Cell F59:

```
+$D$59*F27
```

This formula multiplies the annual marketing expense figure by the seasonal index for January, returning the marketing budget for January in Cell F59.

Now copy the formula from Cell F59 into cells G59 through Q59, placing your cell pointer on Cell F59 and enter the following /Copy command:

```
/C    <Return>    [point to Cell
G59] . [point to Cell Q59]   <Return>
```

Step 34. Enter the following formula in Cell F60:

```
+$D$60/12
```

This formula divides annual maintenance and repair expenses evenly among the twelve months of the year.

Now copy the formula from Cell F60 into Cells G60 through Q60, placing your cell pointer on Cell F60 and entering the following /Copy command:

```
/C    <Return>    [point to Cell
G60] . [point to Cell Q60]   <Return>
```

Step 35. Enter the following formula into Cell C62:

```
+D62/D35
```

This formula divides total annual controllable expenses by total revenue, returning the annual average percentage of sales taken up by total controllable expenses in Cell C62.

Step 36. Enter the following formula into Cell D62:

```
@SUM(D53..D61)
```

This formula sums annual controllable expenses.

Now copy the formula from Cell D62 into cells F62 through Q62, placing your cell pointer on Cell D62 and entering the following /Copy command:

```
/C    <Return>    [point to Cell
F62] . [point to Cell Q62]   <Return>
```

Step 37. Enter the following formula into Cell C68:

```
+D68/D35
```

This formula divides the total operating profit before expenses by total revenue, returning the overall average percentage of sales taken up by total operating profit before occupation and noncontrollable expenses in Cell C68.

Step 38. Enter the following formula into Cell D68:

```
+D47-D62
```

This formula subtracts total controllable expenses from gross profit, returning total operating profit before occupation and noncontrollable expenses in Cell D68.

Now copy the formula from Cell D68 into cells F68 through Q68, placing your cell pointer on Cell D68 and entering the following /Copy command:

```
/C    <Return>    [point to Cell
F68] . [point to Cell Q68]   <Return>
```

Step 39. Enter the following formula into Cell C74:

```
+D74/$D$35
```

This formula divides total annual fixed rent by total revenue, returning fixed rent as a percentage of total revenue in Cell C74.

Now copy the formula from Cell C74 into cell C75 through C78, placing your cell pointer on Cell C74 and entering the following /Copy command:

```
/C    <Return>    [point to Cell
C75] . [point to Cell C78]   <Return>
```

Step 40. Enter the following formula into Cell F74:

```
+D74/12
```

This formula divides annual rent evenly among the twelve months of the year.

Because all remaining noncontrollable expenses—including insurance, property taxes, other taxes, and interest—are fixed expenses divided evenly throughout the months of the year, you can save time and steps by copying the formula in Cell F74 into the cells for all these noncontrollable expenses, for each month. You can accomplish this by performing the three parts of Step 41.

Step 41. Copy the formula from Cell F74 into cells F75 through F78, placing your cell pointer on Cell F74 and entering the following /Copy command:

```
/C    <Return>    [point to Cell
F75] . [point to Cell F78]    <Return>
```

Edit the formulas you just copied to make the cell references in the cells involved absolute, as shown in table 9-8.

Copy the formulas from cells F74 through F78 into Cell Range G74..Q74, placing your cell pointer on Cell F74 and entering the following /Copy command:

```
/CF74..F78    <Return>    G74..Q74
<Return>
```

Step 42. Enter the following formula into Cell C80:

```
+D80/D35
```

This formula divides annual total noncontrollable expenses by total revenue, returning the overall average percentage of sales taken up by total noncontrollable expenses in Cell C80.

Step 43. Enter the following formula into Cell D80:

```
@SUM(D74..D79)
```

This formula sums annual noncontrollable expenses from annual totals for each subcategory.

Now copy the formula from Cell D80 into cells F80 through Q80, placing your cell pointer on

TABLE 9-8. STEP 41 IN THE CELLS INVOLVED FORMULAS.

Cell	Formula
F74	+$D$74/12
F75	+$D$75/12
F76	+$D$76/12
F77	+$D$77/12
F78	+$D$78/12

Cell D80 and entering the following /Copy command:

```
/C    <Return>    [point to Cell
F80] . [point to Cell Q80]    <Return>
```

Step 44. Enter the following formula into Cell C84:

```
+D84/D35
```

This formula divides total annual profit before depreciation by total revenue, returning the overall average percentage of sales taken up by profit before depreciation in Cell C84.

Step 45. Enter the following formula into Cell D84:

```
+D68-D80
```

This formula subtracts total noncontrollable expenses from total operating profit before occupation and noncontrollable expenses, returning profit before depreciation in Cell D84.

Now copy the formula from Cell D84 into cells F84 through Q84, placing your cell pointer on Cell D84 and entering the following /Copy command:

```
/C    <Return>    [point to Cell
F84] . [point to Cell Q84]    <Return>
```

Step 46. Enter the following formula into Cell C90:

```
+D90/$D$35
```

This formula divides total annual fixed depreciation by total revenue, returning annual depreciation as a percentage of total revenue in Cell C90.

Now copy the formula from Cell C90 into Cell C91, placing your cell pointer on Cell C90 and entering the following /Copy command:

```
/C    <Return>    [point to Cell
C91]    <Return>
```

Step 47. Enter the following formula into Cell F90:

```
+D90/12
```

This formula divides annual depreciation evenly among the twelve months of the year.

Because amortization is also divided evenly among the months of the year, you can save time and steps by copying the formula in Cell F90 into Cell F91, as explained in Step 48.

Step 48. Place your cell pointer on Cell F90, and enter the following /Copy command:

```
/C    <Return>    [point to Cell
F91]    <Return>
```

Edit the formulas you just copied to make the cell references absolute, as shown in table 9-9.

TABLE 9-9. STEP 48 FORMULAS.

Cell	Formula
F90	+$D$90/12
F91	+$D$91/12

Copy the formulas from cells F90 and F91 into Cell Range G90..Q90, placing your cell pointer on Cell F90 and entering the following /Copy command:

```
/CF90..F91    <Return>
G90..Q90    <Return>
```

Step 49. Enter the following formula into Cell C93:

```
+D93/D35
```

This formula divides the annual total depreciation and amortization by total revenue, returning the annual average percentage of sales taken up by total depreciation and amortization in Cell C93.

Step 50. Enter the following formula into Cell D93:

```
@SUM(D90.D92)
```

This formula sums annual depreciation and amortization from annual totals for each.

Now copy the formula from Cell D93 into cells F93 through Q93, placing your cell pointer on Cell D93 and entering the following /Copy command:

```
/C    <Return>    [point to Cell
F93] . [point to Cell Q93]    <Return>
```

Step 51. Enter the following formula into Cell C96:

```
+D96/D35
```

This formula divides total annual net profit before taxes by total revenue, returning the annual average percentage of sales taken up by net profit before taxes in Cell C96.

Step 52. Enter the following formula into Cell D96:

```
+D84-D93
```

This formula subtracts total depreciation and amortization from profit before depreciation, returning net profit before taxes in Cell D96.

Now copy the formula from Cell D96 into cells F96 through Q96, placing your cell pointer on Cell D96 and entering the following command:

```
/C    <Return>    [point to Cell
F96] . [point to Cell Q96]    <Return>
```

Saving BUDGET.WK1

If you would like to stop and take a break at this point, save the spreadsheet you are working now in accordance with Step 53. Otherwise, go on to Step 54.

Step 53. You can save the BUDGET spreadsheet you have created so far, by entering the following /File Save command:

```
/FSB:BUDGET    <Return>
```

If you saved BUDGET in Step 6 or Step 14, you must tell Lotus to overwrite the existing BUDGET.WK1 file on disk, replacing it with your latest version, as follows:

```
/FS [point to BUDGET.WK1]
<Return>    R
```

If you issue the /Quit and Exit commands to leave Lotus after saving your spreadsheet, you will have to retrieve the BUDGET file from disk before you can go on to Step 54. To retrieve your Daily Purchases Register spreadsheet, enter the following /File Retrieve command:

```
/FR [point to BUDGET.WK1]    <Return>
```

If only one file is listed on the third line of the control panel, you need not point to a file name; you may simply hit <Return> after entering /FR.

Budget Analysis Formulas

Step 54. Enter the following formula into Cell D105:

```
+D43/7000
```

This formula divides the annual total cost of goods sold by $7,000.00, which is assumed in this sample budget to be the average inventory value of food and beverage. When you create your actual budget, you will need to calculate or estimate your own average inventory value—the average value of all the food and beverage on hand at any moment during the year. If you take a monthly physical inventory, you can calculate the average inventory value by summing the ending inventory value for each month and then dividing by twelve. Dividing the total cost of goods sold by the average inventory value gives you an approximation of how many times over the course of the year your inventory turns over.
Step 55. By copying this formula so that it applies to each month, you can see how many times per month (rather than per year) your inventory turns over.

Copy the formula from Cell D105 into cells F105 through Q105, placing your cell pointer on Cell D105 and entering the following /Copy command:

```
/C    <Return>    [point to Cell
F105] . [point to Cell
Q105]    <Return>
```

Step 56. Enter the following formula into Cell D106:

```
(D8+D14)/(95*6*52)
```

This formula divides the total annual customer count for lunch and dinner combined by the total number of seats available per day for the year (in the example, the figures used are ninety-five seats times 6 days per week times 52 weeks per year), returning the annual average seat turnovers per day in Cell D106. When planning your actual budget, you will have to adjust the figures used in the spreadsheet example to reflect your facility's actual number of seats and the number of days of the year your facility is open.
Step 57. To calculate the seat turnovers per day for each month, you must adjust the formula you entered in Step 56. Instead of dividing by the number of seats available for the entire year, the formula must be adjusted to divide by the number of seats available for a month. In the example, the facility is assumed to be open an average of 26 days per month. Therefore, you should enter the following formula into Cell F106:

```
(F8+F14)/(95*26)
```

Now copy the formula from Cell F106 into cells G106 through Q106, placing your cell pointer on Cell D96 and entering the following /Copy command:

```
/C    <Return>    [point to Cell
G106] . [point to Cell
Q106]    <Return>
```

Step 58. Enter the following formula into Cell D108:

```
(D53+@SUM(D57..D61)+@SUM(D74..D78)
+@SUM(D90..D91))/(1-($C$43
+@SUM($C$54..$C$56)))
```

Although this is a lengthy formula, it is theoretically simple. It is easiest to understand when considered in parts. The part to the left of the division symbol (/) is as follows:

```
(D53+@SUM(D57..D61)+@SUM(D74..D78)
+@SUM(D90..D91))
```

If you look up (in figure 9-1) the cells and cell ranges used in this part of the formula, you will

TABLE 9-10. VARIABLE COSTS CONSIDERED BY THE FORMULA IN STEP 58.

Cell	Description	Percent	Decimal
C43	total cost of goods sold	34.75%	.3475
C54	hourly wages	21.00%	.2100
C55	employee benefits	5.00%	.0500
C56	direct operating	5.50%	.0550
	Total Variable Costs:	66.25%	.6625

notice that these cells reference all of the fixed expenses in the **ANNUAL** column (column D) and add them up. Thus the first part of the formula simply adds all the fixed expenses, which are all the ones marked with an *F* in column A of the operating budget. Added together, all of these fixed expenses equal $299,232.00. This is an important figure for calculating a break-even point.

The total of all fixed expenses (the first part of the formula) is divided by the following terms of the formula:

```
(1-($C$43+@SUM($C$54..$C$56)))
```

This part of the formula calculates the difference between variable costs (expressed as a percentage) and 100 percent (expressed in decimal notation as 1). The variable costs, marked in column A with a V, are described in table 9-10.

When the variable costs (expressed as a percentage) are subtracted from 100 percent, the figure that remains equals the portion of each dollar of sales that goes to pay off total fixed expenses:

$$1 - .6625 = .3375 = 33.75 \text{ cents per dollar}$$

When you divide total fixed costs by the portion of each dollar that is used to pay off total fixed costs, you get the break-even point in dollars—that is, the amount of sales (in dollars) needed to pay off total fixed costs at the proportion of cents per dollar calculated earlier in this step:

$$\$299,232.00/.3375 = \$886,613.33$$

The formula to calculate the break-even point of your operation can be expressed very simply as:

Break-even = Total Fixed Costs/(1 − % of Total Revenue consumed by Total Variable Costs)

Note that break-even and total fixed costs in this formula are always expressed in dollars, while total variable costs are always expressed as a percentage of total revenue.

To review, break-even is the point at which sales, after paying for your per-dollar variable expenses, leave you just enough money to pay for your fixed expenses—no more and no less. Thus, the break-even computation is a way of asking yourself, "How many cents of each dollar in sales must go to pay for variable expenses (food costs, beverage costs, hourly wages, employee benefits, and direct operating expenses) and how many remain to pay for fixed expenses?" and, "How many dollars in sales must my operation register before all of its fixed expenses are paid off and I can start realizing the 'fixed expenses' portion of each subsequent dollar of sales as profit?"

Do not oversimplify and make the frequent mistake of imagining that the break-even point is defined by your total expenses (that is, by your fixed expenses plus your variable expenses). Total expenses are not the break-even point. The break-even point is total fixed expenses divided by the percentage of each dollar that remains for fixed expenses after deducting the percentage that must go to pay variable expenses. Remember, variable expenses never cease to exist until you go out of business; fixed expenses cease to exist once you reach the break-even point.

Step 59. Copy the formula from Cell D108 into cells F108 through Q108, placing your cell pointer on Cell D108 and entering the following /Copy command:

```
/C    <Return>    [point to Cell
F108] . [point to Cell
Q108]    <Return>
```

Step 60. Enter the following formula into Cell D109:

```
+D108/(12*6*52)
```

This formula divides the break-even figure for total annual sales in Cell D108 by the total number of hours the facility is open per year, returning the break-even figure for sales per hour in Cell D109. In the present example, the formula assumes that the facility is open 12 hours per day, 6 days per week, and 52 weeks per year. Multiplying 12 hours times 6 days times 52 weeks gives you the total number of hours the facility in the example is open per year. When planning your actual budget, you will have to adjust the figures used in the spreadsheet example to reflect your facility's actual number of hours per day open, days per week open, and weeks per year open.

Step 61. To calculate the break-even per hour figure for each month, you must adjust the formula you entered in Step 60. Instead of using the number of weeks open for the entire year, the formula must be adjusted to use the number of days open for a single month. In the example, the facility is assumed to be open an average of 26 days per month. Therefore, you should enter the following formula into Cell F109:

```
(F108)/(12*26)
```

Now copy the formula from Cell F109 into cells G109 through Q109, placing your cell pointer on Cell F109 and entering the following /Copy command:

```
/C    <Return>    [point to Cell
G109] . [point to Cell Q109]
<Return>
```

Step 62. Enter the following formula into Cell D110:

```
+D108/95
```

This formula divides the figure for total annual break-even sales in Cell D108 by the total

number of seats in the restaurant (in the spreadsheet example, the facility is assumed to have ninety-five seats), returning the break-even figure per seat in Cell D110. When planning your actual budget, you will have to adjust this figure to reflect your facility's actual number of seats.

Now copy the formula from Cell D110 into cells F110 through Q110, placing your cell pointer on Cell D110 and entering the following /Copy command:

```
/C    <Return>    [point to Cell
F110] . [point to Cell Q110]
<Return>
```

Step 63. Enter the following formula into Cell D111:

```
+D35/95
```

This formula divides the total revenue figure in Cell D35 by the total number of seats in the restaurant, returning the figure for sales per seat in Cell D111. (Note that Sales per Seat is not a break-even cost but is included here in the spreadsheet for easy comparison with Break-even per Seat.) Here, again, the facility in the example is assumed to have ninety-five seats. When planning your actual budget, you will have to adjust this assumption to reflect your restaurant's actual number of seats.

Now copy the formula from Cell D111 into cells F111 through Q111, placing your cell pointer on Cell D111 and entering the following /Copy command:

```
/C    <Return>    [point to Cell
F111] . [point to Cell
Q111]    <Return>
```

Step 64. Enter the following formula into Cell D113:

```
(D11*$C$32*(1-$C$40))/D8
```

This formula calculates gross profit per customer in the LUNCH FOOD category. *Gross profit* is defined as the difference between sales and the cost of goods. The first cell reference in the formula, Cell D11 contains the total estimated lunch sales figure, which unfortunately includes beverage sales as well as food sales. Because you only want to determine the per-customer gross profit on food, you first need to isolate food sales. You can do this by multiplying the total estimated lunch sales by the overall percentage of food sales (given in Cell C32 as 75 percent):

Total Estimated Lunch Food = `D11*C32`
$$= \$342,600.00 \times 75\%$$
$$= \$256,950.00$$

Next, you need to isolate how much of the lunch food sales figure represents gross profit. Cell C40 tells you that 38 percent of sales goes to pay the cost of goods for food. If you subtract that figure from 100 percent (or in decimal notation, 1), the result represents the gross profit percentage for food:

Gross Profit % for Food = `(1-C40)`
$$= (1 - .38)$$
$$= .62 \text{ or } 62\%$$

By multiplying the gross profit percentage for food by the total estimated lunch food sales, you can compute the total annual gross profit on lunch food sales:

Total Gross Profit on
    Lunch Food = $62\% \times \$256,950.00$
$$= \$159,309.00$$

Now you can calculate the gross profit per customer for lunch food, by dividing the total gross profit on lunch food by the total lunch customer count (expressed in Cell D8):

Lunch Food:
Gross Profit per Customer = `$159,309.00/D8`
$$= \$159,309.00/51,250$$
$$= \$3.11$$

Now copy the formula from Cell D113 into cells F113 through Q113, placing your cell pointer on Cell D113 and entering the following /Copy command:

```
/C    <Return>    [point to Cell F113]
.  [point to Cell Q113]    <Return>
```

Step 65. Enter the following formula into Cell D114:

```
(D17*$C$32*(1-$C$40))/D14
```

The calculations in this formula are based on the same procedures as those explained in Step 64. Only the following two references differ:

1. Total estimated dinner sales (Cell D17) are used instead of total estimated lunch sales (Cell D11).
2. Dinner customer count (Cell D14) is used instead of lunch customer count (Cell D8).

Now copy this formula from Cell D114 into Cells F114 through Q114, placing your cell pointer on Cell D114 and entering the following /Copy command:

```
/C    <Return>    [point to Cell F114]
.  [point to Cell Q114]    <Return>
```

Protecting Your Spreadsheet

Step 66. Use the /Worksheet Global Protection Enable command sequence, followed by Unprotect commands for the shaded areas of the spreadsheet, to protect the cells in the nonshaded areas of the spreadsheet from accidentally being filled (by you or by other spreadsheet users) with unwanted data. Begin by entering the following command string:

```
/WGPE
```

This string is an abbreviated expression for /Worksheet Global Protection Enable command, which protects every cell in the spreadsheet from entry and alteration.

The next step is to unprotect the cells in the shaded areas of the spreadsheet by means of the /Range Unprotect commands listed in table 9-11. Before entering each command, place your cell pointer on the first cell of the corresponding cell range that is to be unprotected.

TABLE 9-11. STEP 66 /RANGE UNPROTECT COMMANDS.

Cells to Unprotect	Command to Enter	
A29..A97	/RU [point to A97]	<Return>
F8..Q9	/RU [point to Q9]	<Return>
F14..Q15	/RU [point to Q15]	<Return>
C32..C33	/RU [point to C33]	<Return>
C40..C41	/RU [point to C41]	<Return>
D53	/RU <Return>.	
C54..C56	/RU [point to C56]	<Return>
D57..D61	/RU [point to D61]	<Return>
D74..D78	/RU [point to D78]	<Return>
D90..D91	/RU [point to D91]	<Return>

Saving Your Spreadsheet

Step 67. You can save the BUDGET spreadsheet you have created, by entering the following /File Save command:

```
/FSB:BUDGET     <Return>
```

If you saved BUDGET in Step 6, Step 14, or Step 53, you must tell Lotus to overwrite the existing BUDGET.WK1 file on disk, replacing it with your latest version, as follows:

```
/FS [point to BUDGET.WK1]
<Return>    R
```

Printing Your Spreadsheet

Step 68. Turn your printer on, align the paper in it, place your cell pointer on Cell A1 by pressing the <Home> key on your cursor/arrow keypad, and print your spreadsheet by issuing the following command:

```
/PPR.    <End>    <Home>
<Return>    AGPQ
```

This abbreviated command language means: "Print to the printer the spreadsheet range A1 to Q115. The paper is aligned in the printer, so the spreadsheet should begin printing at the top of the page. Go and print the spreadsheet. Then page-eject the paper in the printer to the top of a new page, and quit the print commands."

You may need to consult your Lotus manual for information on how to adjust Lotus's printer settings for footers, margins, borders, page length and special set-up strings.

Using the Information in This Spreadsheet

"What If" Budget Analysis

Your BUDGET spreadsheet easily allows you to change the following budgetary factors:

- Customer counts
- Average lunch and dinner checks
- Percentages of food and beverage sales to total sales
- Food cost percentage
- Beverage cost percentage
- Fixed dollar expenses
- Percentage of sales taken up by variable expenses

This enables you to see the effect that one or more changes may have on:

- Forecast lunch and dinner sales
- Revenue
- Dollar cost of goods sold
- Gross profit
- Controllable expenses
- Noncontrollable expenses
- Profit before taxes
- Analysis ratios and statistics for:
  – Turnover
  – Break-even
  – Gross profit per customer

Feel free to play with and adjust these variables until you are confident that your budgetary goals are achievable and until you are satisfied with the bottom line.

This chapter has already covered the input in the shaded areas of figure 9-1—the cornerstones for setting your financial goals. Now consider the ratios and statistics on the bottom of the spreadsheet (see figure 9-4).

Inventory Turnover

Inventory turnover (calculated by the spreadsheet) equals total revenue divided by average inventory value. This ratio has several uses:

1. Use it to measure how quickly inventory is sold. Generally, the higher the inventory turnover, the better your operation is performing.
2. Use it to measure how well you are managing your inventory. Generally, the higher the inventory turnover, the better you are managing your inventory and purchasing. This formula emphasizes the advantages of maintaining a minimum inventory.
3. Use it to compare to your actual inventory turnover ratio.
4. Use it to compare your operation's performance to industry averages.

Seat Turnovers per Day

Seat turnovers per day (calculated by the spreadsheet) equal the total customer count divided by the total number of seats available per day. Use this ratio to measure how quickly your serving staff can turn over the available seating in your establishment. You may want to achieve greater accuracy than the spreadsheet example in this chapter allows, by calculating separate ratios for lunch and for dinner; use these separate ratios to plan your labor schedule to suit the number of turnovers anticipated for each meal period. The seat turnovers per day ratio can also be used to compare budgeted turnovers to actual seat turnovers, and to compare your business's numbers to industry averages for your type of operation. Use your actual seat turnover ratio to calculate customer counts when doing sales forecasting.

Break-even Sales

Break-even sales (calculated by the spreadsheet) equal the dollar amount of fixed expenses divided by the result of 100 percent minus the total variable expense percentage. Use this ratio as a measurement and floor for minimum sales. Use it in "what if" analyses to see how changes in sales

and expenses can cause drastic changes in the break-even point and in potential profits. For instance, if you test to see how a 50¢-per-hour increase in hourly wages affects your operation's break-even point and potential profit, you will find that it detrimentally changes the figures for break-even sales and for profits.

This example emphasizes the importance of controlling costs (particularly, variable costs) in a foodservice operation. A slight increase in variable costs may be extremely harmful to bottom-line profit, eating up a few cents on each sales dollar that otherwise would have gone to pay for fixed expenses and thereafter would have contributed to profit.

Break-even analysis emphasizes the importance of maintaining planned goals once you have set them in the budget. Irresponsible veering from planned goals may increase the figure for break-even sales to a point at which bottom-line losses are inevitable.

Break-even per Hour

Break-even per hour (calculated by the spreadsheet) equals break-even sales divided by the total number of hours your facility is open. Use this ratio to measure hour-to-hour sales in your operation on a here-and-now basis, gauging your operation's daily and hourly performance as you work. Use this ratio to give you an ongoing feeling for your operation's sales performance. This ratio also underscores that many of your open hours may be slow hours and that, in order to break-even, you must do considerably better than this dollar ratio indicates during busy hours.

Break-even per Seat

Break-even per seat (calculated by the spreadsheet) equals break-even sales divided by the number of available seats in your facility. Use this ratio to measure the effect of changes in revenue, variable expenses, and fixed expenses on a break-even per seat basis (as compared with the effect of changes in sales per available seat).

Sales per Available Seat

Sales per available seat (calculated by the spreadsheet) equals total sales divided by number of seats. Use this ratio to measure how efficiently available seating space is being utilized. The higher the sales per available seat figure is, the better your operation utilizes available seating space—until you reach a point at which customers are turned away because there are not enough seats. This ratio is also used in planning new units to determine whether available seating space is being properly utilized, underutilized, or overutilized. In addition, this ratio can be compared with your facility's actual performance ratio as a means toward developing an indicator of maximum seating space utilization—the point at which you are maximizing sales per available seat, without losing customers. Finally, the sales per available seat for your operation can be compared to industry averages and to your operation's break-even per seat figure.

Lunch Food or Dinner Food Gross Profit per Customer

This ratio (calculated by the spreadsheet) equals the lunch or dinner dollar gross profit on food divided by the lunch or dinner customer count. This ratio is used primarily in calculating menu prices by means of the Gross Profit method or one of its derivatives. See chapter 10 for an explanation of recipe costing and pricing, to see how this ratio is used to price menu items.

Use this ratio as a reference to compare against actual gross profit per customer during the year. Differences between actual and budgeted figures may indicate a divergence from the goals you have set for menu prices, customer counts, food costs, labor costs, or other variable costs.

Problems

1. List five reasons for preparing and using a budget.
2. What are some different types of budgets?
3. What are the three phases of budget creation?
4. Explain how the FORECASTS section of the spreadsheet at the top of figure 9-1 projects sales for the year. Include in your explanation an account of all of the factors involved that are used as sales-projection criteria.
5. What are some of the methods that can be used to calculate projected expenses in a budget?
6. What is the difference between controllable expenses and noncontrollable expenses?
7. What is a variable expense?
8. What is a fixed expense?
9. Why is it important to differentiate between fixed and variable expenses?
10. What is a seasonal index? How is the seasonal index used in the spreadsheet shown in figure 9-1?
11. Explain how variable and fixed expenses are used to calculate break-even sales.
12. Explain why the sum of all expenses is not the break-even sales point.

Cases

1. Assume that the budget outlined in figure 9-1 is your last year's budget. Recalculate the budget, given the following sales forecasts for this year:
   a. Customer counts will increase 5 percent this year for lunch and will increase 7 percent this year for dinner.
   b. The average lunch check will increase by $.50 in January, by $.50 in April, and by $.35 in October.
   c. The average dinner check will increase by $.75 in January, by $.50 in April, and by $.75 in October.
   Write a brief summary of the effects of these changes on the budget outlined in figure 9-1.
2. Assume that the budget outlined in figure 9-1 is your last year's budget. Recalculate the budget, given the following sales forecasts for this year:
   a. Customer counts will decrease 10 percent this year for lunch and will decrease 7 percent this year for dinner.
   b. The average lunch check will increase by $.50 in January, by $.50 in April, and by $.35 in October.
   c. The average dinner check will increase by $.75 in January, by $.50 in April, and by $.75 in October.
   Write a brief summary of the effects of these changes on the budget outlined in figure 9-1. How is the figure for break-even sales affected?

10. Recipe Costing and Pricing

Recipe costing is central to food cost control; it is where food cost control begins, embodying such basic principles and procedures of foodservice operations as portion control, menu pricing, contribution margin, menu/sales analysis, and the setting of profit goals.

Suppose that your operation's lunch menu is not producing as much profit as you think it could (or should). Nearby competitors offer lunch specials that are attracting some of your regular customers, and these customers have commented that you ought to offer some variety with lunch specials, too.

So you sit down and begin calculating current menu statistics manually. One of your first objectives is to see if your lunch menu prices are high enough to generate the profit you expect. To determine this, you need to calculate the true cost of each lunch menu item. Assuming that sandwiches are your most popular lunch menu items, you start with the cost of the lunch sandwiches on your menu, to find out if these lunch offerings are priced properly in relation to their cost. For no particular reason, you decide to tackle the ham sandwich first. After some pondering and looking up of prices, you compile the following data:

There are sixteen slices of bread per loaf, and a loaf costs $1.60. Therefore, a slice of bread costs 10¢.

A pound of ham costs $3.20, which is 20 cents an ounce.

Each sandwich uses two slices of bread (20¢) and 4 ounces of ham (80¢).

Each sandwich comes with two slices of tomato (12¢), some lettuce (8¢), mayo (10¢), mustard (5¢) and pickles (7¢).

Each sandwich is served with a paper napkin (2¢) and a side of french fries or cole slaw (45¢).

Altogether, that comes to a cost of $1.89 for a ham sandwich, and the menu price for it is $4.50.

This leaves a contribution to profit, or *contribution margin* (the menu price minus the cost), of about $2.60, and a *food cost* (the cost of the sandwich divided by the menu price of the sandwich) of 42 percent.

So much for the first sandwich. Now, as you proceed (rather laboriously) through the same calculations from BLT sandwich to egg salad sandwich to reuben sandwich, you begin to notice some patterns in your above hypothetical manual menu costing.

First, you notice that sandwiches (your lunch staple) have an overall average food cost (dollar cost per serving divided by current menu price) of about 40 percent, significantly higher than the ideal average food cost of 38 percent you planned when you opened for lunch.

Second, you notice that the average profit contribution margin of a sandwich (the menu price of the sandwich minus the cost of the sandwich) is only about $2.50, 50¢ off the $3.00 average gross profit per menu item you set when you opened for lunch.

Understanding How the Recipe Costing and Pricing Spreadsheet Works

The Recipe Costing and Pricing spreadsheet uses the information in the Physical Inventory and Valuation spreadsheet described in chapter 4. Compare the recipe ingredients in figure 10-1 with the ingredients listed in the inventory spreadsheet in figure 4-1. Notice that the inventory items in the inventory spreadsheet are used as ingredients in the meat loaf plate recipe, that the inventory count unit from the inventory spreadsheet is used as the RECIPE UNIT OF MEASURE in column D, and that the price per count unit from the inventory spreadsheet is used here as the ingredient COST PER UNIT OF MEASURE in column E.

The information in the Physical Inventory and Valuation spreadsheet is automatically transferred (by means of macro commands) to the Recipe Costing and Pricing spreadsheet, where it can be seen in columns I through L under the heading LOOK-UP TABLE #1 #2 #3.

The inventory information in columns I through L of the Recipe Costing and Pricing spreadsheet illustrated in figure 10-1 is arranged in numerical order by inventory item number so that it can be accessed as a look-up table. The Physical Inventory and Valuation spreadsheet data from chapter 4 should be in this order before they are transferred to the recipe costing spreadsheet. If the data are not already so ordered, you can rearrange them by means of the \V macro described in chapter 4.

Look at the inventory item numbers entered under the heading INVENTORY ITEM NUMBER in column A of either figure 10-1 or figure 10-2. When you enter an inventory item number in this column (rows 22 through 42), the spreadsheet looks up the item number in LOOK-UP TABLES #1 #2 #3 (columns J, K, and L), to return the RECIPE INGREDIENT DESCRIPTION, the RECIPE UNIT OF MEASURE, and the COST PER UNIT OF MEASURE (columns B, D, and E, respectively).

Besides automating the costing of recipes as you create them, this scheme automates future updating of recipe costs. Once you have created a recipe using the Recipe Costing and Pricing spreadsheet, you can execute the macro shown at the bottom of figure 10-1 to transfer the latest data from your INVENTORY.WK1 spreadsheet to your RECIPES.WK1 spreadsheet, automatically updating the inventory information in the Recipe Costing and Pricing spreadsheet and recalculating recipe costs on the basis of the latest inventory pricing information. As long as you maintain inventory prices in the Physical Inventory and Valuation spreadsheet, you can easily update recipe costs to stay on top of your menu pricing.

If your computer has a lot of memory, you may want to put the inventory data look-up table in a far corner of your recipe costing spreadsheet, enabling you to place several recipes in the spreadsheet instead of a single recipe as the example in this chapter does.

Before starting Step 1 of this chapter, make sure that you have completed the INVENTRY.WK1 spreadsheet described in chapter 4. The RECIPES.WK1 spreadsheet will not work properly without INVENTRY.WK1.

```
: A ::   B    :: C :: D :: E :: F ::   G   :: H ::  I  ::    J    :: K :: L :: M :: N :
 1  RECIPE COSTING WORKSHEET                                          LOOK-UP TABLE #1  #2    #3
 2  ============================                                      ==================  ====  ========
 3                                                                             RECIPE
 4              RECIPE NAME:  MEAT LOAF PLATE                                  UNIT  COST PER
 5      DATE OF LAST UPDATE:  October 19, 1985                     INGREDIENT   OF   UNIT OF
 6  RECIPE TYPE (1=SUBMENU;2=MENU;3=BOTH):    2 MENU               DESCRIPTION MEASRE MEASURE
 7                 COMMENTS:  This lunch plate includes 1 slice of meat loaf,  ==========  ====  =======
 8                           a salad of 1/4 head of lettuce and 4 slices  1000 COFFEE          LB    $2.95
 9                           of tomato, broccoli, and a side of 6 raviolis.  1001 ORANGE PEKOE TEA  BOX   $2.15
10                                                                 1002 ROOT BEER         TANK  $15.00
11          NUMBER OF SERVINGS:      12                            1003 APPLE JUICE       GAL   $5.25
12          CURRENT MENU PRICE:    $6.50                           1999 =================TOTAL BEVERAGES:
13     DOLLAR COST PER SERVING:    $2.53                           2000 MOZZARELLA        LB    $2.15
14  FOOD COST AS A PERCENT OF MENU PRICE:  38.89%                  2001 AMERICAN CHEESE   LB    $1.89
15         DOLLAR GROSS PROFIT:    $3.97                           2002 MOZZARELLA        LB    $2.15
16                                                                 2003 WISCONSIN CHEDDAR LB    $3.25
17                                                                 2099 =================TOTAL CHEESES:
18  INVENTORY                      RECIPE  COST PER  EXTENDED      2100 HOMOGENIZED MILK  1/3PT $0.27
19   ITEM   RECIPE INGREDIENT      UNIT OF UNIT OF INGREDIENT      2101 HOMOGENIZED MILK  1/2GL $0.94
20  NUMBER  DESCRIPTION   QUANTITY MEASURE MEASURE   COST          2102 COTTAGE CHEESE    LB    $1.10
21  ----------------------------------------------------------     2103 SOLID BUTTER      LB    $1.47
22  MEAT LOAF INGREDIENTS:                                         2197 =================TOTAL DAIRY:
23    7500 GROUND BEEF - BULK  5.00 LB    $2.75    $13.75          2198 EGGS              DOZ   $0.90
24    6000 WHITE RICE          0.50 LB    $1.23     $0.62          2199 =================TOTAL EGGS:
25    6200 YELLOW ONIONS       0.50 LB    $0.15     $0.08          2200 CHOPPED SPINACH   BOX   $0.98
26    3003 CATSUP - 33%        0.10 CAN   $4.89     $0.49          2201 CABBAGE ROLLS     CASE  $11.50
27    2200 CHOPPED SPINACH     1.00 BOX   $0.98     $0.98          2202 RAVIOLIS          CASE  $10.00
28  VEGIS:                                          $0.00          2203 LASAGNA           CASE  $12.00
29    6203 BROCCOLI            3.00 LB    $0.98     $2.94          2999 =================TOTAL FROZEN FOODS:
30  SALAD:                                          $0.00          3000 TUNA              CANS  $8.99
31    6202 TOMATOES            0.17 CASE  $17.65    $3.00          3001 COTTONSEED OIL    TIN   $18.22
32    6201 ICEBERG LETTUCE     0.13 CASE  $9.89     $1.29          3002 SUGAR PACKETS     CASE  $7.57
33  CARBOS:                                         $0.00          3003 CATSUP - 33%      CAN   $4.89
34    2202 RAVIOLIS            0.72 CASE  $10.00    $7.20          5999 =================TOTAL GROCERIES:
35                                                  $0.00          6000 WHITE RICE        LB    $1.23
36                                                  $0.00          6001 LENTILS           LB    $1.10
37                                                  $0.00          6002 SMALL WHITE BEANS LB    $1.56
38                                                  $0.00          6003 BLACK BEANS       LB    $1.75
39                                                  $0.00          6199 =================TOTAL GRAINS:
40                                                  $0.00          6200 YELLOW ONIONS     LB    $0.15
41                                                  $0.00          6201 ICEBERG LETTUCE   CASE  $9.89
42                                                  $0.00          6202 TOMATOES          CASE  $17.65
43  ----------------------------------------------------------     6203 BROCCOLI          LB    $0.98
44            TOTAL RECIPE COST:           $30.34                  7499 =================TOTAL PRODUCE:
45  ============================================================   7500 GROUND BEEF - BULK LB  $2.75
46                                                                 7501 SAUSAGE LINKS     LB    $1.75
47     Suggested selling price to achieve a 30% FOOD COST:  $8.43  7502 BACON             LB    $2.10
48     Suggested selling price to achieve a 35% FOOD COST:  $7.22  7503 GROUND BEEF - BULK LB  $2.75
49     Suggested selling price to achieve a 40% FOOD COST:  $6.32  8999 =================/POULTRY:
50  Suggested selling price to achieve a $3.00 GROSS PROFIT: $5.53 9000 PAPER FOOD DIVIDERS BOX $2.25
51                                                                 9001 #6 BROWN BAGS     CASE  $25.00
52                                                                 9002 12 OZ PAPER CUPS  CASE  $48.99
53  MACRO                                                          9003 STRAWS            BOX   $3.25
54  NAME    MACRO COMMANDS              COMMAND EXPLANATION         9999 =================TOTAL PAPER/PLASTIC:
55  ======= ========================  ==============================  9999999 _____
56   \U     /WGPD~                     * Unprotect the entire worksheet.    9999999 _____
57          {GOTO}I8~                   * Go to Cell I8.               9999999 _____
58          /FCCNDESCRIPTIONS~INVENTRY~  * Transfer DESCRIPTION data from INVENTRY.WK1.  9999999 _____
59          {GOTO}L8~                   * Go to Cell L8.
60          /FCCNPRICES~INVENTRY~       * Transfer PRICES data from INVENTRY.WK1.
61          /WGPE~                      * Protect the entire worksheet.
62          {CALC}                      * Recalculate the entire worksheet.
63          {HOME}                      * Go to Cell A1.
64                                      * END OF MACRO
```

10-1. *Recipe Costing and Pricing spreadsheet before execution of the \U macro.*

Formatting, Headings, and Labels

Step 1. Reformat columns A through L from the normal, default Lotus column width of nine characters to the widths given in table 10-2.

Step 2. Begin re-creating the example in figure 10-2 by entering the headings and labels for columns A through L, rows 1 through 63, exactly as specified in table 10-3.

You may need to pad some of your cell entries with blank spaces to get your headings to look like those pictured in figure 10-2. Any heading beginning with one of the three Lotus label alignment prefixes (', ", and ^) signifies a label to be padded with blank spaces or to be given a special cell alignment. Remember that the prefix ' aligns text to the left margin of the cell, the prefix " aligns text to the right margin of the cell,

```
   I  A  II    B        II     C     II  D  II   E    II   F    II   G     II H II   I   II       J       II K II L II
 1  RECIPE COSTING WORKSHEET                                                              LOOK-UP TABLE #1  #2  #3
 2  ===================  =========                                                        ==================== ==== ========
 3                                                                                                        RECIPE
 4                       RECIPE NAME:  MEAT LOAF PLATE                                                      UNIT  COST PER
 5                DATE OF LAST UPDATE:  October 19, 1985                                    INGREDIENT       OF   UNIT OF
 6  RECIPE TYPE (1=SUBMENU:2=MENU:3=BOTH):        2 MENU                                   DESCRIPTION    MEASURE MEASURE
 7                          COMMENTS:  This lunch plate includes 1 slice of meat loaf,     ==================== ==== ========
 8                                     a salad of 1/4 head of lettuce and 4 slices
 9                                     of tomato, broccoli, and a side of 6 raviolis.
10
11                 NUMBER OF SERVINGS:        12
12                CURRENT MENU PRICE:     $6.50
13           DOLLAR COST PER SERVING:
14   FOOD COST AS A PERCENT OF MENU PRICE:
15               DOLLAR GROSS PROFIT:     $6.50
16
17
18  INVENTORY                              RECIPE  COST PER  EXTENDED
19    ITEM    RECIPE INGREDIENT            UNIT OF UNIT OF   INGREDIENT
20   NUMBER     DESCRIPTION      QUANTITY  MEASURE MEASURE    COST
21  ------------------------------------------------------------------
22  MEAT LOAF INGREDIENTS:
23    7500                         5.00
24    6000                         0.50
25    6200                         0.50
26    3003                         0.10
27    2200                         1.00
28  VEGIS:
29    6203                         3.00
30  SALAD:
31    6202                         0.17
32    6201                         0.13
33  CARBOS:
34    2202                         0.72
35
36
37
38
39
40
41
42
43  ------------------------------------------------------------------
44                      TOTAL RECIPE COST:
45  ==================================================================
46
47      Suggested selling price to achieve a 30% FOOD COST:
48      Suggested selling price to achieve a 35% FOOD COST:
49      Suggested selling price to achieve a 40% FOOD COST:
50   Suggested selling price to achieve a $3.00 GROSS PROFIT:      $3.00
51
52
```

10-2. *Recipe Costing and Pricing spreadsheet, showing the \U macro and the effects of executing this macro.*

TABLE 10-2. STEP 1 FORMATTING COMMANDS.

Column	Width	Command to Enter	
B	20	/WCS20	\<Return\>
C	12	/WCS12	\<Return\>
D	8	/WCS8	\<Return\>
E	10	/WCS10	\<Return\>
F	12	/WCS12	\<Return\>
G	15	/WCS15	\<Return\>
J	20	/WCS20	\<Return\>
K	6	/WCS6	\<Return\>
L	10	/WCS10	\<Return\>

and the prefix ^ centers text within the cell. Unless a label alignment prefix is indicated in table 10-3, do not use one of these prefixes to begin a label or heading.

Step 3. Enter dashed lines and double-dashed lines into the spreadsheet as indicated in table 10-4. Use the backslash (\) key at the beginning of each cell entry to signal to Lotus that the character immediately following it is to be repeated across the cell from end to end.

To repeat a character across several individual cells, use Lotus's /Copy command, as indicated in table 10-4. Use the pointing method described

TABLE 10-3. STEP 2 HEADINGS.

Cell	Heading
A1	RECIPE COSTING WORKSHEET
B4	' RECIPE NAME:
B5	' DATE OF LAST UPDATE:
A6	'RECIPE TYPE (1=SUBMENU;2=MENU;=BOTH):
C7	' COMMENTS:
B11	' NUMBER OF SERVINGS:
B12	' CURRENT MENU PRICE:
B13	' DOLLAR COST PER SERVING:
A14	' FOOD COST AS A PERCENT OF MENU PRICE:
B15	' DOLLAR GROSS PROFIT:
A18	^INVENTORY
A19	^ITEM
A20	^NUMBER
B19	^RECIPE INGREDIENT
B20	^DESCRIPTION
C20	^QUANTITY
D18	''RECIPE
D19	''UNIT OF
D20	''MEASURE
E18	''COST PER
E19	''UNIT OF
E20	''MEASURE
F18	''EXTENDED
F19	''INGREDIENT
F20	''COST
C44	TOTAL RECIPE COST:
A47	' Suggested selling price to achieve a 30% FOOD COST:
A48	' Suggested selling price to achieve a 35% FOOD COST:
A49	' Suggested selling price to achieve a 40% FOOD COST:
A50	' Suggested selling price to achieve a $3.00 GROSS PROFIT:
J1	^LOOK-UP TABLE #1
K1	^#2
L1	^#3
J5	^INGREDIENT
J6	^DESCRIPTION
K3	^RECIPE
K4	^UNIT
K5	^OF
K6	^MEASRE
L4	^COST PER
L5	^UNIT OF
L6	^MEASURE
K2	^====
L2	^========
K7	^====
L7	^========

TABLE 10-4. STEP 3 REPEAT AND /COPY COMMANDS.

Cell	REPEAT Command to Enter	/Copy Command to Enter			
A2	\=	/CA2	<Return>	B2..B2	<Return>
A21	\-	/CA21	<Return>	B21..F21	<Return>
A43	\-	/CA43	<Return>	B43..F43	<Return>
A45	\=	/CA45	<Return>	B45..F45	<Return>
J2	\=				
J7	\=				

on page 34 to define the last cell of a cell range when performing the /Copy operation. Remember to place the cell pointer on the originating cell (the cell being copied from) before you begin to enter each command listed in table 10-4.

Step 4. Format the cells and cell ranges identified in table 10-5, as indicated there. Enter each command given in the far right-hand column of the table exactly as it appears by typing the characters shown and then hitting the <Return> key. When formatting a cell range, use the pointing method to define the last cell in each indicated cell range. Be sure to place the cell pointer on the first cell indicated in the far left-hand column of table 10-5 before entering the associated command.

Three look-up tables are used in the Recipe Costing and Pricing spreadsheet. Look-up tables 1, 2, and 3 are shown on the right-hand side of figure 10-1. These tables are used to look up the recipe ingredient description, the recipe unit of measure, and the cost per unit of measure, respectively. The values returned from these look-up tables correspond to the number you enter in the INVENTORY ITEM NUMBER column (column A) of the worksheet when creating your recipe. Look-up tables 1, 2, and 3 consist of information transferred from the

INVENTRY.WK1 spreadsheet described in chapter 4. The transfer of this information is accomplished automatically, by means of the macro described later in this chapter; you do not have to enter any data for these look-up tables.

It is necessary, however, for you to name the area to which the look-up data will be automatically transferred. This area, Cell Range I8..L59, will be given the range name INVENTORY (by which it will be identified in functions and formulas that look up data) in Step 5.

Step 5. Place your cell pointer on Cell I8, the first cell of the range that is to be named (Cell Range I8..L59), and enter the following /Range Name command:

/RNCINVENTORY   <Return>   I8..L59
<Return>

Operator Input

Step 6. Enter the specific data that appear in the shaded areas of figure 10-2. Table 10-6 describes the standard input for this portion of the spreadsheet. This is the only information you normally have to enter; the remainder of the spreadsheet is calculated automatically.

TABLE 10-5. STEP 4 /RANGE FORMAT COMMANDS.

Cell(s)	Format/Alignment	Command to Enter			
D12..D13	currency	/RFC2	<Return>	D12..D13	<Return>
D14	percent	/RFP2	<Return>	D14..D14	<Return>
D15	currency	/RFC2	<Return>	D15..D15	<Return>
C23..C42	fixed—two decimal places	/RFF2	<Return>	C23..C42	<Return>
E23..F44	currency	/RFC2	<Return>	E23..F44	<Return>
F47..F50	currency	/RFC2	<Return>	F47..F50	<Return>

TABLE 10-6. DATA INPUT INTO THE RECIPE COSTING AND PRICING SPREADSHEET.

Cell(s)	Input
D4	`RECIPE NAME.` Enter the name of the recipe.
D5	`DATE OF LAST UPDATE.` If this is a new recipe, enter the date on which you are creating the recipe. If you are modifying an existing recipe, change the date in this cell to the date of modification.
D6	`RECIPE TYPE.` Enter the recipe type (1 for submenu, 2 for menu, or 3 for both).
D7..D9	`COMMENTS.` Enter comments, a recipe description, or a serving description.
D11	`NUMBER OF SERVINGS.` Enter the number of servings produced by the recipe.
D12	`CURRENT MENU PRICE.` Enter the current menu price.
A22..A42	`INVENTORY ITEM NUMBER.` Enter the inventory item number for each ingredient in the recipe.
C22..C42	`QUANTITY.` Enter the quantity—the number of recipe units of measure—of each ingredient to be used in the recipe. You may enter fractions of units of measure, expressed as decimal numbers with up to two decimal digits.

Formulas

Some of the steps that follow contain instructions about making cells absolute when copying formulas and cell references. The meaning of absolute and relative cells is discussed on pages 34–35.

Before proceeding to Step 7, you should understand recipe types and how they are used.

Most restaurants create two types of recipes. One, called a *submenu recipe,* is a recipe for an item such as salad dressing that is not listed as a menu offering in itself but is used as part of a larger recipe for an item, such as a salad that is listed on the menu. Submenu recipes describe such things as sauces, batters, soup stocks, and fillings. Each submenu recipe should be entered as a single inventory item in the inventory spreadsheet described in chapter 4; it can then be

looked up and used in menu recipes or in other submenu recipes.

The other type of recipe, called a *menu recipe,* is a recipe composed of inventory ingredients and/or submenu recipes that have been entered as ingredients in your inventory spreadsheet. Its distinguishing characteristic is that it describes a menu item listed as an offering on the menu to customers.

Some menu recipes may also be submenu recipes—if they are used as ingredients in other recipes. For example, a dinner salad may be listed as a menu offering (with its own price) and may also be used as a submenu item that forms part of a full-course dinner on your menu.

It is important that you indicate in your spreadsheet the recipe type of each recipe you create, to remind yourself to enter submenu recipes in your inventory spreadsheet.

Step 7. Enter the following function, which returns the recipe type into Cell E6:

```
@CHOOSE(D6,'' '',''SUBMENU'',
''MENU'',''BOTH'')
```

For an explanation of the @CHOOSE function, see page 67.

Step 8. Enter the following formula into Cell B23:

```
@IF(@ISERR(@VLOOKUP(A23,$INVENTORY,
1)),'' '',@VLOOKUP(A23,$INVENTORY,1))
```

Rendered in English this formula reads: "If Cell A23, when looked up in the look-up table that has the range name INVENTORY, causes an `ERR` message, display a blank space (`'' ''`) instead of the `ERR` message in Cell B23. If, however, Cell A23 does not cause an `ERR` message, look up the value of A23 in the range of cells named INVENTORY, and return the label from the first column adjacent to the value looked up—the `INGREDIENT DESCRIPTION` column."

The @IF function is used in this formula to avoid a problem with the simpler and more direct formula, `@VLOOKUP(A23,$INVENTORY,1)`. Used by itself, the @VLOOKUP expression will invoke an `ERR` message from Lotus any time the cell looked up (A23) does not contain a numerical value. Because `ERR` messages make your spreadsheet look unsightly, the @IF expression is used to perform a preliminary test to see if the user has entered an inventory item number in the named cell before invoking the @VLOOKUP expression.

The @ISERR function is used to test for an impending ERR message from Lotus before Cell A23 is looked up in Look-up Table 1. Here, again, an ERR message may be caused by the presence of a nonnumerical value or by the absence of any value in Cell A23. In the spreadsheet example illustrated in figure 10-1, Cell A23 contains a numerical value and, therefore, does not produce an ERR message. When this formula is copied to Cells B24 through B42, however, problems will be caused by cell contents such as those in Cells A33 and A37, which contain a label or no value at all.

Placing a dollar sign in front of the INVENTORY range name designates the cell range defined by INVENTORY as absolute. This means that, when the formula is copied, INVENTORY (Cell Range I8..L59) will consist of cells I8 through L59 in each formula that contains a reference to it; in contrast, the reference to Cell A23 will change as it is copied.

Now copy this formula from Cell B23 into cells B24 through B42, placing your cell pointer on Cell B23 and entering the following /Copy command:

```
/C    <Return>    [point to Cell
B24].  [point to Cell B42]    <Return>
```

Step 9. Enter the following formula into Cell D23:

```
@IF(@ISERR(@VLOOKUP(A23,
$INVENTORY,2)),'' '',
@VLOOKUP(A23,$INVENTORY,2))
```

Rendered in English, this formula reads: "If Cell A23, when looked up in the look-up table that has the range name INVENTORY, causes an ERR message, display a blank space (' ' ' ') instead of the ERR message in Cell D23. If, however, Cell A23 does not cause an ERR message, look up the value of A23 in the range of cells named INVENTORY, and return the value from the second column opposite the value looked up— the RECIPE UNIT OF MEASURE column."

See Step 8 for a detailed account of the use of the @IF, @VLOOKUP, and @ISERR functions in a virtually identical formula.

Now copy the formula from Cell D23 into cells D24 through D42, placing your cell pointer on Cell D23 and entering the following /Copy command:

```
/C    <Return>    [point to Cell
D24].  [point to Cell D42]    <Return>
```

Step 10. Enter the following formula into Cell E22:

```
@IF(@ISERR(@VLOOKUP(A23,
$INVENTORY,3)),'' '',
@VLOOKUP(A23,$INVENTORY,3))
```

Rendered in English, this formula reads: "If Cell A23, when looked up in the look-up table that has the range name INVENTORY, causes an ERR message, display a blank space (' ' ' ') instead of the ERR message in Cell D23. If, however, Cell A23 does not cause an ERR message, look up the value of A23 in the range of cells named INVENTORY, and return the value from the third column opposite the value looked up—the COST PER UNIT OF MEASURE column."

See Step 8 for a detailed account of the use of the @IF, @VLOOKUP, and @ISERR functions in a virtually identical formula.

Now copy the formula from Cell E23 into cells E24 through E42, placing your cell pointer on Cell E23 and entering the following /Copy command:

```
/C    <Return>    [point to Cell
E24].  [point to Cell E42]    <Return>
```

Step 11. Enter the following formula into Cell F23:

```
@IF(@ISERR(C23*E23),0,C23*E23)
```

Rendered in English, this formula reads: "If Cell C23 multiplied by Cell E23 returns an ERR message, display a zero (0) instead of the ERR message in Cell F23; but if Cell C23 multiplied by Cell E23 does not return an ERR message, display the product of Cell C23 times Cell E23."

The result returned to Cell F23 is either zero or the extended ingredient cost, which is equal to the quantity times the cost per unit of measure.

See Step 8 for a detailed account of the use of the @IF and @ISERR functions.

Now copy the formula from Cell F23 into cells F24 through F42, placing your cell pointer on Cell F23 and entering the following /Copy command:

```
/C    <Return>   [point to Cell
F24].  [point to Cell F42]   <Return>
```

Step 12. The formula entered in Step 11 creates another unsightliness problem, by displaying $0.00 in cells and making the spreadsheet look cluttered. Suppress the display of zeros in these cells by entering the following /Worksheet Global Zero command:

```
/WGZY
```

Notice how this command acts to suppress the display of zeros in the cells of column F under EXTENDED INGREDIENT COST.

Step 13. Enter the following formula into Cell F44:

```
@SUM(F21..F43)
```

This formula sums the entries in the EXTENDED INGREDIENT COST column and returns the total recipe cost.

Calculating Menu Selling Prices

Several methods of calculating a selling price for menu items can be used. The most popular (but not necessarily the best) method is called the *Food Cost method* and is based on achieving a preset average food cost percentage, as illustrated by the formulas in cells F47, F48, and F49.

The next most popular method of calculating menu selling prices is called the *Gross Profit method* and is illustrated by the formula in Cell F50. The Gross Profit method sets an actual dollar goal rather than an abstract percentage goal (which may be misleading), as the Food Cost method does. The following advantages of the Gross Profit method can be enumerated:

1. It is based on actual dollar goals, not on abstract target percentages. It recognizes that you bank dollars, not percentages.
2. Relatively expensive menu items may be more attractively priced, allowing you to offer them at more competitive prices.
3. Budgeted costs of operation, budgeted sales, profit, and overhead, forecast customer demand, and menu mix—all of which are important factors not considered in setting percentage goals by the Food Cost method, must be considered in determining your overall gross profit goals.

Step 14. Enter each formula given in table 10-7 into the corresponding cell. These formulas calculate a per-serving selling price based on a preset food cost percentage goal.

Rendered in English, these formulas read: "Divide the total recipe cost in Cell F44 by the number of servings in Cell D11; then divide that result by the food cost percentage goal." Thus the first part of each formula, (F44/D11), calculates the cost per serving. When the cost per serving is divided by the food cost percentage goal (expressed as a decimal number), the result is the selling price per serving that yields the desired food cost percentage of 30 percent, 35 percent, or 40 percent.

Step 15. Enter the following formula into Cell F50:

```
(F44/D11)+3.00
```

This formula calculates a selling price per serving, by adding a preset gross profit goal of $3.00 to the cost per serving, (F44/D11).

Step 16. Enter the following formula (which calculates the cost per serving) into Cell D13:

```
+F44/D11
```

Step 17. Enter the following formula into Cell D14:

TABLE 10-7. STEP 14 FORMULAS.

Cell	Formula
F47	(F44/D11)/.3
F48	(F44/D11)/.35
F49	(F44/D11)/.4

```
+D13/D12
```

This formula calculates the achievable food cost percentage, based on the current menu price and the actual dollar cost per serving.

Step 18. Enter the following formula (which calculates the actual dollar gross profit per serving, based on the current menu price" and the dollar cost per serving) into Cell D15:

```
+D12-D13
```

Protecting Your Spreadsheet

Step 19. Use the /Worksheet Global Protection Enable command sequence, followed by Unprotect commands for the shaded areas shown in figure 10-2 to protect the cells in the nonshaded areas of the spreadsheet from accidentally being filled (by you or by other spreadsheet users) with unwanted data. Begin by entering the following command string:

```
/WGPE
```

This string is an abbreviated expression for the /Worksheet Global Protection Enable command, which protects every cell in the spreadsheet from entry and alteration.

The next step is to unprotect the cells in the shaded areas of the spreadsheet by means of the /Range Unprotect commands listed in table 10-8. Before entering each command, place your cell pointer on the first cell of the cell range that you want to unprotect.

TABLE 10-8. STEP 19 /RANGE UNPROTECT COMMANDS.

Cells to Unprotect	Command to Enter
D4..D13	/RU [point to Cell D13] <Return>
A22..A42	/RU [point to Cell A42] <Return>
C22..C42	/RU [point to Cell C42] <Return>

Saving RECIPES.WK1

Step 20. You can save the RECIPES spreadsheet you have created so far, by entering the following /File Save command:

```
/FSB:RECIPES  <Return>
```

RECIPES is the file name for the Recipe Costing and Pricing spreadsheet and will be written onto the disk in drive B. If you have a hard disk or a single floppy drive system, save the RECIPES spreadsheet onto the appropriate drive and directory. When you save this file under the name RECIPES Lotus will automatically add a period and the file name extension WK1 to the name RECIPES. When you look at a directory of files on disk drive B, you will see this file displayed as RECIPES WK1. The WK1 extension identifies this file to you and to Lotus as a file in a spreadsheet format.

You are not finished creating your recipe costing spreadsheet, but saving the Recipe Costing and Pricing spreadsheet now enables you to suspend creation of your recipe costing spreadsheet for the next several steps while you modify the INVENTRY.WK1 spreadsheet that you created in Chapter 4. These modifications add two new range names to the INVENTRY.WK1 spreadsheet that will serve to reference the inventory data in the spreadsheet prior to their being transferred to the RECIPES.WK1 spreadsheet (as the data in Look-up tables 1, 2, and 3).

WARNING: Be sure to save your RECIPES spreadsheet as instructed in Step 20 before executing the command in Step 21. If you fail to do so, you will lose all the work you have done so far to create the RECIPES.WK1 spreadsheet.

Step 21. Erase the Recipe Costing and Pricing spreadsheet from your screen and from your computer's memory by entering the following /Worksheet Erase command:

```
/WEY
```

Step 22. Retrieve the INVENTRY.WK1 worksheet that you created in chapter 4, by issuing the following command:

```
/FRB:INVENTRY    <Return>
```

TABLE 10-9. STEP 23 /RANGE NAME COMMANDS.

Cell Range	Range Name	/Range Name Command to Enter
C9..E59	DESCRIPTIONS	/RNCDESCRIPTIONS <Return> C9..E59 <Return>
G9..G59	PRICES	/RNCPRICES <Return> G9..G59 <Return>

Step 23. Create the two range names given in table 10-9 by entering the corresponding commands identified there.

Step 24. Resave the INVENTRY.WK1 spreadsheet with its new range names, by entering the following /File Save command:

```
/FSB:INVENTRY     <Return>
```

Step 25. Erase the INVENTRY.WK1 spreadsheet from your screen and from your computer's memory (so that you can retrieve the RECIPES.WK1 spreadsheet and resume work on it) by entering the following /Worksheet Erase command:

```
/WEY
```

Step 26. Retrieve the RECIPES.WK1 spreadsheet that you saved in Step 20 by issuing the following command:

```
/FRB:RECIPES     <Return>
```

Using a Macro to Transfer Data to the Recipe Costing and Pricing Spreadsheet

Your next task is to create a macro that will use the /File Combine command to bring together inventory data from the INVENTRY.WK1 spreadsheet in your Recipe Costing and Pricing spreadsheet.

The macro, named \U (for *update*), will specify where in the INVENTORY.WK1 spreadsheet the data are to be retrieved from, and where in the Recipe Costing and Pricing spreadsheet the data are to be placed.

Step 27. Begin creating the \U macro (see figure 10-2) by entering each macro command into the appropriate cell, as indicated in table 10-10. The command explanation in the far right-hand column of the table documents the action initiated by the macro command; each command explanation should be entered into column D of the spreadsheet in the cell corresponding to each macro command cell in column B.

The \U macro twice uses Lotus's /File Combine Copy command to transfer selected data from INVENTRY.WK1 to RECIPES.WK1 automatically. For this command to work, however, you must already have used the /File Retrieve command to retrieve the spreadsheet that you want to transfer the data to, so that it is the current spreadsheet you are using. In addition, the cell pointer must be positioned on the receiving cell or on the cell that forms the upper left-hand corner of the receiving range (the cell or range to which the data are being transferred). The /File

TABLE 10-10. STEP 27 MACRO COMMANDS AND COMMAND EXPLANATIONS.

Cell	Command	Command Explanation
B56	'/WGPD~	* Unprotect entire worksheet.
B57	{GOTO}I8~	* Go to Cell I8.
B58	'/FCCNDESCRIPTIONS~B:INVENTRY~	* Transfer DESCRIPTIONS data from INVENTRY.WK1.
B59	{GOTO}L8~	* Go to Cell L8.
B60	'/FCCNPRICES~B:INVENTRY~	* Transfer PRICES data from INVENTRY.WK1.
B61	'/WGPE	* Protect entire worksheet.
B62	{CALC}	* Recalculate entire spreadsheet.
B63	{HOME}	* Go to Cell A1.

Combine Copy command has the following form and sequence:

```
/FCC [originating cell/cell
range]  <Return>  [receiving file
name]  <Return>
```

Notice how the /File Combine Copy command works (according to the command explanation in table 10-10) and how each of these commands is preceded by a {GOTO} command to ensure that the cell pointer is properly positioned to receive the data in the appropriate cell.

Step 28. Name the \U macro you have just created, by placing the cell pointer on Cell B56 (the first cell of the macro) and entering the following /Range Name command:

```
/RNC\U  <Return>  <Return>
```

Now execute the macro by pressing the <Alt> key and the U key simultaneously.

When the macro has finished executing, look at columns I through M, rows 8 through 59, to see how the inventory data have been transferred from the spreadsheet file INVENTRY.WK1. Notice how the formulas in the Recipe Costing and Pricing spreadsheet looked up the ingredient name, the unit of measure, and the cost per unit of measure for each recipe ingredient. Notice, too, that all the menu pricing formulas and food cost formulas have been calculated.

Saving RECIPES.WK1

Step 29. Save the RECIPES spreadsheet (including the \U macro) by entering the following /File Save command:

```
/FSB:RECIPES  <Return>  R
```

Printing Your Spreadsheet

Step 30. Turn your printer on, align the paper in it, place your cell pointer in Cell A1 by pressing the <Home> key on your cursor/arrow keypad, and print your spreadsheet by issuing the following series of commands:

```
/PPR.  <End>  <Home>
<Return>  AGPQ
```

This abbreviated command language means: "Print to the printer the spreadsheet range A1 through N63. The paper is aligned in the printer, so the spreadsheet should begin printing at the top of the page. Go and print the spreadsheet. Then page-eject the paper in the printer to the top of a new page, and quit the print commands."

You may need to consult your Lotus manual for information on how to adjust Lotus's printer settings for footers, margins, borders, page length, and special set-up strings.

Periodic Updating of Recipe Costs and Menu Prices

As food prices fluctuate with the commodities market, so will your recipe costs. In response, all restaurants periodically have to redo their menu to raise or lower prices and to add, eliminate, or change menu items.

Having your recipes stored in a spreadsheet makes this chore much easier. It is important, however, that you maintain and consistently update price information in your physical Inventory and Valuation spreadsheet. With prices maintained, all you need to do to update your recipes is to issue a /File Retrieve command for your Recipe Costing and Pricing spreadsheet and then execute the \U macro. The macro will automatically retrieve all inventory information (with updated prices) from the INVENTRY.WK1 spreadsheet, place the data in look-up tables 1, 2, and 3, and automatically recalculate all new recipe costs and menu prices based on updated food prices in inventory the INVENTRY.WK1 spreadsheet.

Use the following guidelines when updating your recipes:

1. Be sure to print a copy of all old recipes before updating them. Once you save your modified recipe with new food costs, the old recipe will be overwritten on your disk storage medium.
2. Be sure to print a copy of all updated recipes.
3. Be sure to save all updated recipes onto your disk storage medium.
4. Be sure to change the date of last update for each updated recipe before you save it, so you

will not have to remember when you last updated a recipe.

Using the Information in This Spreadsheet

"What If" Recipe Analysis

Your RECIPES.WK1 spreadsheet easily allows you to change the following:

- Recipe ingredients
- Ingredient portions
- Number of servings
- Current menu price

As a result, it is easy for you to see the effect that one or more changes may have on the following:

- Dollar cost per serving
- Food cost as a percentage of menu price
- Per-serving dollar gross profit
- Suggested selling prices needed to achieve predetermined goals

Feel free to experiment and be creative with recipes within the guidelines of the financial goals you set for your foodservice operation. Because manual recipe costing is tedious for many chefs and foodservice operators, they may tend to consider only the culinary, artistic side of recipe creation and not the financial side. Using a spreadsheet makes the financial aspect of recipe costing easier and more fun.

Recipe Ingredient Quantities and Recipe Units of Measure

Use these totals (preset by the user) to set recipe preparation guidelines for all employees involved in preparing recipes.

Number of Servings

Use the number of servings (preset by the user) to set portion control guidelines for all employees who prepare, portion, or serve recipe/menu items.

Current Menu Price

Use the current menu price (preset by the user) as a basis for determining the new price of the recipe if this recipe is a menu type. Use it to calculate food cost as a percentage of menu price, to calculate dollar gross profit per serving, and to calculate suggested selling prices.

Dollar Cost per Serving

Dollar cost per serving (calculated by the spreadsheet) equals the total recipe cost divided by the number of servings. Use this cost to set and calculate the current menu price. The spreadsheet uses it to calculate the following:

- Food cost percentage
- Per-serving dollar gross profit
- Suggested selling prices

Food Cost as a Percentage of Menu Price

Food cost as a percentage of menu price (calculated by the spreadsheet) equals dollar cost per serving divided by current menu price. This ratio is used by many foodservice operators as a theoretical indicator of how well food costs could or should be managed in their restaurant. If actual food cost percentages (calculated from actual dollar sales and food purchases) vary from this theoretical food cost percentage, one of the following food control problems may be responsible:

- Inconsistent serving portions
- Food wastage
- Food spoilage
- Theft
- Fluctuating ingredient costs
- Improper menu pricing
- Irregular portion control in food preparation

Per-serving Dollar Gross Profit

Per-serving dollar gross profit (calculated by the spreadsheet) equals current menu price minus dollar cost per serving. Use this gross profit figure as a reference for comparison in efforts to meet financial goals set by budget guidelines.

As a simple example, when you determine your yearly budget, you may calculate that your gross profit after cost of goods sold should be $600,000. This gross profit will pay operating, general, and administrative expenses and leave you (you hope) with a pretax net profit. Suppose that you estimate an annual customer count of 200,000 customers; by dividing the $600,000 gross profit by 200,000 customers, you calculate that you need to earn an average gross profit of $3.00 per customer:

$600,000 / 200,000 customers = $3.00 per customer

Use this $3.00 average gross profit per customer as a guideline when setting menu selling prices. You may establish, as a rule for recipe pricing, that the minimum menu selling price for any recipe will not be less than the per-serving recipe cost plus the per serving dollar gross profit (in this case, $3.00).

Suggested Selling Prices

Use suggested selling prices (calculated by the spreadsheet) as guides to assist you in determining menu prices for recipes. By no means does this spreadsheet contain all the information necessary to set a menu price. For example, it does not include answers to the following questions:

1. How popular is the menu item?
2. How labor-intensive is the preparation of the recipe?
3. What is your intuitive feeling about how much you can reasonably charge for the item in your particular market area?
4. What price is the competition charging?
5. What customer preferences are discernable?

All of these factors must be considered when setting a menu selling price. However, you may want to use one of the suggested selling price

formulas on the spreadsheet to set a floor or minimum selling price and a ceiling or maximum selling price for the recipe.

Problems

1. How does recipe costing assist in establishing portion control?
2. How does recipe costing help set menu prices?
3. What is meant by the terms *contribution margin* and *gross profit* as they apply to recipe costing?
4. How does recipe costing help determine contribution margin?
5. What factors other than the cost of the menu item recipe are involved in setting menu prices?
6. How is a recipe's food cost as a percentage of menu price used as a theoretical guide for actual food costs in a restaurant? How can the difference between the theoretical and actual food costs be an indicator of problems in a foodservice operation?
7. How can the Budget spreadsheet in Chapter 9 (see figure 9-1) be used to set menu prices? What item or items in that budget would you use, and how would you use them?
8. What is the difference between a menu recipe and a submenu recipe? Give examples of each.
9. How can a menu item be both a menu recipe and a submenu recipe? Give examples of such items.
10. How do the recipe unit of measure, the inventory count unit and the delivery count unit differ?

Cases

1. Explain in detail how the statistics calculated from the **MEAT LOAF PLATE** special illustrated in figure 10-1 compare to the hypothetical lunch menu goals set in the introductory paragraphs of the chapter.

Glossary

ABSOLUTE CELL REFERENCE. A cell reference that remains the same in a formula even when the formula is copied to other cells.

ACTIVE CELL. *See* CURRENT CELL.

ANOMOLY. A deviation from what you would expect; an inconsistency in the calculated result of a formula or function.

ARGUMENT. An independent variable of a function. You provide arguments as variables to Lotus 1-2-3 functions; these functions then supply arguments to a built-in formula, which processes the arguments to return a value. Depending on the function, an argument may be a number, a text string, an expression, another function, or a cell reference.

AVERAGE CHECK. Net food and beverage sales (not including sales tax and other non-food/beverage sales) divided by the total number of customers. Average check is used as a measure of the average number of dollars spent by each customer and as a measure of server productivity.

BREAK-EVEN. A dollar amount representing the amount of sales needed to pay off total fixed costs at a fixed proportion of cents per dollar; computed by dividing total fixed costs by the difference between 100 percent and the percentage of total revenue consumed by total variable costs.

CELL. One of the individual boxes on a spreadsheet that holds input information; defined by the vertical column and horizontal row that intersect at it.

CELL CURSOR. The bar of light on the Lotus 1-2-3 screen that highlights the current, active cell.

CELL POINTER. Another name for the cell cursor.

CELL RANGE. One or more contiguous cells that may be defined as a square or rectangular block of cells. You specify a cell range to Lotus 1-2-3 by entering (or pointing to) the upper left-hand cell address and the lower right-hand cell address of the cell range, separating the addresses with two (or one) periods.

COMMAND. An instruction to Lotus 1-2-3 chosen from the Command Menu, which is displayed when the slash key (/), also called the MENU key, is pressed. Some commands display subcommand menus or command-modification menus when selected from the main Command Menu.

COMMAND MENU. A menu of Lotus commands that is displayed in the Lotus 1-2-3 screen control panel when the slash key (/) is pressed from the READY mode. The command menu may call subcommand menus depending on which command is chosen.

CONTRIBUTION MARGIN. The result of subtracting all variable expenses from net sales; represents the amount of net sales that goes toward profits.

CONTROLLABLE EXPENSES. Expenses that can be directly controlled or influenced by management.

CONTROL PANEL. The top three lines of the Lotus 1-2-3 screen; used to display status information, mode of operation, current cell contents, user entry and edit of cell contents, commands, command menus, and Lotus 1-2-3 prompts and messages.

COST CONTROL. The implementation of rules, systems, and policies that are used to establish and maintain control over the costs incurred by normal, ongoing business activity; generally, all efforts to minimize the costs and maximize the profits of a business.

COST OF GOODS SOLD. The cost of food and beverage in a foodservice operation; usually calculated for a period by subtracting the period's ending inventory from the total of all goods available for sale during the period (the period's purchases plus the period's beginning inventory).

CURRENT CELL. The cell currently highlighted by the cell cursor.

CUSTOMER COUNT. The total number of customers patronizing an establishment for a given period of time.

DATA. Information entered into a Lotus 1-2-3 spreadsheet, including text, numbers, formatting specifications, range names, definitions, formulas, and functions.

DEFAULT. A Lotus 1-2-3 action, command setting, or configuration that is normally in existence when Lotus 1-2-3 is first retrieved from disk and that remains in existence until changed by the user or by a retrieved spreadsheet data file.

DEPARTMENT KEYS. Keys on a cash register that may be configured to accumulate dollar totals for specifically defined sales categories.

DISK. A storage medium used to store computer programs and data permanently. Common types are floppy disks and hard disks.

DISK DRIVE. A device comprised of several major components: a controller, read/write head(s), and a motor. The controller consists of electronic components and microchips that allow the disk drive to communicate (interface) with the other computer chips when you want to access information on a disk or store information on a disk. The read/write head(s) read and write data onto the disk. The motor spins the disk in the disk drive and makes the data on the disk in the disk drive available to the read/write heads.

DOS (DISK OPERATING SYSTEM). A collection of software programs that are used to manage computer data and program files, memory, storage, and screen use, and that allow other software programs to use these computer components.

ECR (ELECTRONIC CASH REGISTER). A stand-alone device whose architecture is based on integrated circuit design. An ECR typically cannot communicate with another ECR.

EDIT/ENTRY CURSOR. The narrow underscore of light that marks your place on the edit/entry line of the control panel (the third line).

EXPRESSION. A combination of mathematical symbols, operators, and/or values that represents a value and/or returns a result.

FILE EXTENSION. An optional part of the identifying name given to a file stored on disk, consisting of up to three characters added to the right side of the period following the file name.

FILE NAME. The required part of the identifying name given to a file stored on disk, consisting of from one to eight alphanumeric characters.

FIFO (FIRST IN, FIRST OUT). A method of valuing inventory; based on using the last price paid for each inventory item, on the theory that the oldest products are sold first, leaving the most recently purchased goods in inventory.

FIXED EXPENSES. Expenses that do not vary directly with sales, but remain constant regardless of sales.

FORMATTING. Establishing the appearance of data, headings, and labels in cells and columns in a spreadsheet.

FORMULA. A mathematical expression that performs calculations, using values and numbers in the formula and/or in other spreadsheet cells.

FUNCTION. A formula that is built into the Lotus 1-2-3 program and may be accessed using a Lotus 1-2-3 @ function. The function passes variables to these built-in 1-2-3 formulas, using arguments that are provided by the user.

GLOBAL. Describes a Lotus 1-2-3 setting or command that, when executed, performs its actions on the entire spreadsheet.

GOOD-FAITH AGREEMENT. A formula for tip allocation agreed on by owners, managers, and employees.

GROSS PROFIT. The difference between cost of goods sold and sales.

HEADING. The title or label of a spreadsheet column; created exactly as other labels are.

HISTORICAL RECORD. Printed spreadsheets that are stored in chronological order and used as a paper record of business activity.

INFORMATION. Data that have been input, stored, and/or processed in a computer; the specific data entered and stored in a spreadsheet file.

INVENTORY VALUATION. The aggregate dollar value of all inventory items at a specific date and time.

ISSUING. The act of distributing food, beverage, and other inventory within a foodservice operation.

JULIAN NUMBER. The number of days from a specific date; derived from the Julian calendar, which uses 365 days per year and 366 days every fourth year. Lotus calls this a *serial number* and begins counting from January 1, 1900.

LABEL. A text entry beginning with a letter or with a label prefix character (', ", or ^); same as text, a text string, or a heading.

LOOK-UP TABLE. A spreadsheet table used with Lotus's @VLOOKUP or @HLOOKUP function to look up a value and return a corresponding or adjacent value.

LOTUS. Lotus 1-2-3 spreadsheet application software.

MACRO. One or more Lotus 1-2-3 commands and/or keystrokes that can be executed automatically by assigning the first command or keystroke in the sequence of commands and keystrokes to a specially named macro key.

MAN-HOUR. An hour of work by one person; used as a unit of time.

MEAN AVERAGE. The sum of a list divided by the number of items in the list.

MEMORY. The microprocessor chips in a computer, used as a temporary but volatile holding place for all data and programs.

MENU CURSOR. The bar of light on the Lotus 1-2-3 screen that highlights a command option on the Command Menu.

MENU RECIPE. A recipe composed of inventory ingredients and/or submenu recipes that describes a menu item listed as an offering on the menu to customers.

MILITARY TIME. Time based on a 24-hour clock, where the hours of the day range from 0 to 24.

NET PROFIT. The actual profit made on a business transaction after deducting all costs involved in gross sales or revenue.

NONCONTROLLABLE EXPENSES. Expenses over which management has no direct control or influence.

NUMERICAL VALUE. A number used as a number (not as a heading or label).

OPERATOR. A symbol used to express a mathematical operation, such as + for add, − for subtract, × for multiply, and / for divide.

OVERAGE. The amount by which actual cash exceeds cash reported by a cash register or ECR/POS system.

PERIOD-TO-DATE. Describes a category of data consisting of accumulated totals for a specific interval of time.

PERPETUAL INVENTORY. An inventorying method that involves maintaining, for each item of inventory, a record that shows quantities received, quantities issued, and quantities on hand. An entry is recorded each time inventory is increased or decreased.

PHYSICAL INVENTORY. An inventorying method that involves determining on-hand quantities for each inventory item by physically counting and recording these quantities.

POINTING. Using a cell cursor to indicate or select a cell or cell range to be used in Lotus 1-2-3 formulas, functions, and commands.

POS (POINT-OF-SALE) SYSTEM. A system for entering and processing sales transactions at the time the sale occurs, using terminals that employ integrated circuits and are capable of interterminal communication of data.

PRIMARY SORT. The first key field in a Lotus 1-2-3 spreadsheet on which data are sorted in numerical or alphabetic order.

PROTECT. To lock a 1-2-3 spreadsheet cell or cell range to disallow entry and alteration of cell contents.

PTD. *See* PERIOD-TO-DATE.

RAM (RANDOM ACCESS MEMORY). *See* MEMORY.

RECEIVING. The purchasing activity of inspecting the weight, quality, and count of delivered merchandise.

RECIPE. A list of the ingredients of a menu item or submenu item, indicating quantities of ingredients.

RECONCILE. To resolve or find cause for inconsistencies between actual cash count and cash/vouchers reported by a cash register, ECR, or POS system.

RELATIVE CELL REFERENCE. A cell reference that changes in a formula when the formula is copied to other cells.

REPLICATE. To copy.

REQUISITIONING. The purchasing activity that consists of having a person or department (such as the kitchen) make a formal written request for supplies.

SALARY. Fixed compensation paid periodically to an employee; usually remains fixed in relation to sales.

SCRATCH PAD FEATURE. A Lotus software feature that enables you to use the numerical keypad of your keyboard as an adding machine to add, subtract, multiply, and divide numbers that, when entered in a single cell, are displayed as the final result of these operations. For instance, instead of adding numbers in your head to calculate a single number to enter in a spreadsheet cell, you can use this feature—entering your addition in a single cell and letting Lotus 1-2-3 add the numbers.

SEASONAL INDEX. Each month's percentage share of total annual sales.

SECONDARY SORT. The second key field in a Lotus 1-2-3 spreadsheet on which data are sorted in numerical or alphabetic order. All data sorted using a secondary key field will remain arranged according to the primary sort order, but within that will be rearranged in the order of the secondary sort.

SERIAL NUMBER. A Lotus-derived number that represents the number of days that have passed since January 1, 1900.

SETTLEMENT. Whatever method of payment a restaurant customer uses to pay (settle) a bill.

SHORTAGE. The numerical deficiency in cash on hand relative to the amount of cash reported by a cash register, ECR, or POS system.

SHORTFALL. A deficiency of reported tips by a tipped employee.

SORT. To rearrange spreadsheet data in alphabetic or numerical order.

SPREADSHEET. A computer software work space designed to allow orderly analysis, modeling, and presentation of numerical and financial data by column and row.

STANDARD DEVIATION. A measure of acceptable variance from a norm.

STANDARD TIME. The standard 12-hour clock that divides the day into two 12-hour periods—A.M. and P.M.

STORING. The purchasing activity of storing and protecting inventory items from damage and spoilage.

SUBMENU RECIPE. A recipe that is used in other submenu recipes and/or in final menu recipes.

TENDER. The types of payment or settlement accepted by a particular foodservice operation in payment of a bill.

TEXT STRING. One or more letters, numbers, or characters strung together and intended as text (not as numbers on which mathematical operations will be performed).

TIP ALLOCATION. A process of allocating reported tips among tipped employees, using a predefined formula to determine if an employee has a deficiency of reported tips.

TOTAL REVENUE. The total monies derived from the sale of goods and services minus any allotted to discounts, returns, and allowances.

TRUE SALES. A net sales dollar amount that is calculated by subtracting items that are not sales of food and beverage from gross sales.

UNDERSCORE. The character and key on your keyboard that makes an underline.

UNPROTECT. To open up specified portions of a previously protected spreadsheet to allow entry and alteration of data.

VALUE. The result of a formula or function. A value may be text or a number.

VARIABLE EXPENSES. Expenses that vary directly with sales.

WAGE. Compensation paid to an employee based on a short time period, such as per hour, per day, or per week; often varies in relation to sales.

WORKSHEET. *See* SPREADSHEET.

Appendix Trademarks

Lotus 1-2-3 is a trademark of Lotus Development Corporation.

MS-DOS is a trademark of Microsoft Corporation.

PC-DOS is a trademark of International Business Machines Corporation.

IBM is a trademark of International Business Machines Corporation.

SuperCalc 3 is a trademark of Computer Associates.

AT&T is a trademark of AT&T Information Systems.

COMPAQ is a trademark of COMPAQ Computer Corporation.

INDEX